THE FORGOTTEN NINTH AMENDMENT

A CALL FOR LEGISLATIVE AND JUDICIAL RECOGNITION OF RIGHTS
UNDER SOCIAL CONDITIONS OF TODAY

By

BENNETT B. PATTERSON
of the Texas Bar

THE BOBBS-MERRILL COMPANY, INC.
PUBLISHERS
INDIANAPOLIS

INTRODUCTION

Mr. Patterson does the law and juristic and political thinking a real service in calling attention specifically to the Ninth Amendment, in recalling and making conveniently accessible the debates over the Bill of Rights which led to the formulation and adoption of the first ten amendments, substantially contemporary with the Constitution, and in bringing out how a change in numbering of paragraphs led to confusion as to the nature and application of the amendment. Nothing in the Constitution should be taken to be idle and of no moment. The declaration of natural rights in the Ninth Amendment is not something to be relegated to a lumber room of outworn juristic or political ideas. The task is rather to make the natural law and natural rights as believed in by the founders of our polity effective political and legal instruments in the society of today.

In the time in which Anglo-American legal and political ideas, which were set forth in the Bill of Rights took form men held to a doctrine of a universal law of nature of which the law of the time and place was only declaratory. The law of nature as understood in the seventeenth and eighteenth centuries and received in America in the formative era of our law went into eclipse at the end of the eighteenth century and gave way to quite different modes of thought in the nineteenth century. It was a mode of thought for a period of growth in the law and was not suited to what in that century men took complacently for "the maturity of law." Today, in a world which is transforming through the achievements of science, there is a marked revival of natural law ideas throughout the world. Interest in the Ninth Amendment is a symptom of that revival.

But unlike the law of nature of the eighteenth century the revived natural law is not a fixed system of precisely formulated rules to stand fast forever. It is rather a reasoned body of starting points for legal reasoning worked out from a conception of justice as the ideal relation among men. The

iii

ideal is not given in detail. It is shaped as to details by the
conditions and circumstances of life in civilized society. The
conditions of life in a pioneer society, struggling to establish
itself against savage tribes or in a wilderness, those of a rural
community of farms and small towns in an agricultural society,
those of a commercial society of traders and sailors, those of a
complex society of farmers, traders, mechanics, and laborers
in a society of rising industrial centers and metropolitan cities,
and those of a primarily industrial society in which men live
under threats of injury by machinery attending their everyday
activities, raise constantly expanding pictures of an ideal relation in the conflicting and overlapping expectations of men
in continually changing relations.

Adjustment of social control to the ideal, achieving a balance of individual expectations to the exigencies of a har-
monious whole, to accord with an ideal of human relations,
calls for what has been called a "natural law with a growing
content."

From this standpoint the Ninth Amendment is a solemn
declaration that natural rights are not a fixed category of
reasonable human expectations in civilized society laid down
once for all in the several sections of the Constitution. Those
not expressly set forth are not forever excluded but are, if
the Ninth Amendment is read with the Tenth, left to be
secured by the states or by the people of the whole land by
constitutional change, as was done, for example, by the Fourteenth Amendment.

Both the original text of the Constitution in more than
one place, and the first ten amendments as a whole proceed
upon an idea of recognized and secured rights.

It must be borne in mind that the formative era of our
institutions was one of confidence. Men believed that they
could do things by application of reason to the conditions of
social existence. It called itself an age of reason. The men
of that time were not believers in a closed scheme of historical
development or evolution in which all institutions were beyond
their control and were bound inexorably to unfold along a fixed
course from what was given by history. Nor was human
existence to be a regulated Darwinian struggle for existence.
The mode of thought of the time is stamped upon the Great

Seal of the United States: *Novus ordo seclorum*—a new order of the ages.

There is need of this type of confident thinking today, in contrast to the idea which prevailed in the last half of the nineteenth century that all conscious attempts at creative making or shaping of institutions or laws were futile. The historical jurists, who dominated juristic thought in America in the last quarter of the nineteenth century denied the efficacy of effort to improve the law. They conceived that legislation sought to achieve the impossible—to make what could not be made but could only grow. We could do no more than await the process of unfolding or self-realizing of the idea of justice in customs, judicial decisions, and doctrinal writing. The world today moves too fast for such a program.

Economic unification of the whole country has gone very far in the present century. Economic unification of the world has been going forward steadily. Aerial transportation, radio and television, have been making every community the neighbor of every other everywhere. Two attempts have been made toward universal political organization. In what is becoming a crowded world the immunities of land owners are giving way and duties of care not to create or maintain risks in the way they operate their property are coming to be recognized. In the growing bigness and complexity of things simple maxims of the past no longer give workable solutions of problems of overlapping expectations. In the mechanizing of everyday activities our lives are "with dangers compassed round." The expectations of men in civilized life are becoming varied and multiplied. A pronouncement of the claims of humanity to revise and add to the category of recognized and secured expectations is timely today even if it was felt negligible in the latter part of the last century.

If we believe in fundamental inherent rights, they are not, says the Ninth Amendment, a fixed category of definitely formulated precisely defined expectations of individuals, fixed finally for all times, places and men in the texts of the Bill of Rights.

Now comes the question, having drawn attention to the scope and purpose of the Ninth Amendment, what can it do for us today?

As I said above, nothing in the Bill of Rights can or ought to be ignored, though some provisions, such as the right to bear arms have a much altered significance under the conditions of popular uprising against oppression under the conditions of military operations today. Shall we not say that the Ninth Amendment is a pronouncement of a solemn warning to the agencies of government that there are reasonable expectations of individual men living in civilized society which the people retain and for which recognition and security may be demanded? Though not set forth in terms in the Constitution, they should be borne in mind in the process of government. Where rights are defined and secured expressly by the Constitution, there is simply a question of interpretation. But where rights not declared in terms are "reserved" there is a question as to where is the power of defining them, and where is the power of securing them when defined. The Tenth Amendment seems to preclude definition and enforcement by the federal government except as committed to that government by the Constitution. It would seem, therefore, that these reserved rights may be defined and enforcement of them may be provided by the states, except as may be precluded by the Fourteenth Amendment, or may be defined and acquire secured enforcement by the people of the United States by constitutional amendment.

Assuming that the Ninth Amendment is a general recognition of inherent or natural rights, it does not purport to secure them. It lays down no rules such as are provided in articles I to VIII inclusive. It declares that there are natural rights but makes no attempt to define those not expressly provided for in the Bill of Rights nor to provide for securing them. But the states have the attributes and powers of sovereignty so far as they have not been committed to the federal government by the Constitution. So far as inherent rights are not committed to the federal government, defining and securing them is left to the states or to be taken over by the people of the United States by constitutional amendment. Are not the Ninth and Tenth Amendments authority for state legislation to define and secure inherent reasonable expectations in life in civilized society as it is today and is not the Ninth

Amendment a challenge to the states to undertake that work as the conditions of American life today may demand it?

At any rate, we owe much to Mr. Patterson for bringing it to our notice.

ROSCOE POUND

TABLE OF CONTENTS

————

The Forgotten Ninth Amendment

PART I

CHAPTER 1

FOREWORD

"The Enumeration in the Constitution of certain rights, shall not be construed to deny or disparage others retained by the people."

The Ninth Amendment to the Constitution of the United States of America, if given its proper meaning and construction, could be the most significant and forceful clause in the entire Constitution. To this date it has been the "stone which the builders refused", but it is in fact the cornerstone of the Constitution.

Individual freedom, and the recognition and development of the spiritual nature of mankind are the essence of democracy; indeed, they are the essence of life itself. We believe that by nuturing and encouraging the natural development of the individual to the point that he will achieve his greatest work, society, as a whole, will profit in the greatest measure.

There is no clause in the Constitution, except the Ninth Amendment, which makes a declaration of the sovereignty and dignity of the individual.

Since individual freedom is the basis of democracy, and is the virtue which marks the excellence of our form of government over all other forms of government, then the Ninth Amendment immediately takes its place as the most important declaration in our Constitution, because such a declaration is nowhere else therein to be found.

The Ninth Amendment announces and acknowledges in a single sentence that (1) the individual, and not the State, is

1

the source and basis of our social compact and that sovereignty now resides and has always resided in the individual; (2) that our Government exists through the surrender by the individual of a portion of his naturally endowed and inherent rights; (3) that everyone of the people of the United States owns a residue of individual rights and liberties which have never been, and which are never to be surrendered to the State, but which are still to be recognized, protected and secured; and (4) that individual liberty and rights are inherent, and that such rights are not derived from the Constitution, but belong to the individual by natural endowment.

Up to this date no real purpose for the Ninth Amendment has been found. In our entire legal and legislative history it has never been used as the basis for the announcement, protection, or vindication of any human right or inherent liberty. Indeed, as we shall later see, it has been invoked by litigants as a defense of human rights only ten times in our entire jurisprudence, and on each occasion our courts have held that it was inapplicable. The unenumerated rights are yet to be discovered and defined. Since the time it became a part of the Constitution it has rested in a state of meaningless desuetude. The value of this amendment has been lost through the failure of our courts, historians and constitutional writers to recognize that it is a broad declaration of right, and was not intended solely as a restrictive inhibition against the Federal Government.

The real force and effect of the Ninth Amendment has been most unfortunately lost through a series of decisions by our Courts which have placed it in the same category and classification as the first eight amendments in the Bill of Rights. The first eight amendments were intended as restrictions upon the Federal Government, and our Courts have fallen into error, when discussing the Bill of Rights, in holding that "the first ten articles of amendment were not intended to limit the powers of State Government in respect to their own people, but to operate on the National Government alone." This language should have been applicable only, to the first eight amendments to the Constitution, because there is a great distinction between the meaning of the first eight amendments and the meaning of the Ninth Amendment. This distinction has been later recognized by our Courts.

We have approached the study of this amendment in a spirit of research, endeavoring to find whether it was intended to have a useful meaning. It may be that this discussion and research will be considered by some as being purely academic. We do not believe so.

If there are unenumerated inherent human rights with which individuals are naturally endowed, then it is highly important that any clause in our Constitution which recognizes such rights should be brought to light in its real meaning. The recognition of such rights in the Constitution should constitute a guarantee of the protection of such rights.

Nevertheless, we shall trace the origin and history of the Ninth Amendment, and try to establish the truth as to its meaning and intent. If the truth as to its meaning and intent is once established, we believe that this research will be fully justified. The practical value and utility of this discovery must be left for future determination.

CHAPTER 2

OUTLINE OF THIS DISCUSSION

We propose in this discussion of the Ninth Amendment, to establish seven general propositions, which we now enumerate.

(1) The Ninth Amendment to the Constitution is a basic statement of the inherent natural rights of the individual. It is a recognition and re-statement that individuals are endowed by their Creator with certain natural and inalienable rights. As such it is a statement of the essence of the aspirations of a democratic form of government. It is the declaration and recognition of individualism, which is the cardinal virtue of democracy, and is nowhere else to be found in the Constitution.

(2) Its great meaning has never been recognized and construed. It has never been treated as a great declaration of individual liberty, but has been robbed of its meaning through an erroneous classification as a restriction upon the power of the Federal Government, whereas it is not a restriction at all, but is a fundamental *declaration* of human rights.

(3) It represents a growing and living philosophy, and should stand as a protection of individual human rights as such rights are now known, and also as such rights shall later appear.

(4) This declaration of unenumerated human rights implies that there is an obligation on the part of the government to protect such rights.

(5) Since the Constitution has recognized unenumerated natural rights, or rights of natural endowment, then such rights inhere in the individual and should be protected from infringement against all persons and all departments of government; such rights are not inherent or natural rights, if they are not universally recognized and protected. An inherent human right is good anywhere, anytime, any place, and against any person or department of government who would seek to destroy such a right.

(6) If, however, this amendment should be classified only as a restrictive clause against the Federal Government, it is a recognition and declaration of inherent human rights and liberties. There is nothing in the amendment, nor in the Constitution that would prevent the protection of individual rights and liberties, and if the Ninth Amendment should be

narrowly construed as a restriction upon the power of the Federal Government, it only prevents the Government of the United States from destroying such inherent and natural rights, and this declaration would authorize appropriate action upon the part of the Government of the United States for the protection of such rights.

(7) The Ninth Amendment was intended as a covenant between our Government and the individual and it was intended that the unenumerated inherent rights, which were to be protected by the Ninth Amendment, were the personal rights and liberties of the individual rather than public or collective rights which are protected under the General Welfare Clause of the Constitution.

We shall later discuss each of these topics in detail. Before doing so, however, we will trace the historic background of the Ninth Amendment, and the treatment that has been accorded this amendment by our Federal and State Courts.

CHAPTER 3

THE LEGISLATIVE HISTORY OF THE NINTH AMENDMENT

In order to understand the legislative birth of the Ninth Amendment, it is necessary to study and understand the historic background of the first ten Amendments to the Constitution which, many years after their adoption, came to be known as the Bill of Rights.

The suggestion of a Bill of Rights first arose in the Constitutional Convention.

In the closing days of the Convention, Mr. Gorham of Massachusetts remarked that he wished that the plan of Government which had been prepared for submission, had been prefaced with a Bill of Rights. He further stated that if a motion to that effect were made, he would second the motion, and that he felt that it would give great quiet to the people. He suggested that with the aid of the Declaration of Rights of the several States, which were then in existence, in the Constitutions of the States, a Bill of Rights might be prepared in a few hours. Mr. Gerry of Massachusetts thereupon immediately moved that a committee be appointed to prepare a Bill of Rights, and Colonel Mason of Virginia seconded the motion. Mr. Sherman of Connecticut spoke against the necessity or propriety of a Bill of Rights, and after some discussion the vote on the appointment of a committee to prepare a Bill of Rights was put to the Convention. The motion, however, lost without the support of a single State. Ten States voted "no", one State was absent, but no State voted for the Amendment. The proposal was later introduced into the discussions and deliberations of the Convention on several other occasions, but never again came to a vote.

Probably the principal reason for the omission of the Bill of Rights, in the original draft of the Constitution, was due to the fact that the Government of the United States of America was conceived solely as a Government of delegated powers, and nothing more. Freedom of the individual and personal lib-

6

erty were considered a part of the natural law, and were considered so basic and established, that there was no necessity of even mentioning them in the Constitution. As stated in the Declaration of Independence, these rights were deemed to be "self-evident", taken for granted, and unquestioned, while the Constitution was nothing more than a body of specific powers which had been surrendered and yielded by individuals in the interest of the formation of a general Government. We bear in mind that the framers of the Constitution, as well as the signers of the Declaration of Independence, were Englishmen, although colonial Englishmen, by birth, and were greatly influenced by the English constitutional system of Government, in which the basic liberties and freedoms of individuals were recognized even though all of them were not contained in any document which is found in the written part of the British Constitution. The English tradition undoubtedly influenced the framers of the Constitution to believe that basic, natural and fundamental individual rights were protected whether enumerated specifically in the Constitution or not.

The general attitude of the Convention is probably best expressed in a letter from George Washington to Lafayette written from Mount Vernon on April 28, 1788, as follows:

"For example: there was not a member of the convention, I believe, who had the least objection to what is contended for by the Advocates of a Bill of Rights and Tryal by Jury. The first, where the people evidently retained everything which they did not in express terms give up, was considered nugatory as you will find to have been more fully explained by Mr. Wilson and others:— And as to the second, it was only the difficulty of establishing a mode which should not interfere with the fixed modes of any of the States, that induced the Convention to leave it, as a matter of future adjustment."

Max Farrand, in his incomparable work "The Proceedings of the Constitutional Convention", sets out the debates in the Constitutional Convention with respect to the inclusion of a Bill of Rights in the original draft of the Constitution. It is impossible to read these debates without coming to the certain conclusion that a Bill of Rights was not included because these rights were so inherent and fundamental that they need no constitutional recognition. These rights pre-dated the Constitution and the members of the Constitutional Convention did not have the least thought of surrendering these rights to either the State or the Federal Governments. Members of the Constitutional Convention who signed the Constitution had already signed the Declaration of Independence, in which they had declared that their Creator was the source of the "unalienable rights". They had no intention of surrendering these rights in the interest of forming a government. In a word, their inherent rights existed before either State or Federal Constitutions, and were intended to exist independent of such constitutions, subject only to the degree in which such rights were surrendered for regulation in forming a more perfect union.

At the final signing of the Constitution on September 17, 1787, we find that Gerry, Randolph, and Colonel Mason all refused to subscribe their names to the document, and one of the principal reasons assigned by each of them was that the Constitution did not carry any Bill of Rights or guarantee of certain human freedoms which they considered essential.

Consequently, when the Constitution came up for ratification by the Convention of the several states, it ran into some hard sailing, particularly in the States of Virginia, Massachusetts, New York, Maryland, and North Carolina. The State of Virginia did not ratify until the essential nine states for the formation of the government had ratified. Virginia was the tenth State. Neither North Carolina nor the State of Rhode Island ratified the Constitution of the United States, until after Congress had submitted the twelve proposed Amendments to the Constitution to the several states for ratification.

The conventions of Virginia, Massachusetts, Maryland, New York, and North Carolina each had large opposition groups, and this opposition was based principally upon the fact that the Constitution contained no Bill of Rights, such as the declarations contained in several of the constitutions of the various States. However, not all of the State constitutions did actually contain such a Declaration or Bill of Rights.

At that time the constitutions of the States of New York, New Jersey, Virginia, South Carolina, and Georgia had no bills of rights, because no one at that time thought bills of rights necessary to secure liberty.

However, as a result of this opposition, and particularly in the State of Virginia, which was then the largest and most important State, and without whose ratification the new Government and Constitution would in all probability have been a failure, there was an implied, if not an express agreement, on the part of the leaders of the proponents of the Constitution, that if the Constitution should be ratified immediately, the Federalist Party, or the party which was the proponent of the Constitution, would, at the first session of Congress, propose appropriate amendments to the Constitution which would meet the objections of the opposing groups. This gentlemen's agreement, no doubt, greatly influenced the ratification of the Constitution by the Virginia Convention. The Virginia Convention therefore proposed several amendments, and the Conventions of several of the other States also proposed amendments. Not all of these amendments, however, related to the Bill of Rights, but covered other unrelated subject matter.

In an effort to reassure the people that their personal liberties were not endangered through the omission of a Bill of Rights in the Constitution, Alexander Hamilton in The Federalist made the following comment:

"I go further, and affirm that the bills of rights, in the sense and to the extent in which they are contended for, are not only unnecessary in the proposed Constitution, but would even be dangerous. They would contain various exceptions to powers not granted; and, on this very account, would afford a colorable pretext to claim more than were granted. For why declare that things shall not be done which there is no power to do? Why, for instance, should it be said that liberty of the press shall not be restrained, when no power is given by which restrictions may be imposed? I will not contend that such a provision would confer a regulating power; but it is evident that it would furnish, to men disposed to usurp, a plausible pretense for claiming that power."

This reasoning on the part of Alexander Hamilton did not reassure the opposition, nor did it allay the fears of those who were proponents of a Bill of Rights. On the other hand, it seemed to excite their suspicions to a greater degree, and to reinforce their determination. This statement on the part of Hamilton was, in all probability, the actual cause of the insertion of the Ninth Amendment in the Constitution of the United States. It was this statement by Hamilton which caused

Madison to include within his proposals of amendments, the clause which when rewritten ultimately became the Ninth Amendment. Madison at the time of the introduction of his resolution containing the proposals of amendment assigned this very reason himself. In passing, however, we might say that Alexander Hamilton's prophesy may have already come true. If we do not recognize the existence of the "unenumerated" rights, then we must look solely to the Constitution as the source of human rights and liberties, and can only expect the protection of those specifically enumerated therein. Alexander Hamilton may have been right after all. We may, at this time, look to the Constitution and to the Fourteenth Amendment alone as the source and protection of natural and human rights. Madison, in a statesmanlike manner attempted to assure the people of their enumerated rights as requested, but at the same time heeded the warning of Hamilton by proposing the amendment which later became the Ninth Amendment.

Our view with respect to this matter is shared by Story who makes the following comment:

"This clause was manifestly introduced to prevent any perverse or ingenious misapprehension of the well known maxim, that an affirmation in particular cases implies a negation in all others; and a converso, that a negation in particular cases implies an affirmation in all others. The maxim, rightly understood, is perfectly sound and safe; but it has often been strangely forced from its natural meaning into the support of the most dangerous political heresies. The amendment was undoubtedly suggested by the reasoning of 'The Federalist' on the subject of a general Bill of Rights."

According to the Journals of the House of Representatives and the Senate, the First Congress of the United States had a quorum for the first time on Wednesday, April 6, 1789, and got down to business on that date.

Madison did not wait long in fulfilling his agreement with respect to the Bill of Rights, and accordingly on May 4, 1789, gave notice that he intended to bring on for discussion the subject of amendments to the Constitution on the fourth Monday in May thereafter. This announcement was made in compliance with the rules of the House of Representatives.

The House of Representatives did not take up the business on the fourth Monday in May, and as a result Madison was required to wait until the 8th day of June, 1789, before he could get the business before Congress. On June 8, Madison stated that he was "in honor and duty bound" to bring before Congress the matter of the amendments to the Constitution. He made a motion that the House of Representatives resolve itself into a committee of the whole for the purpose of giving consideration to the proposals of amendments. The business of the organization of the new Government was so pressing at that time, that Madison found little or no support for the introduction and discussion of the business at that particular time. In fact, only one of his colleagues from Virginia supported him, while nine other members of Congress, one after another, Federalists and anti-Federalists alike objected and spoke against the motion.

The committee of the whole was a method resorted to at that time for the discussion of matters that justly deserved and commanded the consideration of every member of the House of Representatives, and which permitted a free discussion of the subject in an informal manner, without the usual parliamentary formalities and procedure. Madison realized that he could not obtain the consideration of the House of Representatives as a committee of the whole. He therefore withdrew his motion for a committee of the whole, and stated that he would be content to have his proposals considered by a select committee, because he would not in that manner delay the other important business pending before Congress. While making this motion for a select committee, Madison then "took the bull by the horns" and proceeded then and there to state his proposals and discuss the same.

Madison's amendments were grouped into nine proposals. These proposals will be found in the reprint of Gales and Seaton's Annals of Congress on page 93 of this volume.

In his opening remarks in explanation of the proposed amendments, Madison stated that "the first of these amendments relates to what may be called a Bill of Rights." Madison had attempted to take all of the proposals of amendments, proposed by the ratification conventions of the various states, and combine those which he considered appropriate into one resolution to be submitted to the Congress. It is noteworthy that his proposals did not exclusively relate to the Bill of Rights, but included several other matters of amendment which related to other parts of the Constitution.

It is also important to note that Madison did not intend that the amendments would appear as an appendage to the Constitution, but would be interwoven into the Constitution in the Articles and Sections as set out in the proposals. We emphasize this fact because it shows that the last clause of the fourth proposal, which later became the Ninth Amendment, was not intended by Madison at the time of its introduction as being solely an integral part of the Bill of Rights, but was intended by him to be inserted into the body of the Constitution and have general application to the Constitution as a whole. We bear in mind that there were numerous other specific individual rights protected in the main body of the Constitution which were not enumerated in the first eight amendments included in the Bill of Rights. Madison proposed to insert his fourth proposal into the Constitution under Article 1, Section 9, between the provisions relating to a "Bill of Attainder", and the clause with respect to a "capitation or other direct tax". Madison's conception of a Bill of Rights was not a separate document or an appendage to the Constitution, but he believed that the particular rights that were named in his proposals should merely be included in the Constitution, and enumerated along with other individual rights that had already been included in the Constitution and protected thereby. There can be no mistake with respect to this intention in so far as the Ninth Amendment is concerned, as we can see from the exact wording of the Ninth clause of his fourth proposal, which is the first draft of the Ninth Amendment to the Constitution of the United States; this proposal was as follows:

"The exceptions here or elsewhere in the Constitution, made in favor of particular rights, shall not be so construed as to diminish the just importance of other rights retained by the people, or as to enlarge the powers delegated by the Constitution; but either as actual limitations of such powers, or as inserted merely for greater caution." (Gales and Seaton's "Annals of Congress," page 93 herein).

Madison's reason for the introduction of this clause into the proposed amendments was stated on June 8, 1789 in his explanation of his proposals in the following language:

"It has been objected also against a bill of rights, that, by enumerating particular exceptions to the grant of power, it would disparage those rights which were not placed in that enumeration; and it might follow, by implication, that those rights which were not signaled out, were intended to be assigned into the hands of the General Government, and were consequently insecure. This is one of the most plausible arguments I have ever heard urged against the admission of a bill of rights into this system; but, I conceive, that it may be guarded against, I have attempted it, as gentlemen may see by turning to the last clause of the fourth resolution." (Gales and Seaton's "Annals of Congress," page 93 herein).

According to most historians, this clause was inserted out of an abundance of caution. And this is evident from the last clause in the first draft of the resolution "or as inserted merely for greater caution." This clause was undoubtedly used to clarify the "just importance of other rights retained by the people."

The language "the exceptions *here or elsewhere* in the Constitution" definitely demonstrates that the clause was intended as a general declaration of human rights, and that this clause was not to be narrowly limited to the specific rights named in his proposed amendments, but related to any other rights enumerated or unenumerated in the Constitution. In other words, it was his intention that the clause would be a general clause relating to the entire Constitution, and not a specific clause relating only to the proposed amendments.

The foregoing considerations are important when it comes to a final determination as to whether or not the Ninth Amendment shall be construed narrowly as a limitation upon the powers of the Federal Government, and inapplicable to the governments of the various States, or whether it should be construed, not as a limitation at all, but as a great declaration of natural and endowed human liberty which no government, either State or Federal, can destroy. The language of Madison, who was the father of the Ninth Amendment, shows conclusively in the original draft that he did not intend this narrow limitation upon his proposals.

After Madison had finished the discussion of his proposals, upon motion of John Lawrence of New York, his report was referred to a committee of the whole on the State of the Union instead of giving the matter consideration through a select committee.

Other business engaged the session of Congress until Tuesday, July 21st, when Madison moved that the House resolve itself into a committee of the whole as previously agreed in order to consider his proposals of amendments. On this date the House voted to discharge the committee as a whole, and the proposals of amendments offered by Madison, and all amendments suggested by State Conventions were referred to a select committee consisting of a member from each State, with instructions to give all of the proposed amendments consideration, and to report to the House. Of the eleven members appointed, Madison was fortunate to have associated with him Baldwin, Sherman and Clymer, who were all original signers of the Constitution, and were sympathetic towards Madison's point of view. The special committee did not deliberate long, because one week later, on July 28th, the committee made its report to the House of Representatives, but the House ordered that the report be laid on the table.

In the eighth clause of the fourth proposal in the Special Committee's report we find for the first time the exact language of the Ninth Amendment to the Constitution as follows:

"The enumeration in the Constitution of certain rights shall not be construed to deny or disparage others retained by the people." (Gales and Seaton's "Annals of Congress", page 93 herein).

It is important to observe that the exact language was never changed thereafter by either the House of Representatives or the Senate. It is further most important to observe that at the time the report of the Special Committee was prepared and submitted to the House of Representatives for approval it was intended, and the House of Representatives had so voted, that the clause was to be incorporated in the body of the Constitution and not as an appendage, and undoubtedly for this reason the committee omitted the language "here or elsewhere". The omission of this language from the final draft of the Ninth Amendment, as prepared by the First Special

Committee, has caused this amendment to be interpreted far differently from the interpretation originally intended. There was no need to insert the words "here or elsewhere" if the clause was intended to be inserted in the body of the Constitution itself. The meaning of the Amendment was therefore obscured when, as we shall later see, the House of Representatives reversed itself and added the amendments as an appendage to the Constitution. The committee on style did not then reinsert the words "here or elsewhere", and the meaning of the final draft as an appendage, without the inclusion of these words, became less obvious. The omission of these words in the final draft partly caused the ultimate error in the narrow construction and interpretation of the amendment as not relating to the State governments but solely as a restriction upon the Federal Government.

We also bear in mind that the twelve proposed amendments to the Constitution were not called the "Bill of Rights" at that time, and the business before Congress was not merely the preparation of a Bill of Rights but the preparation of "Amendments to the Constitution". As we shall later see in the first relevant opinion by the Supreme Court, the first ten amendments were not called the Bill of Rights but were referred to as "Articles of Amendment." Neither the Constitution nor the resolution which proposed the amendments contain any time limit in which the necessary three fourths of the States should adopt the same. Therefore, when the Seventh Amendment relating to jury trial was discussed by the Supreme Court, it was referred to as the Ninth Article of Amendment because at that time it was the ninth of the twelve amendments proposed. This thought further establishes that the eleventh proposed amendment which later became the Ninth Amendment was not dependent upon or did it relate exclusively to the first eight amendments. The twelve proposals for amendment did not relate exclusively to a Bill of Rights, and this is a strong argument that the Ninth Amendment was just an amendment to the Constitution as were the first, second, and twelfth proposed amendments which were independent of the third to the tenth, inclusive, of the original proposals.

The report was next given consideration on August 13, 1789 when Richard Bland Lee of Virginia, a colleague of

Madison, moved that the House resolve itself into a committee of the whole for the purpose of discussing the amendments. After debate the House did resolve itself into a committee of the whole, and Mr. Elias Boudinot of New Jersey was named chairman.

The question arose as to whether the proposed amendments would be blended into and interwoven into the main body of the Constitution, or would appear as an appendage to it. Roger Sherman of Connecticut led the fight against weaving the amendments into the body of the Constitution. However, Sherman's motion was voted down at this time only to be adopted at a later session of the House of Representatives.

The House of Representatives, as a committee of the whole, then proceeded to a discussion of all of the proposals, and this discussion carried on through the 18th day of August. The Committee of the whole reported to the House of Representatives on the 19th day of August, and the House of Representatives on August 19th reversed its previous vote, and by a two-thirds majority adopted a resolution of Sherman that the said amendments would be added to the Constitution by way of a supplement.

Thereafter, on August 21st, after further discussion and debate, the amendments with an introductory resolution, were referred to a committee of Messrs. Benson, Sherman, and Sedgwick, who were directed to arrange the said amendments and make report thereof. This committee evidently acted as a committee on style. The Ninth Amendment was the fifteenth of seventeen proposals sent to the Senate. (Appendix I hereto.)

We find that the only discussion had with respect to the Ninth Amendment was had in the House of Representatives on August 17, 1789, when the House as a committee of the whole considered the report of the special committee.

The particular clause which was later to become the Ninth Amendment was at that time the eighth clause of the fourth proposition in the special committee's report and the discussion was as follows:

"The eighth clause of the fourth proposition was taken up, which was 'The enumeration in the Constitution of certain rights shall not be construed to deny or disparage others retained by the people.'

"Mr. Gerry said, it ought to be 'deny or impair', for the word 'Disparage' was not of plain import; he therefore moved to make that alteration, but not being seconded, the question was taken on the clause, and it passed in the affirmative."

When the report of the committee of three to arrange the amendments for submission to the Senate was submitted to the House of Representatives on August 24, 1789, seventeen proposals, including the fifteenth proposal in said report, (the Ninth Amendment), were approved and sent along to the Senate for approval with a proper resolution prefixed to the same.   (Appendix I hereto).

The reports with respect to the treatment which the proposals of amendment received in the Senate are very meager. This is because the legislative and the executive sittings of the Senate were held behind closed doors until the Second Session of the Third Congress. However, the text of the Ninth Amendment was unchanged by the Senate.

When the Senate received the seventeen proposals of amendments from the House of Representatives, some of them were eliminated and some were combined, and the Senate returned twenty-six proposals to the House for consideration. The House of Representatives rejected some of those that were proposed by the Senate, but it is sufficient to say for the purposes of this discussion, that the final draft of twelve proposed amendments was approved by the House of Representatives on September 25, 1789.

However, the Senate added a preamble to the resolutions submitting the twelve proposed amendments to the State Legislatures. This preamble was as follows:

"The conventions of a number of the States having, at the time of their adopting the constitution, expressed a desire, in order to prevent misconstruction or abuse of its powers, that further *declaratory* and restrictive clauses should be added; and as extending the ground of public confidence in the government will best insure the beneficent ends of its institution:

"Resolved, by the Senate and House of Representatives, etc." (Emphasis ours).

The important language of this preamble are the words "further declaratory and restrictive clauses." This language clearly shows that the Senate of the United States, and the

House of Representatives in concurring in this preamble, fully realize and understood that at least a part of the twelve proposed amendments were not restrictive provisions, but were declaratory provisions. This is the part which we want to forcibly drive home. The present Ninth and Tenth Amendments to the Constitution, which were the Eleventh and Twelfth proposed amendments, were not considered in the same light as proposals three to ten, inclusive, and were not considered as restrictive clauses, but on the other hand were regarded as declarations of principles.

The twelve proposed amendments that were ultimately submitted to the several states and to the legislatures of Rhode Island and North Carolina are found as Appendix II hereto on page 89.

As we know, the first and the second proposed amendments were never ratified by the legislatures of three-fourths of the States of the Union, and consequently, never became a part of the Constitution.

Thus, we find that the eleventh proposed amendment became the Ninth Amendment to the Constitution of the United States.

As we shall see, a certain degree of confusion has been caused in the interpretation of the Ninth Amendment due to the fact that the Seventh Amendment (which was originally submitted as the ninth proposal) has through error been referred to in an opinion by the Supreme Court of the United States of America as the Ninth Amendment.

Although we have gone a considerable length to outline the history of the Ninth Amendment as a part of the Bill of Rights; nevertheless, the history of the Ninth Amendment is comparatively simple. It was first proposed in the last paragraph of Madison's fourth article of proposals. It was then changed by the special committee to the identical language in which it now appears. It passed the House and the Senate with little or no debate. It is truly the work of Madison, and for this reason his language with respect to the amendment, and his explanation of the same, should be controlling.

CHAPTER 4

OBVIOUS MEANING OF THE NINTH AMENDMENT

There should really be little or no doubt with respect to the intended meaning of the Ninth Amendment, because from its language, its purpose and intent is obvious.

The Ninth Amendment to the Constitution is a basic statement of the inherent natural rights of the individual. On its face this amendment states that there are certain unenumerated rights that are retained by the people. It is a mere assertion that while certain enumerated rights have been expressly protected by the Constitution, the reservation in the Constitution should not be taken to deny or disparage any unenumerated right which was not so apparently protected. Nothing could be clearer than this statement. It is a declaration and recognition of individualism and inherent right, and such a declaration is nowhere else to be found in the Constitution. Its absence elsewhere in the Constitution accounts for its very presence in this Amendment.

The concept of individual sovereignty, and supremacy in the realm of natural and inherent rights and liberties was not a creature of the Constitution of the United States. This basic concept of individual liberty was absolute in the theory of American Government from the very beginning of American Government. This theory was carried over from the English Constitution, and as we have remarked before, the framers of the Constitution and the signers of the Declaration of Independence were Englishmen by blood, tradition, and citizenship until the signing of the Declaration of Independence. Therefore, the framers of the Constitution and the Bill of Rights carried with them into their work the English concept of individual liberties, as being inherent in the individual irrespective of the form of government. The last thought in their minds was that the Constitution would ever be construed as a grant to the individual of inherent rights and liberties. Their theory of the Constitution was that it was only a body of powers which were granted to the government, and nothing more than that.

It might be said that the theory of individual inherent rights is a part of our unwritten Constitution, in the same manner in which portions of the unwritten English Constitution are recognized and enforced. But we feel that it is much more than the unwritten Constitution; the individual inherent rights and liberties antedate and are above constitutions and may be called pre-constitutional rights.

This idea has been aptly expressed in 16 C. J. S. page 578, paragraph 199, as follows:

"The Constitutions are not the sources of our personal rights. Our theory of government is that the people, in full possession of inherent, inalienable rights, have formed the government in order to protect these rights, and have incorporated them into the organic law as a shield against unwarrantable interference by any department of governments."

John Adams, the second great President of the United States, assured the people as follows:

"You have rights antecedent to all earthly governments; rights that cannot be repealed or restrained by human laws; rights derived from the Great Legislator of the Universe."

In Gow vs. Bingham, 107 N.Y.S. 1011 (Supreme Court of New York), the court held that we possess certain rights which have their origin as natural rights independent of any express provision of law, and that constitutional provisions are not the sources of these rights. The right "to be let alone" was one of the rights sustained by the court.

In a relatively recent decision of the Supreme Court of Texas (Spann vs. City of Dallas, 111 Texas 350, 212 S. W. 513) this same confidence in natural rights is expressed:

"To secure their property was one of the great ends for which men entered into society. The right to acquire and own property, and to deal with it and use it as the owner chooses, so long as the use harms nobody, is a natural right. It does not owe its origin to constitutions. It existed before them. It is a part of the citizen's natural liberty—an expression of his freedom, guaranteed as inviolate by every American Bill of Rights."

In City of Pineville vs. Marshall, 299 S. W. 1072, 222 Ky. 4, by the Court of Appeals of Kentucky, the court held that:

"While the Bill of Rights declares and secures certain inherent rights, it does not create them, nor does it license an individual to ignore and defy the correlative rights of other individuals or of society."

In the City of Dallas vs. Mitchell, 245 S. W. 944 (error refused, which gives this case Supreme Court authority in the State of Texas), we find the modern restatement of the faith of our forefathers:

"The rights of the individual are not derived from the governmental agencies, either municipal, state or federal, or even from the Constitution. They exist inherently in every man, by endowment of the Creator, and are merely reaffirmed in the Constitution, and restricted only to the extent that they have been voluntarily surrendered by the citizenship to the agencies of government. The people's rights are not derived from the government, but the government's authority comes from the people. The Constitution but states again these rights already existing, and when legislative encroachment by the nation, state, or municipality invade these original and permanent rights, it is the duty of the courts to so declare, and to afford the necessary relief. The fewer restrictions that surround the individual liberties of the citizen, except those for the preservation of the public health, safety, and morals, the more contented the people and the more successful the democracy."

As great as is our reverence, gratitude, and respect for the Constitution of the United States, the undoubted and fundamental belief of the people of the United States in the security of their individual liberties existed long before the Constitution of the United States was ever thought of. The doctrine of individual liberty was championed in the great liberty documents which preceded the Constitution by many years. The Virginia Resolutions, the various declarations adopted by the other colonies, and the addresses and orations of patriots like Patrick Henry proved without doubt their pre-constitutional belief in individual rights.

This philosophy of government was summarized in the preamble to the Declaration of Independence:

"When, in the course of human events, it becomes necessary for one people to dissolve the political bonds which have connected them with another, and to assume among the powers of the earth the separate and equal station *to which the laws of nature and of nature's God entitle them,* a decent respect to the opinions of mankind requires that they should declare the causes which impel them to the separation.

"We hold these truths to be self-evident: That all men are created equal; that they are endowed by their Creator with certain unalienable rights; that *among these* are life, liberty, and the pursuit of happiness". (Emphasis added).

This statement closely followed the Virginia Bill of Rights adopted by the convention of delegates on June 12, 1776. Article 1 of that document states:

"That all Men are by Nature equally free and independent, and have certain inherent Rights, of which, when they enter into a State of Society, they cannot, by any Compact, deprive or divest their Posterity; namely, the Enjoyment of Life and Liberty, with the Means of acquiring and possessing Property, and pursuing and obtaining Happiness and Safety."

We particularly note that the Declaration of Independence was careful to state that liberties and human rights were not man made. The source of human liberty was not government. The source of individual liberty as stated by the Declaration of Independence is the "Creator" of men. The Declaration of Independence is not only a philosophic document but it is also a legal document. May the day soon come when our courts, in the vindication of individual liberties, will cite the Declaration of Independence as legal authority for the doctrine that individual liberty is natural and inherent, instead of attempting to show that these rights stem from the Constitution of the United States, which was never intended to be anything other than the protector of these rights, and not the creator of them.

The Declaration of Independence was a forerunner of the Ninth Amendment. Note how carefully the words "among these" are used in the enumeration of any human rights.

The only published treatise or legal discussion relating to the Ninth Amendment is found in a brilliant article by the Honorable Knowlton H. Kelsey in Volume 11, No. 4, page 309, of the Indiana Law Journal (1936), in which he states that the colonists waged war, "not for philosophic perfection of any utilitarian doctrine of civil rights, but for the rights of Englishmen."

Then we see that the Ninth Amendment is nothing new in principle, but is merely a restatement of the old.

Basically a right as referred to in the Ninth Amendment is not a right at all unless it is recognized any time, any place, and anywhere.

The real meaning and substance of the Ninth Amendment to the Constitution of the United States has been lost through an erroneous classification of this Amendment in the earlier decisions by the Supreme Court of the United States, as a limitation upon the powers of the Federal Government, and not upon the States.

Typical of these decisions is Fox vs. The State of Ohio, 12 L. Ed. 213, 5 How. 410, in which the Court stated the following:

"The prohibition alluded to as contained in the amendments to the Constitution, as well as others with which it is associated in those articles, were not designed as limits upon the State governments in reference to their own citizens. They are exclusively restrictions upon federal power, intended to prevent interference with the rights of the States, and of their citizens. Such has been the interpretation given to those amendments by this court, in the case of Barron v. The Mayor and City Council of Baltimore (7 Peters 243)."

In sweeping declarations of this type, our Courts have failed to recognize a distinction between the first eight amendments included in the Bill of Rights, and the Ninth Amendment. It is quite true that the first eight amendments to the Constitution were intended as restrictions upon the powers of the Federal Government, arising out of a distrust of the several States of a strong centralized and Federal Government. A careful analysis of the Ninth Amendment will reveal that the Ninth Amendment cannot be classified as a restrictive clause at all, because it is on the contrary a great declaration of the rights of natural endowment.

Irrespective of such decisions as Fox v. Ohio, supra, and the general language contained therein with respect to a general grouping of the first ten amendments to the Constitution as restrictive inhibitions upon the National Government, there has been no specific decision by any Court in the United States that forecloses the utility of further research and study as to the real intent and meaning of this amendment. The rule of stare decisis has not closed the door to the results of research, or to the proper construction of this amendment.

It is not strange that it has never been used as the basis for the vindication of any basic human liberty, because under the cloud of its classification as a restrictive clause, it can have no reasonable meaning whatsoever. Under such construction, this amendment could only mean that "the Federal Government is restricted from denying or disparaging any unenumerated human rights, but the power to deny and disparage such rights are reserved to the States."

It is no criticism of the Supreme Court of the United States that the Ninth Amendment has not been construed. The question has simply never been presented to that Court for review. As we shall later see, the Supreme Court of the United States has in its decisions recognized a difference between the first eight amendments and the Ninth.

The failure to discover the real meaning of the Ninth Amendment is probably due to a mechanical error or misstatement in the early case of Lessee of Livingston vs. Moore et al, 7 Peters 469, 8 Law Ed. 751 (781). In that case, the Constitutional question that was before the Court was the right of trial by jury. In the decision of this case, the Court stated that the legislative acts under consideration were charged with being contrary to the Ninth Article of the amendments of the Constitution of the United States. The Supreme Court overruled this contention holding that it was then settled law "that those amendments do not extend to the States." A careful study of this decision reveals that the Ninth Amendment to the Constitution was not discussed either by counsel or by the Court. The question involved was solely the right of trial by jury, covered by the Seventh Amendment.

This view is best stated in Constitution of the United States of America revised and annotated (1938), page 711, which is the compilation and revision which was authorized by Senate Concurrent Resolution No. 35, adopted May 14, 1936. The volume was compiled in the Legislative Reference Service of the Library of Congress and published by the United States Printing Office. We quote the only annotation of this amendment contained in this volume as follows:

"This amendment is in terms referred to as a ground of the argument in Livingston v. Moore, 7 Pet. 469, 551 (1833), and the Court meets the argument with a general statement that 'the amendments of the Constitution' do not extend to the States. But the context shows clearly that the reference intended was the Seventh Amendment. The whole sentence involved is as follows: 'They (certain laws of Pennsylvania) are charged with being contrary to the ninth article of the amendments of the Constitution of the United States, and the sixth section of the Pennsylvania bill of rights, securing the trial by jury.' The argument of Mr. Ingersoll (p. 482) specifically makes the point to '* * * the Seventh Amendment of the Constitution of the United States'. The discrepancy is doubtless to be explained by the fact that numbers 1 and 2 of the 12 amendments proposed for adoption in 1789 were never ratified, and consequently number 9 became number 7 of the amendments adopted. A similar example of reference to an amendment by its number among the proposed amendments rather than among those adopted, may be seen in Re Burford, 3 Cr. 448, 451 (1806), where counsel referred to the 'Sixth Article' relating to issue of warrants, i.e., Amendment 4."

It might further be stated that there is no provision in the Constitution which sets a definite date for ratification of amendments which are submitted to the several States. There was no such practice at that time as now prevails of fixing a limit of seven years, or some other definite period in which the States shall ratify a proposed constitutional amendment. Therefore, when the case of Livingston v. Moore was decided, the first and second proposed amendments were technically still pending for ratification by the States, since there was no deadline for ratification. The amendments at that time were therefore referred to only as "amendments", and had not at that time been by accepted usage called the "Bill of Rights". This explains why the Court was in all probability referring to the Seventh Amendment to the Constitution, numbered in accordance with their adoption by the States, while referring to it in their opinion as the ninth article of amendment, or ninth proposal. This matter has been detailed in order that it may definitely be established that the case of Livingston v. Moore is not to be considered or construed as a decision by the Supreme Court of the United States definitely and finally classifying the Ninth Amendment solely as a restriction upon the Federal Government similar to the classification of the first eight amendments to the Constitution. However, this decision has been sufficient to creat doubt and confusion. Just how much influence this decision has had upon the subsequent decisions of the Supreme Court in grouping all of the Ten Amendments together in this respect is not known. However, it is certain that when broad statements with respect to the restrictive nature of the first Ten Amendments appear in the decisions of the Supreme Court of the United States, the case of Livingston v. Moore has been usually cited as authority.

We hope that some day our courts, when called upon to do so, in the vindication of one of the unenumerated rights, will find or rediscover the Ninth Amendment with the full force of its meaning.

It is now covered with the "dust of antique time", but it is hoped that the dust may be swept away and the cloud removed, and that the "mountainous error" has not been piled so high that "truth cannot o'er peer it."

We will ultimately find that this amendment is a succinct expression of the inherent dignity and liberty of the individual and a recognition of the soul of mankind, a belief in his spiritual nature, and an humble acknowledgment of the infinity of our Creator and our nature.

We do not find an expression of this philosophy in any other portion of the Constitution. "We, the people" is not an expression of individual rights as much as it is an expression of the collective sovereignty of the people in matters of government.

It is not found in the due process clauses, because the rights protected under due process are not protected because such rights are natural rights, but because they are expressly protected by the Constitution.

How unfortunate it is that with this fundamental expression in our Constitution and in the Declaration of Independence, no occasion has ever been found for any court in the United States to ever utilize the Ninth Amendment or the Declaration of Independence as the basis for the vindication of natural and inherent liberty. Is there such a thing, or do our rights arise out of the Constitution?

CHAPTER 5

JUDICIAL CONSTRUCTION OF THE NINTH AMENDMENT

There has been no direct judicial construction of the Ninth Amendment by the Supreme Court of the United States of America. There are very few cases in the inferior courts in which any attempt has been made to use the Ninth Amendment as the basis for the assertion of a right, but in each of these cases it has been held that this amendment was not applicable.

Beginning with Barron vs. Baltimore, 7 Peters 243, 8 L. Ed. 672, there has been a long line of cases holding that the first ten amendments to the Constitution were exclusively restricttions upon the Federal Government. These cases generally state that the prohibitions contained in the amendments were designed solely as limitations upon the Federal Government, and not as limitations upon State governments.

All of these cases are generalizations, and may be classed as dicta, because they do not specifically relate to the Ninth Amendment, but only to some specific prohibition contained in the first eight amendments. Among these decisions, there is no case which specifically discusses the Ninth Amendment. As we have heretofore pointed out, there is a mechanical error in Livingston vs. Moore, 7 Peters 469, 8 L. Ed. 751, and the court in this case was actually discussing the Seventh, and not the Ninth Amendment.

In the case of Eilenbecker vs. The District Court of Plymouth County, Iowa, 134 U. S. 31, 33 L. Ed. 801 (1890), in an opinion by Justice Miller, the Supreme Court of the United States for the first time announced that only the first *eight* articles of amendment to the Constitution had reference to the powers exercised by the Government of the United States and not to those of the States. No comment is made by the Court as to why this distinction was made, and none of the cases cited by Justice Miller in his opinion throw any light upon this new distinction which the Court made between the first eight amendments and Amendments Nine and Ten. This is very significant. With the background of many cases which made a general grouping of the ten amendments, it definitely showed that the Supreme Court realized that there was a distinction between the Ninth Amendment and the first eight amendments.

We quote from the opinion of Justice Miller in the case of Eilenbecker vs. District Court as follows:

"The first three of these assignments of error, as we have stated them, being the first and second and fourth of the assignments as numbered in the brief of the plaintiffs in error, are disposed of at once by the principle often decided by this court, *that the first eight articles* of the Amendments to the Constitution have reference to powers exercised by the government of the United States and not to those of the States." (Emphasis ours).

This new interpretation limiting the rule of prohibition to the first eight articles of the Amendments was announced thereafter in several other decisions, as follows:

> Brown vs. Walker, 161 U. S. 591, 40 L. Ed. 819 (824); in an opinion by Justice Brown, decided in 1895;
>
> Holden vs. Hardy, 169 U. S. 366, 18 S. Ct. 383, 42 L. Ed. 780 (787); in an opinion by Justice Brown, decided in 1897;
>
> Bolin vs. Nebraska, 176 U. S. 83, 44 L. Ed. 382 (384); in an opinion by Justice Brown, decided in 1899;
>
> Ohio vs. Dollison, 194 U. S. 445, 48 L. Ed. 1062 (1065); in an opinion by Justice McKenna, decided in 1903.

In Palko vs. Connecticut, 302 U. S. 319, 82 L. Ed. 288, Mr. Justice Cardoza, in rendering the majority opinion, stated that the original Bill of Rights consisted of amendments one to eight. (Actually, however, the Bill of Rights consists of amendments, one to nine.)

There is nothing specific in the foregoing cases. As in the older cases the Ninth Amendment is not directly discussed. *We see, however, that the United States Supreme Court is not bound to any construction of the Ninth Amendment which would limit its application to the Federal Government alone.* On the contrary, these decisions may be cited as authority for the distinction which this court makes between the first eight amendments and the Ninth Amendment. The departure from the prior dicta would indicate that the Supreme Court would apply a different rule to the Ninth Amendment.

We will now outline the cases in which the Ninth Amendment is directly discussed.

In United Public Workers v. Mitchell, 330 U. S. 75, 91 L. Ed. 745 (1770), the Hatch Act enacted in 1940, which declared unlawful, certain specified political activities of federal employees, was under attack. One of the grounds of attack was that it violated the Ninth Amendment to the Constitution of the United States. The statute construed was a Federal statute, and not a State statute. This decision construed the Ninth Amendment as it related to the Federal Government. This decision, however, does not define any unenumerated right but does recognize the doctrine of the fundamental inherent unenumerated rights. This decision merely held that the particular Federal statute under construction would not violate an inherent right. In an opinion by Justice Reed, the Supreme Court balanced the guaranty of inherent political freedom against the public interest in preventing the growth of political machines through government employees. The Court held that the power existed in the Federal Government to regulate the situation, and that the United States of America had not infringed upon the individual right of the plaintiff, and upheld the constitutionality of the Act.

In Whelchel v. McDonald, 176 F. 2d 260, affirmed by the Supreme Court, 340 U. S. 122, 95 L. Ed. 141, the contention was made that a court martial proceeding which was composed of officers only, denied an enlisted man the right of trial by jury by his peers. This position was overruled by the Circuit Court of Appeals for the Fifth Circuit, and the Supreme Court commented that courts martial have been composed of officers both before and after the adoption of the Constitution.

In Woods v. Miller, 333 U. S. 138, 92 L. Ed. 596, the contention was made in the briefs, but not discussed by the Court, that the power of the United States Government to regulate rents under the Rent Control Act was an infringement upon the power of the States. The Court overruled this contention without mentioning the same in its opinion.

In Tennessee Electric Power Company v. Tennessee Valley Authority, 306 U. S. 118, 83 L. Ed. 543, it was contended that sale of electricity by the Tennessee Valley Authority was a violation of the Ninth Amendment because it put the Federal authority in competition with privately owned interests, and deprived the people of the States of the right to acquire property and employ it in a lawful business. This contention was overruled by the Supreme Court.

In Aschwander vs. Tennessee Valley Authority, 80 L. Ed. 688, 56 S. Ct. 145, 297 U. S. 288, the Supreme Court of the United States in an opinion by Chief Justice Hughes, denied a contention that this amendment prohibited Congress from disposing of electric power as property of the United States. The court held that there was no inherent limitation which would render invalid the disposition of electric energy generated from water power.

In Clay vs. City of Eustis, 7 F. 2d 141 (D. C. Fla.), The District Court for the Southern District of Florida held that the extension of the boundaries of the City of Eustis, Florida, which subjected the annexed territory to the prior bonded indebtedness of the City was not violative of this amendment. It is interesting to note that this decision construed a State statute and no statement was made by the court that the Ninth Amendment was not applicable to State statutes.

In United States vs. Fujimoto, 102 F. Supp. 890, it was urged that the Smith Act, which provides punishment for one who advocates overthrow of the Government of the United States or any State, was unconstitutional under the Ninth Amendment. This position was overruled by the court without comment.

In Youngstown Sheet & Tube Company vs. Sawyer, 103 F. Supp. 569, in the opinion of Justice Pine, District Judge, the court touched upon the Ninth Amendment in discussing the doctrine of limited enumerated and delegated powers of the Federal Government.

In National Maritime Union v. Herzog, 78 F. Supp. 146, affirmed by the Supreme Court of the United States in a memorandum decision in 92 L. Ed. 1776, the anti-Communist provisions in the Labor-Management Act were contested on the ground that they were in violation of the Ninth Amendment. This contention was overruled by the lower court, which ruling was later affirmed by the Supreme Court.

In the case of Ex Parte Kirth, 28 F. Supp. 258, decided in 1939 by the District Court for the Southern District of California, the Court was considering a deportation case. The right of asylum in the United States of America was asserted under the Ninth Amendment to the Constitution of the United States. The Court was not impressed by the soundness of the argument, and held that the claim was contrary to the principles of international law, and has never been recognized by any civilized nation.

In Commonwealth & Southern v. Securities and Exchange Commission, 134 F. 2d 747, decided in 1943 by the Third Circuit Court of Appeals, the Court held that the entry of an Order requiring a public utility holding company to change its corporate structure was a power that could be exercised by the United States of America under the Commerce Clause, and that therefore it was not a violation of the Ninth Amendment to the Constitution.

In United States v. Painters Local Union No. 481, 79 F. Supp. 516, it was urged that the Corrupt Practices Act prohibiting contributions or expenditures upon certain elections illegal was unconstitutional and in violation of the Ninth Amendment. The Court overruled the contention, holding that Congress had the power to regulate and that the contention was without merit. (This case was reversed on other grounds at 172 F. 2d 854).

In Gernatt v. Huiet, Commissioner of Labor, 192 Georgia 729, 16 S. E. 2d 587 (1941), by the Supreme Court of Georgia, the Unemployment Compensation Act of the State of Georgia was attacked on the constitutional ground that as a whole it was violative of Article Nine of the Amendments to the Constitution of the United States. The Court held that on the whole the Act was not violative of this Amendment, citing as authority Livingston v. Moore, and other cases holding that the first ten amendments were applicable only to the Federal Government. The Court undoubtedly was influenced by the mechanical error in Livingston v. Moore.

In State v. Michel, 46 So. 430, 121 La. 374 (1908) by the Supreme Court of Louisiana, the statute in question was enacted by the State of Louisiana providing that a voter could not vote in both the Democratic and Republican primaries. It was urged that this statute violated the Ninth Amendment, but the Court held that the Amendment was not applicable to the facts involved in the case.

In Johnson vs. Board of Commissioners of Reno County (1938), 147 Kans. 211, 75 Pac. 2d 849 (857), the objection was made that certain legislative statutes of the State of Kansas regulating the sale of 3.2 beer violated the Ninth Amendment to the Constitution of the United States, and a similar provision to the Constitution of the State of Kansas. This contention was overruled by the Supreme Court of Kansas, which held that the contention was governed by certain local decisions and by Brown vs. New Jersey by the Supreme Court of the United States, which was one of the cases which holds that the first ten amendments to the Constitution are inapplicable to acts of a State Legislature.

There are a number of cases which briefly mention the Ninth Amendment by grouping it with the Tenth Amendment. However, these decisions do not actually discuss the Ninth Amendment, but actually discuss the Tenth Amendment. The distinction between the Ninth Amendment and the Tenth Amendment is obvious. The Tenth Amendment is an overall companion amendment which deals with powers. The Ninth Amendment does not relate to *powers* at all; it relates solely to *rights*. The Tenth Amendment is a reservation of powers to the States respectively, or to the people of the States, while the Ninth Amendment is a reservation by the people of their unenumerated rights. The grouping of the Ninth and Tenth Amendments together under the discussion of powers reserved "to the States respectively" is due to the erroneous grouping of the first *ten* amendments (as distinguished from the first *eight* amendments) as solely a restriction upon the National Government. While the contention has been made in these cases that certain enactments violate the Ninth and Tenth Amendments to the Constitution, the discussion actually revolves around the question of the violation of the Tenth Amendment. The Ninth Amendment is not directly discussed.

After a careful search we have not been able to find any other decisions by the courts in the United States, either State or Federal, which directly discuss the applicability of the Ninth Amendment. The decisions of our courts to this date throw very little light upon its meaning.

However, our courts, and particularly the Supreme Court of the United States of America, are deeply concerned over the doctrine of fundamental rights; the common law rights of man; the rights of natural endowment; or by whatever name they may be called. There seems to be no doubt in the minds of nearly all of the Justices of the Supreme Court of the United States in the last few decades that there should be some protection for the "Unalienable rights" with which a citizen is endowed, whether enumerated specifically or not.

Beginning with the case of Ex Parte August Spies et al, 8 S. Ct. 21, 123 U. S. 131, 31 L. Ed. 80 (86), decided in 1887, our courts have been in some confusion with respect to a constitutional means for the protection of these rights.

Actually, the Supreme Court of the United States has for a number of years been applying the doctrine of the Ninth Amendment, as we urge it, under the Due Process Clause in the Fourteenth Amendment to the Constitution. The Due Process Clause has been used as a substitute for the doctrine of rights by natural endowment. It is only reasonable to do so since the Due Process Clause was first announced in the Magna Charta. But there must ever be a doubt as to whether the whole realm of fundamental and inherent human rights is included within the words "due process of law". We also bear in mind that it has always been our theory of individual freedom, as announced in the Declaration of Independence, that our human rights of life, liberty and the pursuit of happiness, among other rights, exist by natural endowment, and are not created by human laws either statutory or constitutional. There is a wide difference in the vindication of fundamental and inherent rights as creatures of enactment through the Fourteenth Amendment, and such rights which are declared to exist in the individual apart from, independent of, and prior to either constitutions or statutes. Also, it seems to require an attenuated enlargement and extension of the words "due process of law" so that they include all native human rights.

The matter has, however, been pointed up in rather recent decisions of the Supreme Court of the United States of America in which some members of the Court have urged that the words "due process of law" in the Fourteenth Amendment, include all of the rights enumerated in the first eight amendments to the Constitution. There seems to be a great deal of doubt in the decisions as to just what rights are protected under the "due process" clause in the Fourteenth Amendment, and as to what rights are not protected. There seems to be no real basis or ground for distinction, except that only fundamental or inherent rights are protected by the Fourteenth Amendment. But still this leaves a large area of uncertainty.

This situation seems to be best illustrated in the recent case of Adamson vs. California, 332 U. S. 46 (68), 67 S. Ct. 1672, 91 L. Ed. 1903. At this time it is most difficult to determine just what is the basis or yardstick employed by the Supreme Court of the United States in the classification of those rights which in their opinion are protected from infringement by the several States by the Fourteenth Amendment and those which are not protected by it.

We believe that our Supreme Court may find a solution of this perplexing problem by making application of the Ninth Amendment, and making it the basis for the protection of rights of natural endowment, rather than trying to find protection for such pre-Constitutional and super-Constitutional rights by justifying their origin and existence through the "due process" clause in the Fourteenth Amendment.

We see, therefore, that there are no decisions by any of the courts, either Federal or State, which are not in agreement with our theory that rights of natural endowment are universal, and since such rights exist, they cannot be destroyed by the Governments of the several States. On the contrary, the later decisions of the Supreme Court of the United States seem, in general language, to support our position.

Most important, however, is the fact that interpretation of the Ninth Amendment to the Constitution is still an open question for our courts. The vital force of this Amendment has not been impaired in the least by judicial construction.

CHAPTER 6

THE NINTH AMENDMENT IS APPLICABLE
TO STATE GOVERNMENTS

From a legal and from a historic viewpoint we must not confuse the underlying meaning and intent of the Ninth Amendment with the reason for its inclusion in the Bill of Rights.

We have seen that long before its inclusion in the Constitution, it was a basic and underlying philosophy of life.

It is true that this amendment was among the first that were added to the Constitution, and the reason for its inclusion was because of the fear of the people of a strong national government. But, it is fallacious and illogical to insist that by expressly protecting our liberties from the force of the Federal Government, the same liberties would not be protected from the force of State governments. Irrespective of whether this provision was included in the original Constitution, in the amendments, or whether it was omitted entirely, its great principle has always existed, and always will exist as long as there is human life. We must not discount or limit its meaning because of the circumstances which made it a part of the Constitution.

We have a choice of the theory of liberty and rights by natural endowment as announced in the Declaration of Independence, and again in the Ninth Amendment, and in the other liberty documents, or we have the choice of the theory that all of our inherent and fundamental rights were surrendered to State Governments and that the governments of the States are the creators of our rights and liberties. We are forced to the position that the States, and the States alone, with forty-eight possible divergent views, have the power and the sole power to define and protect our native human liberties and rights. We believe that no such idea was ever intended. It is impossible to believe that human rights and individual liberties were wrung from tyrants and despots through suffering, sacrifice and death, and announced in the Declaration of

Independence and in other liberty documents, only to be surrendered up to State governments where they could be destroyed by the sovereign people acting en masse, or by a tyranny acting in the name of the people of the several States. The power to destroy or define negatives the idea of natural human rights.

However, the following reasons definitely established that the Ninth Amendment was not intended solely as a restrictive inhibition against the National Government, but as a great declaration of the liberty of mankind:

(1) Opinions of the Supreme Court of the United States beginning with Eilenbecker vs. The District Court of Plymouth County, Iowa, 134 U. S. 131, 33 L. Ed. 801, definitely show that only the first eight amendments to the Constitution were intended to be narrowly construed as inhibitions upon the National Government. Since the decision of this case in 1890, the Supreme Court of the United States has abandoned the dust-covered dictum that the first ten Amendments to the Constitution were intended as restrictions upon the National Government, and now holds that only the first eight amendments were so intended. Since the decision of the Eilenbecker case, there has been no decision of the Supreme Court of the United States and no dictum which has adhered to the old text. The mechanical error in the case of Livingston vs. Moore definitely establishes that it is no precedent or authority for the narrow construction of the Ninth Amendment.

Therefore, the Ninth Amendment is unshackled from its early erroneous classification and the cloud has been removed, and it is now ready for use any time our courts or our people may discover an unenumerated human right.

(2) Our constitutions are not the sources of our liberties. In Calder vs. Bull, 3 Dallas 386, 1 L. Ed. 648, and in Savings and Loan Association vs. Topeka, 87 U. S. 686, 22 L. Ed. 455, cited also in the next succeeding chapter, the Supreme Court of the United States has recognized the doctrine of inherent human rights which are entitled to protection against the legislative acts of the several states, even though such rights may be unenumerated in the Constitution of the United States.

These cases proceed upon the theory that there are rights in every free government which are beyond the control of state governments. These cases recognized the doctrine of the implied reservation of individual rights. This is the doctrine of the Ninth Amendment. Although the decision of Calder vs. Bull has been questioned, these cases have been cited many times with approval, and we do not find any decision which has overruled or distinguished the holding in these cases.

These decisions can be construed in no other way except to establish that inherent rights, whether enumerated in the Constitution of the United States or not, are entitled to protection, not only against the Federal Government, but also as against the government of the several States.

(3) The debates in the Constitutional Convention, and in the First Congress which drew the amendments for submission, and the entire historic background established that the rights of natural endowment were intended to be universal and entitled to protection against all governments, either State or National.

There is nothing in the historic background of the Bill of Rights that even remotely suggests that these liberties were to be protected from abuse by the Federal Government only, but that such rights would be surrendered to the governments of the several States without protection. The entire historic background definitely establishes that our forefathers were merely, through an abundance of caution, protecting their rights against the powers of a strong National Government. There is no suggestion anywhere in any historical document that we have been able to find, that could constitute the slightest indication of the abandonment of their liberties to the control of State Governments. On the other hand, they felt that their individual liberties were safe at the hands of a State government, whether expressly enumerated in State constitutions or not. This thought is forcibly emphasized in a statement made by Mr. Jackson, the Representative from Georgia, in a debate on the floor of Congress on June 8, 1789, in which he opposed the addition of the Bill of Rights as being "dangerous, improper and unnecessary", and in this debate he made the following statement:

"But do gentlemen suppose bills of rights necessary to secure liberty? If they do, let them look at New York, New Jersey, Virginia, South Carolina and Georgia. Those States have no bills of rights, and is the liberty of the citizens less safe in those States, than in the other of the United States? I believe it is not."

Mr. Jackson made the same argument that was made by Alexander Hamilton in "The Federalist". They both feared that by enumerating our present liberties, there would be a disparagement of those liberties not enumerated. Their fears will certainly have been duly justified if the enumeration of certain inherent rights should be construed not only as a disparagement of other enumerated rights, but also construed in such a manner as to strip the individual of inherent rights in so far as State governments are concerned.

If this erroneous construction should prevail, the necessary result is that inherent rights are recognized by neither our National or our State Governments unless they are expressly enumerated and spelled out in both the Federal and State Constitutions. This means, then, that men have no inherent rights and that all of our rights are granted to us by the State. This, of course, was never intended. We might add at this point that our Country is the strong advocate of human dignity and human liberty in the family of nations throughout the earth. Can it be possible that we advocate such natural liberty for others, yet enjoy no such natural liberties ourselves?

(4) The Ninth Amendment as a part of the Constitution must be given some meaning. This construction is the only logical construction that could be given it. Any other construction as an inhibition against the National Government would only lead to an untenable conclusion. Such a construction would mean that the several States reserve to themselves the right to deny and disparage natural rights. This, of course, could not have been the intention of the First Congress.

The meaning which we urge is the only reasonable construction that could be given to this amendment.

(5) The very language of the Amendment negatives such a narrow construction. The words "the enumeration *in the Constitution*" definitely show that the language was language of general import, as applied generally to the Constitution, instead of special import and restricted only to the first ten

amendments. If a narrower construction had been intended, the amendment would have read "the enumeration *in these amendments.*"

We bear in mind the fact that the body of the Constitution spelled out and protected a number of other basic individual rights. It would therefore be unreasonable to hold that this amendment related only to the rights enumerated in Amendments one to eight in the Bill of Rights and did not relate to the other individual rights protected in the body of the Constitution. If it is contended that the Ninth Amendment was required as a safeguard against the infringement of the rights enumerated in the first eight amendments only, it would seem strange that no such safeguard should be thrown around the enumeration of other individual rights protected in the body of the Constitution.

Therefore, its provisions can only be construed as a broad declaration relating to the Constitution as a whole, and it certainly cannot be construed as a narrow limitation to be considered only in connection with the first Ten Amendments to the Constitution.

(6) The historic legislative background of the Amendment shows definitely that Madison, who was the father of both the Constitution and the Bill of Rights, and the particular author of the Ninth Amendment, never intended that it should ever be so narrowly restricted. Without repetition of its historic background, the fact that his original draft included the language "here or elsewhere in the Constitution", coupled with the fact that Madison never intended that the Amendments to the Constitution would appear as an appendage thereto, definitely proves that this Amendment was always intended to be a broad declaration relating to the Constitution as a whole without any narrow or restricted construction.

(7) The preamble to the twelve proposed articles of amendment which states that "further declaratory and restrictive clauses should be added," definitely shows that of the twelve amendments submitted for ratification, some were considered by the Congress of the United States, and particularly the Senate, as being broad declarations rather than restrictive inhibitions. The first and second proposed amendments relat-

ing to per capita representation and salaries of government officers, certainly could not be classified under this language as "declaratory" clauses. Undoubtedly the Senate and the House of Representatives realized the distinction between the first eight amendments to the Constitution, and Amendments nine and ten as ultimately adopted. This introductory clause, which seldom if ever appears on the conventional printing of the Bill of Rights, but which does appear upon the original in the archives of the Library of Congress, is very convincing.

(8) However, we do not need the preamble to immediately recognized the difference between the first eight Amendments and the Ninth and Tenth Amendments. The first eight Amendments are negative in their statements and of course can be classified no other way than with a restrictive intent.

No stretch of the imagination could ever convert a broad declaration of human liberty into any kind of a restriction. It can only be classed as a declaration.

(9) The broad and historic concept of human rights and human liberty establishes such unenumerated rights as pre-constitutional rights, and such rights were not abridged by the Constitution of the United States, or any State constitution, or any power, Government or person whomsoever.

We either believe in inherent human rights, or we do not believe in them; if we believe in such inherent rights, then such rights must be protected against the unwarranted power of either the National or the State Governments, otherwise they fail and cannot be classed as an inherent right at all.

We would like to suggest as a basis for further study that the chief difficulty surrounding the subject of this chapter arises out of the fact that in the colonial days, and under State governments as they existed prior to the adoption of the Constitution, each State had its own method of jury trial and criminal procedure. Each State regarded jury trial, particularly in criminal cases, as an inherent right. As was pointed out in the letter from Washington to Lafayette heretofore quoted (page 8), the framers of the Federal Constitution thought of jury trial as a consideration separate and apart from a Bill of Rights. They desired to leave to the several States their respective methods of jury trial and criminal procedure. There was no thought in their minds that by closing the draft of the Constitution without including a provision guaranteeing jury trial, the several States would be justified in refusing jury trial. It would have been difficult, however, to have included any provision with respect to the manner in which jury trial should be conducted, because the procedure in each of the States was different.

These circumstances may throw some light upon which of the rights enumerated in the first eight amendments to the Constitution shall be classified as fundamental rights and which shall not be so classified.

There is another consideration which is worthy of careful thought. There is no provision in the Constitution which shall prevent the Government of the United States from protecting inherent rights. There is only a restraint upon their impairment or denial by the Federal Government. We believe that there could be no constitutional objection to any national legislation enacted for the purpose of the protection of natural rights.

We feel that American liberties are not less safe in the hands of those who administer the Federal Government than those who administer State Government.

There is no danger in the destruction of our individual liberties through either State or Federal Government, except the danger that exists in the quality of statesmanship of the men who administer both. However, whatever may be the complaints against the administration of a strong centralized national government, the historical fact stands that since 1789 the Federal Government, and in particular the Supreme Court of the United States, has been the greatest champion of individual liberties. We shudder to think what might have been the result if our human liberties had been left to final determination by the courts of forty-eight states. The undisputed truth is that in practically all important instances where human rights have been denied, it has been at the hands of the government of a State or its inferior subdivisions. It is to be expected that more cases would arise out of State action because there are forty-eight more chances for this to occur. However, there have been very few incidents in which it could even be claimed that the Supreme Court of the United States has imposed upon the fundamental liberties of individuals. There is no logical reason why State governments and those who administer State governments are superior either in mentality or integrity to those who administer our National Government. If we have poor administrators in either branch of our government, the fault does not lie so much in the men whom we have chosen to administer, but in ourselves, and in our lack of morale and patriotism.

We believe that in the one hundred and sixty and more years of the history of our Federal Government, the quality of statesmanship of Federal officers has been on the whole of a higher character than those who administer State governments.

However, there is nothing in the Constitution of the United States that gives the Federal Government the right of power to destroy human liberties. There is nothing and should be nothing in any power reserved to the States that gives the States the right to destroy such liberties, and such power was never intended.

CHAPTER 7

WHAT ARE THE UNENUMERATED RIGHTS?

In order that this entire treatise may not be purely academic, and in order that it may have present practical value and purpose, it must be shown that there are unenumerated inherent rights. Since we are without definite legal precedent as a guide, and since rights appear only gradually in the evolution of the human race, and are incapable of classification under any fixed or steadfast rule, the task of presenting the existence of the unenumerated rights is the most difficult chapter to write.

Before beginning the discussion, however, it is believed that if recognition is given to the Ninth Amendment, and it is recognized as announcing a living and vital philosophy, a use will be found for this amendment, and that hereafter it will be given the opportunity to function under the guidance of stable, but spiritual intellect as the course of history shall unfold.

Needless to say, it is our belief that the unenumerated rights permit of no exact definition. To attempt to define these rights would be contrary to the obvious intent and meaning of the amendment. There should be no haste or necessity for immediate application of the great principle involved. If our research has brought to light a truth, then it is a truth of great importance. The idea should first be presented and weighed by those who are qualified through years of experience to make its application. If the idea is as basic and fundamental as we believe it to be, a practical application will be made in the not too distant future.

Therefore, when we discuss the question as to what the unenumerated rights may be, may we preface our remarks by stating that we are more in the attitude of asking questions than expounding, and everything we say should properly be prefaced with the statement that these are our opinions and beliefs.

We believe that the Supreme Court of the United States has, under the due process clause of the Fourteenth Amendment, been defining the unenumerated rights of natural endowment. Thus far the fundamental rights have been confined to those enumerated in the First Amendment to the Constitution. Actually, however, the rights under the Fifth Amendment, such as the protection of life, liberty and property, double jeopardy, protection against self-incrimination in a criminal case, and the taking of private property for public use, are just as fundamental and inherent as the rights under the First Amendment. There are other rights in the first eight amendments that are of equal importance as inherent rights. There are great inconsistencies in the decisions of not only our Supreme Court, but our other great courts, both State and Federal. For some reason the words "due process of law" take on a more expansive and all inclusive meaning when interpreted under the Fourteenth Amendment, than when interpreted under the Fifth Amendment. There would have been no need for the First Amendment to the Constitution if all of the rights and liberties enumerated therein were protected by the due process clause in the Fifth Amendment, even if limited to the National Government alone.

The error seems to lie in the false idea that our constitutions are the only sources of our individual liberty, and that in order to protect a native human or inherent right, we must find the source of its protection in the Constitution. The resolution of this question is the very purpose of this discussion.

We believe that a sounder basis for the protection of the rights enumerated in the First Amendment which have been protected by the Supreme Court of the United States, as fundamental or inherent rights, would be that such rights are rights of natural endowment which should be protected under the Declaration of Independence and the Ninth Amendment to the Constitution, without the necessity of including them within the protection of the due process clause.

There are three decisions of the Supreme Court which are certainly worthy of mentioning which bear out the belief in inherent rights. A most interesting early case is Calder vs. Bull, 3 Dallas 386, 1 L. Ed. 648, decided prior to Marbury vs.

Madison, prior to the Fourteenth Amendment, and prior to Barron vs. Baltimore, which shows the philosophy of the Supreme Court with respect to basic and inherent rights of individuals. In this case, as had been the custom of the State of Connecticut over a period of many years, the Legislature, acting in a capacity very much as the Law Lords of England, had the right to grant new trials in litigation which had been decided by the courts. In this case the trial court had denied probate of a will. The statute passed by the Legislature of Connecticut set aside the judgment of the trial court and granted a new trial, and on the second trial the court probated the will and this decree was affirmed by the highest appellate courts in Connecticut. An appeal was taken to the Supreme Court of the United States on the sole and only ground that the statute was an ex post facto law. Apparently no other constitutional ground of invalidity was asserted by the appellant. The Supreme Court of the United States held that ex post facto law applied only to criminal cases, and then held that it was not applicable to the case in question on that ground. The three concurring opinions further held that since such procedure had been in customary usage in the State of Connecticut from the date of its charter, such usage would not be disturbed.

However, Justice Chase, in the principal opinion of the case, did make certain announcements which are the identical principles which we contend are enunciated by the Ninth Amendment. We quote from this decision as follows:

"Whether the Legislature of any of the states can revise and correct by law, a decision of any of its courts of justice, although not prohibited by the constitution of the state, is a question of very great importance, and not necessary now to be determined; because the resolution or law in question does not go so far. I cannot subscribe to the omnipotence of a state legislature, or that it is absolute and without control; although its authority should not be expressly restrained by the constitution, or fundamental law, of the state. The people of the United States erected their constitutions, or forms of government, to establish justice, to promote general welfare, to secure the blessings of liberty, and to protect their persons and property from violence. The purpose for which men enter into society will determine the nature and terms of the social compact; and as they are the foundation of the legislative power, they will decide what are the proper objects of it: The nature, and ends of legislative power will limit the exercise of it.

This fundamental principle flows from the very nature of our free Republican governments, that no man should be compelled to do what the laws do not require; nor to refrain from the acts which the laws permit. There are acts which the federal, or state, legislature cannot do, without exceeding their authority. There are certain vital principles in our free Republican governments, which will overrule an apparent and flagrant abuse of legislative power; as to authorize manifest injustice by positive law; or to take away that security for personal liberty, or private property, for the protection whereof the government was established. An act of the Legislature (for I cannot call it a law) contrary to the great first principles of the social compact, cannot be considered a rightful exercise of legislative authority. The obligation of a law in governments established on express compact, and on republican principles, must be determined by the nature of the power, on which it is founded. A few instances will suffice to explain what I mean. A law that punished a citizen for an innocent action, or, in other words, for an act, which, when done, was in violation of no existing law; a law that destroys, or impairs, the lawful private contracts of citizens, a law that makes a man a judge in his own cause; or a law that takes property from A. and gives to B. It is against all reason and justice, for a people to entrust a Legislature with such powers; and, therefore, it cannot be presumed that they have done it. The genius, the nature, and the spirit of our state governments, amount to a prohibition of such acts of legislation; and the general principles of law and reason forbid them. The Legislature may enjoin, permit, forbid, and punish; they may declare new crimes; and established rules of conduct for all its citizens in future cases; they may command what is right, and prohibit what is wrong; but they cannot change innocence into guilt; or punish innocence as a crime, or violate the right of antecedent lawful private contract; or the right of private property. To maintain that our federal, or state, Legislature possesses such powers, if they had not been expressly restrained, would, in my opinion, be a political heresy, altogether inadmissible in our free republican governments."

The case of Savings and Loan Association vs. Topeka, 87 U. S. 686, 22 L. Ed. 455, decided February 1, 1875, also announces not only the spirit, but the letter of the Ninth Amendment. We bear in mind that this decision came after the Fourteenth Amendment. The City of Topeka, in an endeavor to build an industrial city, had issued bonds which were payable out of the public treasury for the purpose of inducing King Wrought Iron Bridge Manufacturing & Iron Works Company to establish a factory in the City of Topeka. This constituted the taking of private property through taxation and giving it to

private industry. This was done under the force of a statute
of the State of Kansas which authorized such a procedure, and
the statutes of the State of Kansas had been fully complied with.
The question before the Supreme Court of the United States
was whether or not the statute of the State of Kansas was constitutional or unconstitutional.

In an opinion by Justice Miller, with a dissent by Justice
Clifford which we shall hereafter mention, the Court quickly
disposed of the question and held without specific reference to
any provision in the Constitution of the United States or any
of the articles of amendment thereto that the statute of the
State of Kansas was unconstitutional. The opinion contained
the following language:

"It must be conceded that there are such rights in every free
government beyond the control of the State. A government which
recognized no such right, which held the lives, the liberty and the
property of its citizens subject at all times to the absolute disposition and unlimited control of even the most democratic depository
of power, is after all but a despotism. It is true it is a despotism
of the many, of the majority, if you choose to call it so, but it is
none the less a despotism. It may well be doubted if a man is to
hold all that he is accustomed to call his own, all in which he has
placed his happiness, and the security of which is essential to that
happiness, under the unlimited dominion of others, whether it is
not wiser that this power should be exercised by one man than by
many.

"The theory of our governments, state and national, is opposed
to the deposit of unlimited power anywhere. The executive, the
legislative and the judicial branches of these governments are all
limited and defined powers.

"There are limitations on such power which grow out of the
essential nature of all free governments. Implied reservations of
individual rights, without which the social compact could not
exist, and which are respected by all governments entitled to the
name. No court, for instance, would hesitate to declare void a
statute which enacted that A and B who were husband and wife
to each should be so no longer, but that A should thereafter be the
husband of C, and B the wife of D. Or which should enact that
the homestead now owned by A should no longer be his, but should
henceforth be the property of B. Whiting v. Fond du Lac, 25 Wis.,
188; Cooley, Const. Lim., 129, 175, 487; Dill. Mun. Cor., § 587.

"* * * * To lay, with one hand, the power of the government
on the property of the citizen, and with the other to bestow it upon
favored individuals to aid private enterprises and build up private

fortunes, is none the less a robbery because it is done under the forms of law and is called taxation. This is not legislation. It is a decree under legislative forms."

It is vitally significant and important that the majority opinion was based, not upon the interpretation of any constitutional provision, but upon the basis of the fundamental right of an individual to retain his own property against taxation for the support of private industry.

The question of inherent or fundamental rights was directly before the courts and Justice Clifford dissented, using the following language:

"Courts cannot nullify an Act of the State Legislature on the vague ground that they think it opposed to a general latent spirit supposed to pervade or underlie the Constitution, where neither the terms nor the implication of the instrument disclose any such restriction.

"Such a power is denied to the courts, because to concede it would be to make the courts sovereign over both the Constitution and the people, and convert the government into a judicial despotism.

"* * * because it is not competent for a Federal Court to adjudge a State statute void which does not conflict in any respect with the Constitution of the United States or that of the State whose Legislature enacted the statute."

This case supports us in the very substance of our position with respect to the force and meaning of the Ninth Amendment to the Constitution. The exact question was decided, as demonstrated by the dissenting opinion of Justice Clifford.

We again point out that Justice Miller was a member of the Court which first declared that the Bill of Rights consisted of the first *eight* articles of amendment to the Constitution instead of the first *ten* articles of amendment.

Calder vs. Bull has been cited with approval a number of times by our Supreme Court. The notes to this decision in Volume 1 Law. Edition cite numerous authorities in which the doctrine of the fundamental principles of the social compact are recognized. This case was followed by the Supreme Court of the United States in Gunn vs. Barry, 21 L. Ed. 215, 82 U. S. 540. The Supreme Court of the United States declared void a constitutional provision and a statute of the State of Georgia which increased the amount of property exempt from execution and made the statute applicable to judgments which had been previously rendered and on which the judgment lien had already attached. The Court held that this was contrary to reason and justice. The Court also held that the statute was void as being in conflict with the contract clause of the Constitution, but nevertheless cited Calder vs. Bull as authority.

The case of McVeigh vs. United States, 20 L. Ed. 80, 78 U. S. 260, is a case which cites Calder vs. Bull and gives recognition to the first principles of the social compact.

Savings and Loan Association vs. Topeka, however, in several most recent cases, has been recognized as the law of decision holding that the Supreme Court of the United States can declare an act of a State Legislature void, if the State statute is violative of fundamental rights by exacting taxation and making a gift of tax money to private industry. While our Supreme Court holds that this far-reaching authority must be exercised with extreme caution, nevertheless Savings and Loan Association vs. Topeka is still controlling law. Everson vs. Board of Education, 330 U. S. 1, 91 L. Ed. 711 (718); Thompson vs. Consolidated Gas Utilities Corporation, 300 U. S. 55, 81 L. Ed. 510, 57 S. C. 364; Parkersburg vs. Brown, 106 U. S. 487, 27 L. Ed. 238, 1 S. C. 442.

In Green vs. Frazier, 253 U. S. 233 (240), 64 L. Ed. 878 (881), 40 S. C. 499, The Supreme Court followed the opinion of Justice Miller, but has used the due process clause in the Fourteenth Amendment as the basis of its decision; however, Justice Miller, speaking for the Court in Savings and Loan Association vs. Topeka, made no mention whatsoever of the Fourteenth Amendment or any other amendment, or any portion of the Constitution, but the Court's decision was based solely upon the existence of certain fundamental rights which were beyond the control of the State.

In National Labor Relations Board vs. Jones and Laughlin Steel Corporation, 81 L. Ed. 893 (902), 301 U. S. 1, the Supreme Court of the United States, in an opinion by Justice Hughes, defined one of the fundamental rights. The court held that employees had as clear a right to self-organization and selection of their representatives for lawful purposes as a business has to select its officers and agents. This is Supreme Court authority for the existence of fundamental unenumerated rights.

But we shall try to illustrate the unenumerated rights with some supposed examples. The governors of two states in recent years have threatened that they intended to procure the enactment of statutes controlling newspaper publicity and criticism of executive officers. Such statutes would be construed to be in violation of the Fourteenth Amendment by the incorporation of the First Amendment therein. But such a statute would also be void under the Ninth Amendment. This is true because it is an inherent human right and is one of the basic requirements for the existence of a free people. Such a right is a part of the British Constitution, and is an inherent right of the English people, although such a right is unenumerated in any portion of the British Constitution, and there is not one written word which protects the freedom of the press. Freedom of the press has been recognized as an inherent right protected under the Fourteenth Amendment by the Supreme Court of the United States, but it is also such an inherent right as should be protected under the Ninth Amendment.

Suppose, for instance, that a state should pass an act abolishing jury trial in criminal cases. We believe that such a statute would be void under the Ninth Amendment as destroying an inherent human right. While no effort has been made on the part of the Federal Government to determine the method of jury trial and criminal procedure to be employed by the several States, because the framers of the Constitution preferred to leave the States to the various modes which they had used at the time of the adoption of the Constitution, nevertheless there is no decision which can be construed to uphold the abolition of jury trial in criminal cases.

Suppose a legislature of a State should pass an act fixing punishment of certain crimes by death, and declaring that the means of execution should be inhuman and torturous, such as gradual mutilation of the body, burial alive, or some other form of cruel punishment. Do we have any doubt but that the Supreme Court of the United States would declare such a statute to be void?

Suppose that some of the States should enact statutes providing for imprisonment for ordinary debt, and reestablish the old debtor' prison. There is no guarantee in the Constitution which prohibits imprisonment for debt. In fact, at the time of the adoption of the Constitution this practice prevailed under the statutes of several of the States. To the great shame of the American people, Robert Morris, who was the principal donor of money to finance the American Revolution, and who was a member of the Constitutional Convention, died in a debtor's prison. We believe that this form of punishment is no longer a part of the American concept of morality or justice, and that our Supreme Court would quickly declare unconstitutional any statute enacted by either the Federal or a State Government which provided for imprisonment for ordinary debt at this time.

At the time of the adoption of the Constitution it was common practice in several of the States that a person convicted of crime should be branded with a branding iron as an outward proof of his iniquity. No court would tolerate such a practice at this time, even though it was not considered cruel and unusual punishment at the time of the adoption of the Constitution.

At the time of the founding of this Government, there was still wide-spread belief in witchcraft, and statutes of some of the States punished its practice. After a hundred and sixty-five years of enlightenment, would we now tolerate the punishment of any individual for witchcraft?

These examples are hypothetical. However, the Supreme Court of the United States in Calder vs. Bull and in Savings and Loan Association vs. Topeka have given some other examples of what the unenumerated rights may be.

We believe that the Ninth Amendment was intended to protect the unenumerated rights, not only as they have now appeared, but also as such rights may appear as history and the future shall unfold. As the race becomes more evolved, and as the respect for the dignity of human life increases; as we become more intelligent and spiritual human beings, then we shall learn more of the fundamental truths about human nature.

In my research I have discovered only one treatise on the subject of the Ninth Amendment to the Federal Constitution. This is a learned and scholarly discussion by Honorable Knowlton H. Kelsey published in the Indiana Law Journal in April 1936, entitled "The Ninth Amendment to the Federal Constitution". This author points out that while the human liberties enumerated in the Constitution are imposing, nevertheless they do not exhaust the list of human rights. He urges that the Ninth Amendment was never intended as a mere Mother Hubbard clause which is usually contained in a bill of sale specifying "all articles too numerous to mention on the improbable chance that something worthwhile may have been forgotten." He further urges that no word can be unnecessarily rejected as superfluous and meaningless, and that the Ninth Amendment does have some meaning.

Mr. Kelsey further aptly points out that the American Revolution was not a doctrinary war, or a war for "philosophic perfection of any utilitarian doctrine of rights, but for the rights of Englishmen." He points out that these rights were best expressed in Blackstone's Commentaries, and carefully analyzes the natural rights of men as set out in Blackstone's Commentaries and recommends this authority as a study for their definition.

However, it is our belief that the philosophy of the Ninth Amendment is a living and growing philosophy. It was intended to be so in the same manner that the Magna Charta was intended and has been interpreted as part of a living and growing Constitution. The Magna Charta has not been restricted by English law to the rights of Englishmen as they existed in 1215 on the field at Runnymede. In the same manner the natural rights of Americans should not be static and fixed as of the date of the adoption of the Constitution and the Bill of Rights. To interpret the Ninth Amendment in this manner would take it out of its clearly intended meaning. Such an interpretation would mean that there was a cutoff date at the time of the adoption of the Bill of Rights; that prior to that date rights of natural endowment were recognized, but after said date only such rights as were enumerated or known to exist would be protected. This interpretation destroys the distinction between "enumerated" and "unenumerated", and restricts its meaning to be read as "such enumerated rights as are now known to exist."

We can only see from the stream of history that human rights are the product of the growth of civilization. It was never intended that civilization in other phases of life should

progress, but that human liberty and rights of natural endowment can only be defined as they existed almost two centuries
ago, and that however apparent such a right may become in the
light of current history, such a natural right could never be
recognized except by a statute or constitutional amendment.
We do not believe that it was ever intended that the science
of the law should become so fixed and archaic, while all other
sciences may go forward in the discovery of truth and may
utilize it wherever it is found. We should not attempt to
harness our rights to a civilization as it existed one hundred
and sixty-five years ago, and it was not the intention of the
framers of the Bill of Rights that we should do so.

The law is necessarily built upon retrospect and is founded
upon tradition. It is difficult for such a science to keep abreast
and maintain progress with other business and professions. We
have been, more or less, unjustly compared to the crab who
never looks where he is going but only wants to see where he
has been. There are those who urge that this is a weakness of
the system of the English common law, and that in an expanding world of business and commerce in the machine age, we
must ultimately come to a system of codification or a system
of justice which is more visibly defined and executed.

With this view we do not agree, but we believe that although the demands of a fast moving, business commercial
world require a large degree of codification and visible certainty, and the laws relating to property must in a great manner be
fixed and static, the rule should be different in the field of
human relationships.

As we become more civilized, we learn more about the
natural forces of the world, such as the use and properties of our
elementary minerals, steam, electricity, and other natural forces.
We also increase in spiritual and intellectual growth and are
capable of understanding natural rights and liberties that have
always existed, but which have been beyond our limited intellect to comprehend.

We believe that the great and underlying truths of human
nature are yet to be discovered, in the same manner that we are
from year to year expanding our knowledge of the natural and
physical forces of the universe. The framers of our Constitu-

tion and the signers of the Declaration of Independence actually understood, defended and vindicated human rights to the greatest extent that they had ever been recognized up to that time. However, they had little or no conception of human rights as we understand them today. We ourselves cannot possibly have any conception of what natural and human rights of the future may be, in the light of the progress and development of the race, after a century or two centuries of civilization and intellectual and spiritual growth. We cannot doubt this when we remember that less than a century ago we permitted slavery and human bondage and the majority of our people did not consider slavery as being morally or spiritually wrong; and when we further remember that only a little more than a quarter of a century ago we liberated women from political disfranchisement and gave them the right to participate in the government. These examples illustrate the changes in our moral philosophies that have taken place in the short era of a century.

Our thesis is that human rights which are not enumerated in the Constitution will be revealed and become apparent in the future, and it is within the spirit of the Constitution, and the letter of the Ninth Amendment, that these rights should be recognized and protected.

Some of the rights may now be making their appearance.

The right of privacy may be such a right. If there is such a right, it is difficult to classify it under any right that is enumerated in the Constitution. This is a right which is of comparatively recent recognition. Some courts call it a fundamental right. While the courts seem to feel that it should exist, there is a great timidity and lack of forthrightness in the protection of this right, because its existence is not to be found in the written and enumerated law.

There are many questions surrounding our labor problems that might appropriately come under the classification of rights of natural endowment. Do men have a natural or inherent right to strike? Does an employer have the right or privilege to choose those whom he desires as employees, or can such employer be forced to employ against his will? Is there a fundamental right to work?

Such rights are not discussed in any clause of the Constitution, but if such rights exist, shall they be denied simply because they are not enumerated?

Another possible inherent right is the right to participate in government. This includes the right to have votes counted. The clause insuring to the States a republican form of government has not been effectively interpreted so as to save our States or the various subdivisions and municipalities in our States from virtual dictatorships in matters of franchise and elections, and even the operation and management of government on a few occasions. It may be possible that the Ninth Amendment is a means of insuring the voters in any subdivision of government against the virtual destruction of his franchise and right to participate in government, through fraudulent elections and the usurpation of dictatorial powers by the executive branch of the government.

There are, no doubt, many other rights of natural endowment that have already become apparent to those who possess a richer experience than the writer. We are content if we have established the Ninth Amendment as embodying a living philosophy, and helped the law of human rights to be given an opportunity to grow as other sciences have grown.

We believe that the law should grow, and our Constitution should be interpreted in the light of current history, as was stated by one of the eminent courts of last resort of one of the States,

"The law should be construed in reference to the habits of business prevalent in the country at the time it was enacted. The law was not made to create or shape the habits of business, but to regulate them, as then known to exist."

There must be some unenumerated rights. The amendment must be given some meaning. Its value and meaning should not be lost through disuse. This amendment can only be saved by our courts.

CHAPTER 8

THIS AMENDMENT PROTECTS PERSONAL RIGHTS AND LIBERTIES RATHER THAN PUBLIC OR COLLECTIVE RIGHTS

In any Republican form of government each citizen possesses a dual investiture of rights. The citizen, in fact, possesses a dual civic nature. First, he possesses his fundamental or inherent rights of natural endowment. Secondly, as a member of the public, he possesses public rights which he holds collectively with other citizens. He thus has a private self as well as a public self. Or, we might otherwise say he consists of a private and a governmental self. There is of course a conflict between these dual personalities. This conflict is because of the fact that any form of government must necessarily be a restraint on individual liberty.

Therefore, any democratic form of government must have dual systems of restraints which protect the public interest, and at the same time preserve the liberty of the individual.

As we have heretofore pointed out, the ever present danger in a democracy is the power of the majority to over-emphasize the importance of our collective rights and security, and thus permit our individual selves to become the captives of our public selves.

The "General Welfare" clause in the preamble to the Constitution is a provision of general meaning and inclusiveness. This clause is a guarantee of the protection of our public rights and interests whether they are specifically enumerated in the Constitution or not. The enumeration in the Constitution of certain public rights and interests shall not be construed to deny or disparage other unenumerated public rights and interests. This is the guarantee of the "general Welfare" clause.

The Ninth Amendment in the Constitution is the counterpart of the "general Welfare" clause. It protects the individual in the same manner that the general welfare clause protects the public.

The entire context of the Ninth Amendment, and its historic background, definitely prove that it was intended solely as a protection of our unenumerated personal rights as individuals as distinguished from our public or collective rights. This concept is necessary to maintain an even balance in the Constitution.

We can conceive that there is a possibility that this great declaration of individual liberty might be distorted into support for the advocacy of extreme socialism, such as the right to food, housing, medicine, etc. If, however, the amendment should be used by either the legislative or judicial branches of our Government as the basis of such a public right, then it would be taken out of its natural meaning and setting. The individual Bill of Rights would be distorted into a public Bill of Rights.

It is well for us to review, and keep before us, the proper relationship between government and individual liberty. This nation began with the cardinal principle that individual liberty is paramount, and can only be limited by public necessity. The burden was upon those who claimed public necessity to establish it. In some manner or other, the rule now seems to be changed, and in conflicts between the individual and government, there is a presumption in favor of public necessity when weighed in the balances with individual liberty. Government has grown immense, and the national planning covers immense projects with collective social results as the final goal. We have in a large measure lost sight of the individual except as he is carried along as a part of mass projects.

This is not what individual freedom means in the least, and we seem to somewhat have lost the identity of the religious, spiritual, and noble principles upon which this government was founded.

The founders of this government understood to a greater degree the distinction between sovereignty and government than we understand it today. In 1789 most men were political scientists. They were political scientists because they lived in an age when political science was one of the great cultures of the time. It was an age of unselfish giants among whom patriotism was taken for granted.

The attitude of the founding fathers is well expressed by Dr. C. Edward Merriam in his treatise entitled "American Political Theories" (1906) from which we quote as follows:

"In the formation of state governments, the doctrine of delegated powers was everywhere prevalent. Assuming that the people were, originally, and continue to be the only source of political power, it follows that all governmental authority is only delegated by the people and is held in trust for them. Governmental authority has no inherent force in itself; it is not the creator, but the creature; it is not the master, nor even the partner of the people, but their agent or servant; it acts in the name of and in behalf of some one else and not for itself. Not only is government the servant of the people, but it is an untrustworthy and unreliable servant. It cannot be given a free hand in caring for the affairs of its master; on the contrary, it must be limited in many ways; it must be checked at every possible point; it must be at all times under suspicion. Otherwise, it will cease to be servant and take the place of master. Too much emphasis cannot well be laid upon the fear which the 'Fathers' had of government. *To them the great lesson of history was, that government always tends to become oppressive, and that it is the greatest foe of individual liberty.*" (Pages 76 and 77). (Emphasis added.)

In Poindexter vs. Greenhow (1885), 114 U. S. 270, 29 Law Ed. 185, the Supreme Court of the United States speaking through Mr. Justice Matthews again reaffirmed these great principles in the following language:

"The State itself is an ideal person, intangible, invisible, immutable. The government is an agent, and, within the sphere of the agency, a perfect representative; but outside of that it is lawless usurpation. The Constitution of the State is the limit of the authority of its government, and both government and State are subject to the supremacy of the Constitution of the United States and of the laws made in pursuance thereof. So that, while it is true in respect to the government of a State, as was said in Langford v. U. S., 101 U. S. 341 (Bk. 25 L. Ed. 1010), that the maxim that the King can do no wrong has no place in our system of government; yet it is also true, in respect to the State itself, that whatever wrong is attempted in its name is imputable to its government and not to the State, for, as it can speak and act only by law, whatever it does say and do must be lawful. That which, therefore, is unlawful because made so by the supreme law, the Constitution of the United States, is not the word or deed of the State, but is the mere wrong and trespass of those individual persons who falsely speak and act in its name. * * *

"This distinction is essential to the idea of constitutional government. To deny it or blot it out obliterates the line of demarcation that separates constitutional government from absolutism, free self-government based on the sovereignty of the people, from that despotism, *whether of the one or the many*, which enables the agent of the State to declare and decree that he is the State—to say 'L'Etat, c'est moi.' Of what avail are written constitutions, whose bills of right for the security of individual liberty have been written, too often, with the blood of martyrs shed upon the battle field and the scaffold, if their limitations and restraints upon power may be overpassed with impunity by the very agencies created and appointed to guard, defend and enforce them; and that, too, with the sacred authority of law, not only compelling obedience, but entitled to respect? And how else can these principles of individual liberty and right be maintained, if, when violated, the judicial tribunals are forbidden to visit penalties upon individual offenders, who are the instruments of wrong, whenever they interpose the shield of the State? The doctrine is not to be tolerated. The whole frame and scheme of the political institutions of this country, State and Federal, protest against it. Their continued existence is not compatible with it. It is the doctrine of absolutism, pure, simple and naked; and of communism, which is the twin; the double progeny of the same evil birth." (Emphasis ours).

However, beginning about the date of this decision, or shortly thereafter, there has been a great change in the thinking of our people with respect to the proper relation of government to the individual. Our people, our executives, our legislators, and in many instances our courts, have often come to the point where liberty means the lack of restraint upon the masses of our people, to the extent that any proposal which purports to advance the welfare of the public, or a part of the public, is paramount and justifiable, even though it may impose upon individual liberty. The results which are sought to be accomplished have frequently been used to justify the means of accomplishment. Our individual liberties are in danger of being overwhelmed by public necessities. The trend is now towards expediency, and our executives, administrative bodies, legislatures, and even our courts have been able to rationalize and justify almost any measure which the general public demands, under the theory that it is for the general welfare and common good. This has in a large measure been to the disparagement of private rights and individual genius.

After almost two centuries under our form of government, we are reaching its greatest test. Can we preserve our individual genius and freedom against the demands of our public selves? Will we lose entirely the line of demarcation between private rights and public necessity? Will we ultimately destroy the Constitution and our form of government through the process of gradual attrition without even a constitutional amendment? The question is best stated by Everett Dean Martin in his volume entitled "Liberty" (1930) as follows:

"One hundred years ago the struggle for liberty was a struggle of the average individual against the tyranny of a nobility, a monarchy, a priesthood. Now the enemy of liberty seems to be the crowd itself, operating through the instrumentalities of the Machine Age and its social organization. If this view is correct, then the problem of liberty must be recast in new terms of social psychology. It becomes a challenge to men to understand themselves and to master themselves in new ways in order that they may retain some vestige of their inherited freedom.

"The psychological fact is that to the mass of men, acting as a whole, liberty is primarily the removal of restraint on crowd behavior, and what crowds call liberty is not liberty for the individual; it is liberty for the crowd to act without considering the results of its behavior on other people.

"The old struggle for liberty was, as has been pointed out, a struggle of common men against a sovereign. For several hundreds of years that struggle went on. Every clause in our Bill of Rights, every right that we enjoy was wrung from an unwilling sovereign who sought to impose his will upon the people. When the sovereign is no longer a king but the sovereign people itself, the situation is entirely changed. When the mass becomes sovereign it immediately announces: The voice of the people is the voice of God; and, The people can do no wrong! There is no longer the same reason for protecting the individual against the sovereign when the sovereign happens to be ourselves acting as Mass. The question is, how are we going to protect the personal self of ourselves against the public self of everybody?" (Pages 9 and 10).

Whenever we lose the distinction between individual liberty and the necessities of the general welfare, the virtue of our form of government is lost, and we have nothing but the worst form of tyranny, which is a despotism imposed by the force of and under the name of the people themselves. We will have, then, nothing that is preferable to any other form of tyranny or despotism elsewhere.

It would be a wise thing now for all of the people of the
United States, and particularly those who serve as our representatives in a legislative capacity, to again at this time re-
examine the real meaning of liberty, and to re-examine their
philosophy of government, and see whether or not we have
departed substantially from the basic principles of the democratic process as given to us by the founders of this government.

It is now time for the people of our generation to again
become political scientists. It is now a proper time for a wide-
spread revival of interest in representative and constitutional
government, and to learn that individual freedom is the basis
of democracy, and that individualism is of equal importance
with the public welfare.

We should realize the danger in a public bill of rights, because a public bill of rights implies that there is a duty and
obligation upon others, or upon the public, to fulfill the demands and necessities included. This is just another way of
advocating collectivism, which is the complete opposite of
anything which our individual Bill of Rights advocates.

We believe with Woodrow Wilson that "Liberty has never
come from the government. . . . The history of liberty is the
history of the limitation of governmental power, not the increase of it."

We believe that a careful study and analysis of the meaning
of the Ninth Amendment will be helpful when the time comes
for the casting of our ballots in appraising the issues of the
day and in determining whether any proposal is in keeping
with the true principles of a republican form of government.

FOREWORD TO PART II

In the first part of this work we have attempted to establish that the protection of the individual and his naturally endowed rights are the principal office and purpose of a democratic form of government. We have further tried to demonstrate that the Ninth Amendment is an expression of this basic concept.

We have felt, however, that this discussion would be incomplete without some inquiry as to what we actually mean when we speak of individualism, and whether it deserves the importance we have placed upon it.

Since the individual under our constitutional form of government is sovereign in his sphere, should we not while declaring this sovereignty, at the same time give some thought to the mould of character of the average citizens who must necessarily compose our body politic, if our form of government is to survive. The subject matter of this discussion is merely half covered if we go only far enough to establish our rights of natural endowment without including an analysis of our duties and obligations.

It is with this thought that we offer the following chapters.

PART II

CHAPTER 9

THE IMPORTANCE OF BEING AN INDIVIDUAL

Individualism is a spiritual concept. It is basically and historically the most important element in our national origin, growth, and progress.

It is important and significant in three great respects.

First, it is the very basis of a democratic form of government, the basis of our social and political compact, and the virtue which distinguishes our form of government from the dictatorships, autocracies, and Communism.

We all know that in the totalitarian forms of government, the State demands all; the individual is secondary and is vested with no rights, but only has such privileges as may be granted him by the government. The Ninth Amendment points up the basic differences between these forms of government and ours.

In our government, we begin with the individual who is "endowed" by his Creator with inalienable rights established by "the laws of nature and of nature's God." Some of these rights the individual surrenders, or partly surrenders, by his consent, for the establishment of a government.

The totalitarian forms of government assert that the State is the supreme power and that individuals have no natural or fundamental rights, but all of their privileges are gifts from the State and may be revoked or denied at will by the government.

The real conflict exists because tyrants and despots in the administration of a totalitarian form of government cannot recognize any right that any individual could claim as against the power of government, or any moral or spiritual force which is beyond its control.

Therefore, the despotic forms of government cannot exist with God because it cannot allow its people to maintain a belief in a Supreme Being more powerful than the State. In

64

order to maintain supremacy it becomes necessary for these tyrants to destroy the last vestige of the spiritual life of the individual, and to destroy his faith in Deity because such ideas are a threat to the total government. It further becomes necessary for such a government to destroy the concept of individual liberty or freedom because these are always present threats to total power.

The struggle in the world now is no different than it has been down through the ages.

The question that constantly confronts the world is whether or not the nations of the world will be governed by men without the spiritual guidance of a Supreme Being, or whether we shall live under a system of laws which are inspired through the moral and spiritual guidance of God.

The American people made many early declarations of their allegiance to God which were climaxed in the founding of the government in the Declaration of Independence. From the beginning our greatest leaders have been imbued with a deep sense of humility and worship, and they have always asked for spiritual guidance in the administration of the affairs of government.

The early American people were spiritually inclined. Religious worship and devotion to God have been the greatest building stones in our national structure. This statement is not merely a sentimental or emotional expression, but on the other hand a strongly factual truth and must be considered as elemental in every phase of our national growth.

Of the thirteen colonies there were seven which were founded for the sake of religious freedom alone. All of the colonies were founded either directly or indirectly because of the desire of the colonists for religious freedom or other personal liberties. America has not only been the "land of the free and home of the brave", but it has also been the home of the devout and faithful. We can truly say that God is the soul of America and that freedom to worship God is the most cherished of all our personal liberties.

In the building of this nation, the concept of Deity and the relationship of the Deity to our inherent and natural rights was not a mere abstraction; it was more than mere philosophy or sentiment; it was more than a ritual. It has been the most real, vital, and inspiring force in America.

Neither have we at this time, after more than a century and a half of government under the Constitution, departed from the basic beliefs and teachings of our forefathers.

Today the moral and spiritual nature of the American people is the real strength and power in our national existence. Our love of freedom and our personal liberties are still the basis of our national life. While our material gifts and blessings are immense, these gifts and blessings are the fruit of the inward spiritual graces which characterize us, and the product of three centuries of stimulus through the exercise of natural and inherent liberty and freedom, and living in humility before God. A belief in rights comes from the spiritual development of a people.

The American people as a whole, and with little exception, now recognize that there is a force and power in the universe that is greater than the force and power of man; an intellect that is greater than the human intellect, and a perfection that humans can never attain.

The moral and spiritual resources of our democracy are its greatest national assets.

This would have been impossible, however, under a form of government which did not recognize the essential importance of the freedom of the individual. We see, then, that the office of the Ninth Amendment is fully revealed as announcing in a single sentence our fundamental belief in individual freedom; in a single sentence it is an expression of individualism as the basis of democracy.

Secondly, individualism is important because it is essential to the spiritual nature of a human being. Man is part human and part divine. Our individuality is the part of the Deity that is within us. Our individuality is proof of the infinite part of our beings and our immortality.

God created us as individuals; we should always struggle to live as individuals and help others to live as individuals, because individualism is a part of the Divine plan. We were created as individuals for a purpose. It is not merely an accidental occurrence that of all the millions of people in the world, no two of us should look alike. Could there possibly be more convincing proof of the infinity of our being. If it were intended that we should be identical in thought, in conduct, and in our personalities, then nature would have provided that we all would look alike.

Individualism is the essential basis of human life because human nature demands a spiritual existence. It is only natural for mankind to know the infinity of God and to have faith in the comfort and health that comes to an individual through his belief in a Divine Being. From the beginning of history mankind has realized his own insufficiency, and it has been with few exceptions that any nation or race of people, or any individuals have lived in atheism. The despots or tyrants who have believed in their own self-sufficiency have always within a short time met with destruction.

It is only natural, and it is a part of our individual nature, to believe that there is a Supreme Being that is wiser, greater, and more compassionate than any human can be. It is against human nature for men to worship men. Every individual knows that he has a soul and an infinite nature, and that there is a part within him of a greatness which he is incapable of fully understanding. The greater a person becomes and the richer his experience, the more he realizes the infiniteness of his nature and his inability to fulfill the potential greatness that is within him.

Mankind demands God because being partly divine in his nature, he is incomplete without Him. And what is more, his belief in God is an individual concept. There are as many religions in the world as there are people in the world.

How fortunate we are that we live in a country, whose destinies were so guided by our ancestors, that we as individuals can live in harmony with our soul and our infinite nature, with the recognition of the right to do so as a natural and inherent right. How unfortunate are those who live under a form of government that denies them the right to profess and practice their individual religious and spiritual life except with the consent of the government under which they live.

Thirdly, it is important to be permitted to live as an individual because individual liberty is essential to the happiness of a people in their material life. It is a most elemental natural instinct of mankind to demand to be free.

Liberty or freedom are the equivalents of the right to live as an individual. The desire for freedom is a primary expression of the soul of mankind.

We cannot consider government in an impersonal manner without taking into consideration the natural instincts and impulses of those who are governed. Human relationships are essentially based on human nature. The intricacies of governmental and world affairs are no deeper than the intricacies of human beings. The desire to be an individual, or the desire to be free, is now and always has been the most important and dynamic force in the world's progress.

Democratic forms of government have flourished only because it is the theory of democracy that every one of its citizens, be he ever so humble, is a separate and important personality, and living as such in an atmosphere of freedom, he shall be privileged to develop his natural gifts or personality to the fullest extent.

There is nothing in human nature that tolerates abuse or slavery. There is nothing in human nature which is in conflict with the freedom of the soul. There is no natural human trait or desire which chooses submission over liberty, or abject obedience over freedom. Any such impulse is contrary to the natural instinct of men. If men are not free, it is not because they do not desire to be free.

Much has been written on the much debated subject as to whether or not there are any such things as natural rights or natural freedoms. It is enough to say in this discussion that this government has always been dedicated and committed to the doctrine of the rights of natural endowment and the divine source of these rights. Until the very form of our government is changed, and until the Declaration of Independence and the great liberty documents have been entirely repudiated, and until the Ninth Amendment has been repealed, we shall still be committed to this same philosophy of rights. Those who argue against the existence of natural rights with which individuals are endowed by their Creator, should carefully weigh their arguments and see if they are not inevitably led into a theory that undermines the very basis of democratic government.

Religious freedom, however, is not by any means the only expression of the demand of the soul of an individual for freedom.

The right of individuals to acquire property and to enjoy the fruits of their own labor are natural rights and are essential to the mental and spiritual happiness of the individual. This is true because human nature demands these rights. The right of private ownership of property is one of the freedoms and liberties that makes our system of government preferable to any other. It is one of the greatest sources of the moral strength of our nation.

There has never been a nation in history comparable to the United States of America. It is unique and different because of the heterogeneous nature of our population. When we take time to stop and think of it, this is a tremendous phenomenon. Assembled under one flag and under one loyalty are millions of people from all of the races, creeds, and nations of the world. This is something new in history. It is one of the marvels of the world that a nation composed of such a citizenship could remain united. This flow of population began about one hundred years ago, and yet there has been no ebb in our standard of loyalty and patriotism on the part of our people as a whole. The reason is that most men came to this country in search of freedom of one kind or another. The spirit of brotherly love has cemented our mutual interest in each other and our faith in our country.

This liberty and freedom has also made our land the land of golden opportunity. How often has the immigrant boy beginning at the bottom of the ladder finished his career as the president or owner of the business. Every boy, or possibly every girl, has a chance to be President. Every person who lives in this country has an opportunity for financial success.

The enemies of our standards of life sometimes seek to discount our system of government by calling it capitalism, with an implication that capitalism is unjust or immoral. Capitalism means only that we believe in the right of private ownership of property as a natural and inherent right. Actually our system of government is not only capitalism, but individualism, and the right of private ownership of property is only one of its virtues. It is the system where we can work and retain the fruits of our labor; we can retain the benefits of our thrift, and we can save and make provision for our loved ones for their protection after we have gone.

There are many other examples and illustrations of the liberties with which men are naturally endowed. We have only to search the great liberty documents to find them. The right to religious freedom, and the right of private ownership of property, however, are two of the outstanding liberties with which men are naturally endowed, which forcefully illustrate the importance of the right to live as an individual.

These illustrations make us realize and appreciate the virtues of our system of government, and make us realize that any government which does not have as its basic ideal the enhancement of the life and possibilities of the individual, or which tends to destroy the individual genius of its people, is a force that is contrary to human nature and the natural instincts of men, and is eventually doomed to failure.

The destruction of the genius of the individual cannot possibly lead to anything more than a feeling of futility in men's outlook on life, and this of course will inevitably result more and more in his disregard of the lives and happiness of others. The concept of individuality has led to a high sense of responsibility on the part of our people. As individuals practice and enjoy freedom, the more they desire that other people will be free. Freedom has in our country led to a higher degree of tolerance than exists in any other nation in the world. Individual freedom has always been the highest development of civilization. The greater our intellect, the more desirous are we that we shall live in peace and in charity with other people.

History has proven that the minds of men are more apt to learn the truth when they are spiritually and intellectually free. We believe that the spirit of mankind, with divine guidance and power, is the best means with which to harness and control the powerful forces of evil that are contrived by those who have no belief in the Infinite.

May we always, however, have in our ever present consciousness, the knowledge that our heritage of liberty is handed down to us from generation to generation without any guarantee of survival unless each generation learns and realizes its debt to posterity. May we ever remember that history records the many times that liberties of a free people in a democracy, even when once attained, have been lost.

We should constantly keep in our foremost thoughts the knowledge that individual liberty exists only in a democracy, and has no place in any other form of government. When we speak of individual liberty, we do not realize it but we are actually meaning to speak of individual liberty in a *democracy*. If individual liberty is important and if we love freedom, then we must preserve the democratic processes of government. Natural rights are unknown in a totalitarian government.

May we study and keep fresh in our memories, and the memories of our children, the real meaning of liberty and freedom and the excellence of our heritage. May we ever impress upon those who come after us that our form of government excels because the enhancement of the individual is its cardinal virtue, and the principal reason why it is superior to those forms of government which disregard the individual and fail to recognize his infinite and spiritual nature.

CHAPTER 10

THE RESTRAINTS ON INDIVIDUALISM

While it is true that man is a spiritual being, it is equally true that he is a human being, and the conflict between the human and the spiritual is constant. There must of necessity be restraints on individual behavior. We who believe in democracy realize that not only the government must be restrained, but the individual must be restrained in the interest of maintenance of an orderly society. Those of us who are unwilling to cheerfully consent to the reasonable and necessary restraints that may be placed upon us, do not have a real basic belief in the processes of democratic government. There are some rights and privileges which we must surrender for the common good.

In the letter to Congress dated September 17, 1787, over the signature of George Washington, the President of the Convention, with which the proposed Constitution was sent to Congress, we find the best expression of this thought:

"Individuals entering into society, must give up a share of liberty to preserve the rest. The magnitude of the sacrifice must depend as well on situation and circumstance, as on the object to be obtained. It is at all times difficult to draw with precision the line between those rights which must be surrendered and those which may be reserved."

Government was instituted primarily for the purpose of curbing and restraining the selfish and over-aggressive side of our natures. The ultimate ideal of government is to strike that balance which will encourage and protect the freedom of our individual natures, yet at the same time restrain the unfair and unjust purposes to which the human side of our being is subjected. Individual enterprise is a part of the basis of our natural philosophy, but it is not a free and unrestrained exercise of selfish endeavor. Our belief in private ownership of property and individual enterprise does not mean that we believe in a "dog eat dog" competitive world. Undoubtedly the incentive of individual gain, and the pride and security

72

in the acquisition of property, are all essential for progress and individual morale. On the other hand, if selfishness and aggressiveness are not curbed, there is no end to the hardships that would be suffered by those who cannot equally compete. The moral code of democracy is that we must, by encouraging the individual, retain the stimulus to the genius of our people, yet at the same time learn to apply the restraints that are necessary for social justice. We must always retain the reasonable restraints upon over-aggressiveness and selfishness, but we should never go to the extreme of adopting a policy of sentimental over-generosity and assistance that will in short time weaken our people by doing for them the things which they should be able and willing to do for themselves, and thus stifle genius and destroy their stamina.

Our laws and our system of government must necessarily have restraints and just punishments for those who are so obsessed with greed that they cease to know or feel the natural restraints of conscience.

It is sometimes difficult to reconcile individual enterprise and proper governmental restraints. This problem is one of the greatest problems of the administration of a democracy. The dividing line is not established by any demonstrable theorem and is never fixed or static. The problem is a continuing problem, and will always exist as long as there is a democracy. It was never intended that it should be settled. The loss of balance, however, is the pitfall and the danger that is ever present.

On the one extreme is government through the worship and power of extreme materialism, and on the other extreme is state socialism or even Communism. To this date our national leaders, with the help and morale of the people, have steered the course wisely and well. However, our salvation does not lie in the wisdom of leadership but in the character and temperament of the people. We find daily large groups of people who are on the verge of being classified as "government haters", and on the other hand we find large groups of people who are resentful of the material success of others, even though through heavy taxation our legislators have placed curbs and restraints upon excessive gain. We should never let either of these groups gain the ascendancy. The survival of our system of government depends in a great measure upon the moral force of middle-class psychology.

The continuing course of democratic government depends upon whether or not the rank and file of our people will understand this problem of democratic government, and will cultivate and develop within themselves the most just and sincere parts of their nature.

The question is not whether our leadership is right, so much as whether or not the people are thinking right.

In discussing the Bill of Rights before the First Congress, James Madison, the Father of the Bill of Rights, warned the people that

"The prescriptions in favor of liberty ought to be leveled against that quarter where the greatest danger lies, namely, that which possesses the highest prerogative of power. But this is not found in either the Executive or Legislative Department of the Government, but in the body of the people, operating by the majority against the minority. But I confess that I do conceive that in a government modified like this of the United States, the great danger lies rather in the abuse of the community, than in the legislative body." (Gales and Seaton's "Annals of Congress", page 93).

It was because of the fears of the excesses of the people as well as fears of the administrators of government that the framers of the Constitution set up the system of restraints, checks, and balances, on both officers and the people alike, and in their wisdom saw fit to protect the rights of individuals in the Bill of Rights, and then for further assurance added the Ninth Amendment confirming the basic belief in the rights and dignity of the individual.

Strange as it may seem, however, there are several absolutisms in our system of government. Some of them may be briefly named.

For instance, there is no restraint in some respects upon the power of the Supreme Court of the United States. In many respects it is the sole and final judge of its own powers and authority. Yet this body has always so carefully examined its powers, authority, and its sphere of influence, that it has been recognized as the greatest stabilizing force in our Republic from its beginning up until the present date. This is because our Justices have always possessed a deep sense of responsibility, and strong moral and spiritual fibre.

Another absolutism is the power and privilege of a member of Congress to be entirely unrestrained in any utterance he may desire to make upon the floor of Congress. This power is a sacred public trust, and its abuse has always led to disrepute and ruin because of the moral sense of justice on the part of his constituents.

The freedom of the press is also in many regards in this country an absolutism. This freedom also is one of the most sacred public trusts in a democracy, and without it a free people could not long survive. A breach of this governmental public confidence has always been regarded by the American people as a disgrace. Yet the public press in this country has been a source of inspiration, and has maintained the confidence of our people in democratic government.

However, the greatest absolutism in a democracy resides in the individual citizen himself. The individual is the basic unit of sovereignty in this Republic, and has powers through the ballot box, through his power of free speech and other liberties, that do not inhere in any other people in the world. The proper use or abuse of the powers of the individual are the eventual test of the success or failure of free government. Democracy is an ideal, but it is based upon the theory of the citizen as an ideal citizen. When the importance of this fact dawns upon us, the more we come to a realization that we must use the absolute power that is within our hands in such a manner as to prove that the theory of democracy is sound. The burden upon us is not so much to govern and regulate the conduct of our neighbors and fellow citizens, but to study ourselves and determine whether or not we are actuated by worthy or unworthy traits of human character when we are called upon to exercise the absolute governmental power and authority invested in us. Do we cast our vote and do we exercise our powers of free speech because of a selfish or financial interest? Are we actuated from some gain which we hope to obtain out of the public treasury? Are we actuated with prejudice, or with an open and just mind? Do we ask ourselves how long the democratic system would survive if everyone voted as we vote, or if everyone exerted the same influence that we exert?

The great poet Wordsworth has said "the discipline of tyranny is not known among us; therefore must we practice the discipline of virtue."

We finally realize that the survival of democracy depends not so much upon the agencies of government, but upon the restraints and the self-discipline which we as individuals are willing to impose upon ourselves.

Our forefathers were not dealing in rhetoric or oratory when they signed the Declaration of Independence and said that they pledged "our lives, our fortunes and our sacred honor" to the cause of liberty and freedom. Many unselfish patriots have carried the lighted torch of liberty to our generation and placed it in our hands.

Are we as present day Americans still able to practice self-discipline to the extent that we are able to preserve our heritage and hand the torch of liberty and freedom to the next generation?

CHAPTER 11

OUR BILL OF OBLIGATIONS

The Bill of Rights is not a gift without obligation. The proper corollary of a bill of rights is a bill of obligation. A republican form of government is neither self-executing nor self-perpetuating. Our Bill of Rights will remain with us only as long as we are worthy of them. The survival of democracy depends upon the stamina of the manhood and womanhood of America, and the maintenance of the highest degree of patriotism.

The early demise of democracy may be predicted if our people think of democracy only in terms of their rights and give no thought to their obligations. We learn from history that when the quality of citizenship degenerates, liberty is lost.

Except for the periods of world wars, our people have accepted with a great degree of complaisance and assurance the blessings of liberty under our system of government, and have given only a slight degree of serious thought to what price has been paid and must be paid for these blessings. We are a glorious nation in the way we respond in time of war against a foreign enemy, but we are inclined to be undisciplined, selfish, and uninformed when performing our duty to our country in times of peace. We have grown into a custom or habit of believing that "everything is all right", and that there is not much that we can individually do about it if it were otherwise. We are inclined to get just a trifle bored when we are reminded of our duties and obligations of citizenship. There is a tendency to mildly ridicule the patriotic efforts of our citizens by accusing them of "flag waving". The well-being of our country is taken for granted. This is largely because we have never experienced a national catastrophe or defeat. America has never lost a war. We have never had the will of another sovereign imposed upon us. We have never been as a nation brought to our knees. For these reasons, we have become to a degree apathetic and have lost some of the diligence and political consciousness engendered through hardship and defeat.

We should all remind ourselves, however, that we are living in a world at this time in which there are two principal schools of thought, one of which believes in the rights of the individual, and one of which does not. We should also realize that while we are living in a republic, nevertheless transformations can take place in our country under the name and disguise of the democratic process, which are not at all in keeping with democratic government and individual freedom. At this time we should be watching and guarding against the rise of autocracy in the administrative processes of our government. The separation of the powers of government is the means by which constitutional government is preserved. The over-extension of administrative powers, and the exercise by administrative bodies of legislative, judicial, and executive powers have already become a threat to our republican form of government. It is even suggested by some that we now have a fourth power or division of government, known as the administrative branch of government which is complete within itself through the exercise of a portion of the three great powers of government outlined in our Constitution. Transformations have occurred in the governments of other countries where one branch of the government gains ascendancy over the others, and can, except with our diligence and patriotism, undermine our government.

We believe that when each citizen reads with pride the individual liberties that are secure to him under our Bill of Rights, he should then be conscious of his obligations and duties, which are the price he must pay for his liberties.

Some of the duties and obligations which we owe in exchange for our liberty are the following:

1. Our first duty is to defend our country with our lives if necessary. The signers of the Declaration of Independence pledged "our lives, our fortunes, and our sacred honor." Are we in this day and time willing to measure our patriotism by the same standard?

The fighting forces of this nation have been the greatest that the world has ever known. There have never been any military forces that have ever compared with those of our country, either from a standpoint of loyalty or courage; in this respect we have certainly fulfilled our obligation. Americans have always been willing to fight for and to die for their country.

2. Those of us who are not in the military service and who do not offer to die for our country on the battlefield certainly owe an obligation to our fighting men and to our country to be worth dying for.

3. We owe an obligation to maintain a reverent belief in God as the guide of the destiny of this nation, and to encourage an attitude of gratitude, humility, and worship of the Supreme Being.

4. We owe the duty of fostering and preserving the sanctity of the American family group and family life.

5. We owe the duty of cheerfully paying our taxes and sharing the reasonable expense of the administration of our government.

6. We owe the duty of working and making our lives useful, and to maintain a respect for the dignity of labor.

7. We owe the duty of maintaining the American tradition of integrity in our business and profession, and to stamp out and refrain from the practice of unfair or unethical competition.

8. We owe a duty to participate in government, and in all matters in which we can cast our ballot we should never fail to do so.

9. We owe a duty to be outspoken in praise of the services and accomplishments of public servants and functions of government which are praiseworthy; to be just in our criticism, and never to criticize unless we can do so authentically. We should overcome the tendency to criticize our public officers and our governmental functions more frequently than to praise their virtues.

10. We owe a duty to maintain the efficiency of the system of jury trial in this country and to serve in that capacity always when called upon to do.

11. We owe a duty to enjoy a wholesome leisure, and to support a program that will provide a healthful and wholesome leisure for all of our people.

12. We owe a duty to take such physical care of our bodies that will enable us to fulfill whatever worthwhile possibilities are within us. At all ages, American citizens should be able to compare physically with the citizens of other countries, and particularly any enemy. We owe a duty not to become a public burden through self-indulgence.

13. We owe a duty to be tolerant of the condition of life and opinions of other people.

14. We owe a duty to be charitable, and to contribute within our reasonable means for the maintenance of private charities for those who are unable to maintain themselves.

15. We owe a duty to keep informed on public issues and to learn enough of the background and the platform of aspirants for public office, to enable us to cast an intelligent vote.

16. We owe a duty to support our system of free public schools and to foster the education of our youth.

17. Every citizen owes a duty of practicing the Golden Rule, and to develop a love and consideration for all kinds and conditions of people.

18. Every citizen owes it to himself, to his maker, and to his country to try at all ages in life to develop the powers, talents, and personality with which he is naturally gifted.

Of course, this is by no means an exhaustive list of our duties or obligations. Our duties are as numerous as our rights.

In the proceedings and debates of the First Session of the Eighty-second Congress on Monday, April 9, 1951, under remarks of the Honorable Paul J. Kilday, is outlined a "Bill of Responsibilities" which has been proposed by the American Citizenship Committee of the State Bar of Texas. This is a magnificent document which every citizen should read. Attached to the Bill of Responsibilities is a questionnaire which asks in a series of questions whether or not "you are a full time citizen". This questionnaire enables the citizen to make a practical self-analysis and to rate himself as to whether or not he is living up to his responsibilities as a citizen. We heartily recommend that this test should be taken seriously by every citizen of this country. It is the American tradition, however, that the rights of a citizen are guaranteed and protected, regardless of whether he fulfills his obligations, and even his lack of patriotism does not deprive him of his rights.

The conscience of the American people requires that even the lowest type of criminal is entitled to a square deal. It is one of the hardships of democracy that some of us must bear more than our equal share of the burden and responsibilities of government because there is a minority which is unwilling to do its part.

However, the vast majority of our people are conscious of these obligations and try to fulfill them. This deep sense of responsibility is one of the main reasons why democracy is still working in this country of ours.

CHAPTER 12

CONCLUSION

The United States of America has achieved the highest state of civilization that the world has ever known. This is true not only from a standpoint of economic development, but spiritual development also.

Our economic success is one of the strongest proofs that freedom and democracy are the superior way of life.

What is more important, however, is the fact that the American character is ingrained with love which is not only the greatest force in the world, but the most noble trait of human nature. It is traditional and historic with the American citizen that he believes in practical and applied religion by desiring to share with others the material gifts and comforts with which this nation has been at this time blessed above all others. In addition, a deep sense of justice is a part of the make-up of each one of us.

However, because of our favored position among the people of the world, we must also realize the magnitude of our responsibility. We occupy at this time in the stream of history the most responsible position that any nation has ever known. The future history of this nation will in all probability be the determining factor in the life or death of democracy. The ultimate result of the struggle will determine whether or not the people of our nation, as well as the people of the world, will be governed by love and justice or by fear and tyranny, and whether or not men are capable of self-government.

Is there any question as to whether or not men are capable of self-government? Our answer, of course, is to readily say without a doubt that men are. Actually, however, history reveals that up to the present-day republics, democracy has failed. The shocking part, however, is that they have failed from within and not from forces from without. Our second great President has warned us that "there never was a democracy in all history which did not commit suicide."

A century and three quarters is not a long time when we look far backward and look far forward. The great test of democracy, which is an emblem of the forces for good in the world, may now be at hand. Democracy as we know it is comparatively young, and our marvelous country is one of the very youngest in the family of nations.

There is one vast difference, however, between our country and the old democracies. We live in a country which curbs the powers of the various departments of the government, and this enables the people to keep control of their government. It has stood the test of time so far, and will continue to stand the test of time if we will be constantly aware of the evils and dangers of unrestrained power in any form of government. We must be ever vigilant, lest gradual mutations and transformations become a menace to the separation of the powers of government. It is possible through the relaxation of restraint upon any of the departments of government through necessity or expediency, that our very form of government could actually be changed under our very eyes without even as much as a single constitutional amendment.

We must at all times be impressed with our duty to support and defend our Constitution. Democracy is an ideal. It is an expression of the aspiration for the complete attainment of spiritual truth and justice among men. The best means of attaining this ideal that has yet been formulated is a republican form of constitutional government. The government of the United States of America under our Constitution is superior to all others.

The only real danger is whether or not our people will prove themselves worthy of freedom by maintaining individually the highest degree of character and patriotism.

We must overcome the forces of envy, selfishness, and apathy which have in the past destroyed self-government, and learn more of the lessons of self-discipline.

Certainly there are injustices which must and will be righted. But as long as we maintain our free school system and equality of opportunity for everyone, and as long as we have the universal ballot, our people will become conscious of injustice, and they have always proven that they are ready to provide relief. Law is not perfect. Law is a human attempt to define and dispense justice. Its human quality shows that it must be imperfect in some respects. However, as our people

are self-governing, there is much greater probability of adjustment of wrongs than where justice is dispensed by one or by
a few.

If we believe in private ownership of property, then we
must realize that some of us will have greater material wealth
than others and none of our people can permit themselves
to rankle and become bitter, because it is a part of our system
to believe in private ownership of property.

Oftentimes there is a confusion in the minds of ordinary
people as to what are the true standards of judging success or
failure. Many people are inclined to feel that they have not
lived a successful life because the work which they have
accomplished has gained no public recognition or acclaim, or
because they have not amassed a fortune. Yet these same
people have lived the ordinary and simple life of love and
service. It may be that in the last few decades we have over-
emphasized or vulgarized ambition. Possibly we need to preach
a little more that money and property are not the real source
of happiness, nor the proof of a successful life. The successful
life is a life of service, and happiness comes from unselfish
love and purposeful work. A person does not have to possess
a large bank account, or live in a mansion and possess the
things that go with it, in order to take pride in his life and
accomplishments. A man is a success if he has "the right job
and the right woman."

> "Enough if something from our hands have power
> To live, and act, and serve the future hour,
> And if, as toward the silent tomb we go,
> Through love, through hope, and faith's
>   transcendant dower,
> We feel that we are greater than we know."

The people who are happiest are those who live simply but
have a high standard of thinking. You have done your part if
you have tried your best to develop that personality which is
yours and yours alone.

If you would take time to consider, you would realize that
you are a wonderful and worthwhile person. You have a part
of the Deity in your infinite being. You are the final work of
God, and you are so important in His plan that you have been
created as an individual. You possess a personality that no other

person in the world possesses. You have the opportunity to live a life that no one else can live. You can serve the world in a way that no other person can serve. You have duties and responsibilities that cannot be performed by anyone else. You have a purpose in life that no one else can fulfill. Mankind is the final work of God, and you as an individual are one of God's masterpieces. You have an equal chance of achievement, and your success is limited only by the amount of effort you are willing to expend. As a citizen of the United States of America, you are given the greatest opportunity to live a purposeful life, to develop your native ability and to pursue happiness for yourself and your loved ones that the world has ever known.

The Ninth Amendment to our Constitution is a guarantee of our individual personality. It makes you realize that of all the people in the world, there is no one like you. It impresses upon you that you have been purposely created as an individual, and have been endowed with gifts and personal genius that no one else possesses. You are an important and worthwhile personality and you live under a government that has not forgotten you as an individual. May you always continue to fight for and believe in a government that believes in you.

May all of us be humbly grateful to a Creator who has endowed us with a soul, and a constitutional government which guarantees to us the right to own it.

APPENDIX I

August 25, 1789

The resolve of the House of Representatives of the 24th of August, was read, as followeth:

"CONGRESS OF THE UNITED STATES,

"In the House of Representatives,
"Monday, the 24th of August, 1789.

"Resolved by the Senate and House of Representatives of the United States of America in Congress assembled, two-thirds of both Houses deeming it necessary, That the following articles be proposed to the legislatures of the several states, as amendments to the constitution of the United States; all or any of which articles, when ratified by three-fourths of the said legislatures, to be valid, to all intents and purposes, as part of the said constitution: to-wit:

"Articles in addition to, and amendment of, the constitution of the United States of America, proposed by Congress, and ratified by the legislatures of the several states, pursuant to the fifth article of the original constitution.

"Art. I. After the first enumeration, required by the first article of the constitution, there shall be one representative for every thirty-thousand, until the number shall amount to one hundred; after which the proportion shall be so regulated by Congress, that there shall be not less than one hundred representatives, nor less than one representative for every forty thousand persons, until the number of representatives shall amount to two hundred; after which the proportion shall be so regulated by Congress, that there shall not be less than two hundred representatives, nor less than one representative for every fifty thousand persons.

"Art. II. No law, varying the compensation to the members of Congress, shall take effect, until an election of representatives shall have intervened.

"Art. III. Congress shall make no law establishing religion, or prohibiting the free exercise thereof; nor shall the rights of conscience be infringed.

"Art. IV. The freedom of speech, and of the press, and the right of the people peaceably to assemble and consult for their common good, and to apply to the government for redress of grievances, shall not be infringed.

"Art. V. A well regulated militia, composed of the body of the people, being the best security of a free state, the right of the people to keep and bear arms, shall not be infringed, but no one religiously scrupulous of bearing arms shall be compelled to render military service in person.

"Art. VI. No soldier shall, in time of peace, be quartered in any house, without the consent of the owner; nor in time of war, but in a manner to be prescribed by law.

"Art. VII. The right of the people to be secured in their persons, houses, papers, and effects, against unreasonable searches and seizures, shall not be violated, and no warrants shall issue, but upon probable cause, supported by oath or affirmation, and particularly describing the place to be searched, and the persons or things to be seized.

"Art. VIII. No person shall be subject, except in case of impeachment, to more than one trial, or one punishment, for the same offense, nor shall be compelled, in any criminal case, to be a witness against himself; nor be deprived of life, liberty, or property, without due process of law; nor shall private property be taken for public use without just compensation.

"Art. IX. In all criminal prosecutions, the accused shall enjoy the right to a speedy and public trial; to be informed of the nature and cause of the accusations; to be confronted with the witnesses against him; to have compulsory process for obtaining witnesses in his favor; and to have the assistance of counsel for his defense.

"Art. X. The trial of all crimes (except in cases of impeachment, and in cases arising in the land or naval forces, or in the militia when in actual service, in time of war or public danger) shall be by an impartial jury of the vicinage, with the requisite of unanimity for conviction, the right of challenge, and other accustomed requisites; and no person shall be held to answer for a capital, or otherways infamous, crime, unless on a presentment or indictment by a grand jury; but, if a crime be committed in a place in the possession of an enemy, or in which an insurrection may prevail the indictment and trial may, by law, be authorized in some other place within the same state.

"Art. XI. No appeal to the Supreme Court of the United States, shall be allowed, where the value in controversy shall not amount to one thousand dollars; nor shall any fact, triable by a jury according to the course of the common law, be otherwise reexaminable, than according to the rules of common law.

"Art. XII. In suits at common law, the right of trial by jury shall be preserved.

"Art. XIII. Excessive bail shall not be required, nor excessive fines imposed, nor cruel and unusual punishments inflicted.

"Art. XIV. No state shall infringe the right of trial by jury in criminal cases, nor the rights of conscience, nor the freedom of speech, or of the press.

"Art. XV. The enumeration in the constitution of certain rights, shall not be construed to deny or disparage others, retained by the people.

"Art. XVI. The powers delegated by the constitution to the government of the United States, shall be exercised as therein appropriated, so that the legislative shall never exercise the powers vested in the executive or judicial; nor the executive the powers vested in the legislative or judicial; nor the judicial the powers vested in the legislative or executive.

"Art. XVII. The powers not delegated by the constitution, nor prohibited by it to the states, are reserved to the states respectively."

APPENDIX II

(COPIED FROM THE APPENDIX TO THE JOURNAL OF THE SENATE)

PROPOSED AMENDMENTS TO THE CONSTITUTION

The conventions of a number of the states having, at the time of their adopting the constitution, expressed a desire, in order to prevent misconstruction or abuse of its powers, that further declaratory and restrictive clauses should be added; and as extending the ground of public confidence in the government will best insure the beneficent ends of its institutions:

Resolved by the Senate and House of Representatives of the United States of America in Congress assembled, two-thirds of both Houses concurring, That the following articles be proposed to the legislatures of the several states, as amendments to the constitution of the United States, all or any of which articles, when ratified by three-fourths of the said legislatures, to be valid, to all intents and purposes, as part of the said constitution, viz:

Articles in addition to, and amendment of, the constitution of the United States of America, proposed by Congress, and ratified by the legislatures of the several states, pursuant to the fifth article of the original constitution.

ARTICLE I. After the first enumeration, required by the first article of the constitution, there shall be one representative for every thirty thousand, until the number shall amount to one hundred; after which, the proportion shall be so regulated by Congress, that there shall be not less than one hundred representatives, nor less than one representative for every forty thousand persons, until the number of representatives shall amount to two hundred, after which, the proportion shall be so regulated by Congress that there shall not be less than two hundred representatives, nor more than one representative for every fifty thousand persons.

ART. II. No law, varying the compensation for the services of the Senators and Representatives, shall take effect until an election of representatives shall have intervened.

ART. III. Congress shall make no law respecting an establishment of religion, or prohibiting the free exercise thereof, or abridging the freedom of speech, or of the press, or the right of the people peaceably to assemble, and to petition the government for a redress of grievances.

ART. IV. A well regulated militia being necessary to the security of a free state, the right of the people to keep and bear arms shall not be infringed.

ART. V. No soldier shall, in time of peace, be quartered in any house, without the consent of the owner, nor, in time of war, but in a manner to be prescribed by law.

ART. VI.   The right of the people to be secure in their persons, houses, papers, and effects, against unreasonable searches and seizures, shall not be violated, and no warrants shall issue but upon probable cause, supported by oath or affirmation, and particularly describing the place to be searched, and the persons or things to be seized.

ART. VII.   No person shall be held to answer for a capital, or otherwise infamous, crime, unless on a presentment or indictment of a grand jury, except in cases arising in the land or naval forces, or in the militia when in actual service, in time of war or public danger; nor shall any person be subject, for the same offense, to be twice put in jeopardy of life or limb; nor shall be compelled, in any criminal case, to be a witness against himself, nor be deprived of life, liberty, or property, without due process of law; nor shall private property be taken for public use without just compensation.

ART. VIII.   In all criminal prosecutions the accused shall enjoy the right to a speedy and public trial by an impartial jury of the state and district wherein the crime shall have been committed, which district shall have been previously ascertained by law, and to be informed of the nature and cause of the accusation; to be confronted with the witnesses against him; to have compulsory process for obtaining witnesses in his favor, and to have the assistance of counsel for his defense.

ART. IX.   In suits at common law, where the value in controversy shall exceed twenty dollars, the right of trial by jury shall be preserved; and no fact, tried by a jury, shall be otherwise reexamined in any court of the United States, than according to the rules of the common law.

ART. X.   Excessive bail shall not be required, nor excessive fines imposed, nor cruel and unusual punishments inflicted.

ART. XI.   The enumeration in the constitution of certain rights, shall not be construed to deny or disparage others retained by the people.

ART. XII.   The powers not delegated to the United States by the constitution, nor prohibited by it to the states, are reserved to the states respectively, or to the people.

FREDERICK AUGUSTUS MUHLENBERG,
Speaker of the House of Representatives.

JOHN ADAMS,
Vice President of the United States, and President of the Senate.

Attest,
John Beckley, Clerk of the House of Representatives
Samuel A. Otis, Secretary of the Senate.

AUTHORITIES

Adamson v. California
  332 U. S. 46, 67 S. Ct. 1672, 91 L. Ed. 1003
Aschwander v. Tennessee Valley Authority
  80 L. Ed. 688, 56 S. Ct. 145, 297 U. S. 288
Barron v. Baltimore
  7 Peters 243, 8 L. Ed. 672
Bolin v. Nebraska
  176 U. S. 83, 44 L. Ed. 382
Brown v. Walker
  161 U. S. 591, 40 L. Ed. 819
Calder v. Bull
  3 Dal. 386, 1 L. Ed. 648
City of Dallas v. Mitchell
  243 S. W. 944
City of Pineville v. Marshall
  299 S. W. 1072, 222 Ky. 4
Clay v. City of Eustis
  7 F. 2d 141
Commonwealth and Southern v. Securities
  and Exchange Commission
  134 F. 2d 747
Eilenbecker v. The District Court of
  Plymouth County, Iowa
  134 U. S. 31, 33 L. Ed. 801
Everson v. Board of Education
  330 U. S. 1, 91 L. Ed. 711
Ex Parte August Spies et al
  8 S. Ct. 21, 123 U. S. 131, 31 L. Ed. 80
Ex Parte Kirth
  28 F. Supp. 258
Fox v. State of Ohio
  12 L. Ed. 212, 5 Howard 410
Gernatt v. Huiet, Commissioner of Georgia
  192 Ga. 729, 16 S. E. 2d 587
Gow v. Bingham
  107 N. Y. S. 1011
Green v. Frazier
  253 U. S. 233, 64 L. Ed. 878, 40 S. Ct. 499
Gunn v. Barry
  21 L. Ed. 215, 82 U. S. 540
Holden v. Hardy
  169 U. S. 366, 18 S. Ct. 383, 42 L. Ed. 780
Johnson v. Board of Commissioners of Reno County
  147 Kan. 211, 75 Pac. 2d 849
Lessee of Livingston v. Moore et al
  7 Peters 469, 8 L. Ed. 751

McVeigh v. United States
   20 L. Ed. 80, 78 U. S. 260
National Labor Relations Board v. Jones and Laughlin
   Steel Corporation
   81 L. Ed. 893, 301 U. S. 1
National Maritime Union v. Herzog
   78 F. Supp. 146, 92 L. Ed. 1776
Ohio v. Dollinson
   194 U. S. 445, 48 L. Ed. 1062
Palko v. Connecticut
   302 U. S. 319, 82 L. Ed. 288
Parkersburg v. Brown
   106 U. S. 487, 27 L. Ed. 238, 1 S. Ct. 442
Poindexter v. Greenhow
   114 U. S. 270, 29 L. Ed. 185
Savings and Loan Association v. Topeka
   87 U. S. 686, 22 L. Ed. 455
Spann v. City of Dallas
   111 Tex. 350, 212 S. W. 513
State v. Michel
   46 So. 430, 121 La. 374
Tennessee Electric Power Company v.
   Tennessee Valley Authority
   306 U. S. 118, 83 L. Ed. 543
Thompson v. Consolidated Gas Utilities
   300 U. S. 55, 81 L. Ed. 510, 57 S. Ct. 364
United Public Workers v. Mitchell
   330 U. S. 75, 91 L. Ed. 745
United States v. Fujimoto
   102 F. Supp. 890
United States v. Painters Local Union No. 481
   79 F. Supp. 516
Whelchel v. McDonald
   176 F. 2d 260, 340 U. S. 122
Woods v. Miller
   333 U. S. 138, 92 L. Ed. 596
Youngstown Sheet and Tube Co. v. Sawyer
   103 F. Supp. 569
6 Corpus Juris Secundum 578

REFERENCES

Annotations from the Constitution of the United States, 1938, Revised and Annotated by Senate Concurrent Resolution No. 35, adopted May 14, 1936.

Max Farrand, "The Proceedings of the Constitutional Convention."

Knowlton H. Kelsey, "The Ninth Amendment to the Federal Constitution", Indiana Law Journal, April 1936.

Everett Dean Martin, "Liberty".

Dr. C. Edward Merriam, "American Political Theories" (1906).

Annals of Congress

THE DEBATES AND PROCEEDINGS IN THE
CONGRESS OF THE UNITED STATES
WITH AN APPENDIX

containing

Important State Papers and Public Documents

VOLUME I

COMPRISING (WITH VOLUME II) THE PERIOD FROM
MARCH 3, 1789 TO MARCH 3, 1791, INCLUSIVE.

Compiled from Authentic Materials
BY JOSEPH GALES, SENIOR.

— WASHINGTON —

PRINTED AND PUBLISHED BY GALES
AND SEATON.
1834.

A REPRINT OF THE PORTION OF VOLUME 1 OF GALES AND SEATON'S "ANNALS OF CONGRESS" RELATING TO THE FIRST TWELVE AMENDMENTS PROPOSED TO THE CONSTITUTION OF THE UNITED STATES

FOREWORD

The purpose of this reprint of portions of Volume 1 of The Debates and Proceedings in the Congress of the United States, as printed and published by Gales and Seaton (1834), is to furnish to students of the Bill of Rights access to one of the most important source books which has ever been written upon the subject.

It is believed that the most authentic information with respect to the first ten Amendments to the Constitution, which later came to be known as the Bill of Rights, comes from four publications, which are, the Journal of the House of Representatives, the Journal of the Senate, the reports of Thomas Lloyd in the Congressional Register, and Gales and Seaton's reports of the Debates and Proceedings in the Congress of the United States.

As we know, the Senate of the United States of America sat in executive session up until the Second Session of the Third Congress. Therefore, the Senate Journal which was required by the Constitution shows only official action, and even this record is very meager and sometimes incomplete.

The Journal of the House of Representatives contains a little more information than the Senate Journal, but it contains only a record of official action by the House of Representatives and the official vote on the business before that body, and does not include any of the debates and deliberations of the House of Representatives.

Thomas Lloyd was a shorthand reporter who reported the proceedings and the debates of the first session of the House of Representatives, and these were published in 1789 by Harrison and Purdy (New York). The title of this work is Thomas Lloyd, the Congressional Register or History of the Proceed-

94

ings and Debates of the First House of Representatives of the United States of America (taken in shorthand by Thomas Lloyd). This work is presented in four volumes, with Volumes 3 and 4 in one binding. This publication is very rare and is not available for loan, and is therefore practically inaccessible to the average student. This publication is the only history of the proceedings of the House of Representatives which was reported and published contemporaneously with the first session of Congress. It is an invaluable work. Fortunately, however, it is carried forward almost in its entirety in Volume 1 of Gales and Seaton's Debates and Proceedings in the Congress of the United States, a partial reprint of which volume as related to the proposed Amendments to the Constitution is here offered.

There is no other contemporaneous record of the debates for this period, since there was no verbatim reporting attempted until many years later, and no official verbatim reporting was provided until 1874. The Annals of Congress by Gales and Seaton covered the period from 1789-1824, and this series contained forty-two volumes. The period from 1825-1837 is covered by Register of the Debates in Congress (29 Volumes) also published by Gales and Seaton. The Congressional Globe, published in Washington, D. C., covers the debates and proceedings of Congress for the years 1833-1873, in which year the Congressional Record was officially established by act of Congress.

Volumes 1 and 2 covering the First Congress of the United States bears the date of publication in the year 1834. Apparently the edition of these two volumes was limited to one thousand copies. By joint resolution of March 3, 1849 (Stat. L. v. 9, p. 419), the Secretary of the Senate and the House were authorized to subscribe under the direction of the Joint Library Committee, on behalf of Congress, for one thousand copies of the volumes already published, and by Act approved September 30, 1850, an appropriation was made for the payment of the same.

By Act of September 30, 1850 (Stat. L. v. 9, p. 524), the Secretary of the Senate and Clerk of the House were authorized to subscribe for two thousand sets of Annals of Congress, which authorization included the one thousand volumes previously authorized. By Acts of Congress approved March 3, 1851, (Stat. L. v. 9, p. 543, 599), Congress provided for the distribution of the two thousand copies of the Annals of Congress, as follows:

"One copy to the library of the President of the United States; two copies to each of the executive departments; five copies to the library of Congress; fifty copies to the library of the House of Representatives; twenty-five copies to the document room of the Senate, for the use of the Senate; six copies for the office of the secretary of the Senate; three hundred copies to colleges and literary institutions, and public and incorporated libraries, one to be designated by each senator, representative, and delegate in Congress; twenty-five copies for international exchanges; two copies to the executive office of each State and Territory; sixty copies to supply the several foreign legations of the United States, to be deposited in and distributed under such regulations as may be made by the department of state; two copies for the Military Academy, and two copies to the Naval School; two copies to the Smithsonian Institution; one copy to each Circuit and District Court of the United States; and the residue to be deposited in the department of state, subject to the future disposition of Congress."

Thereafter the remaining volumes were distributed to new members of Congress and the offices of the Department of State until the supply was exhausted.

It is unknown how many of these volumes are now in existence, but they are very rare and unavailable for loan to students ordinarily.

The attached letter from the Library of Congress explains the confusion arising out of the publication of two sets of this work. The inquiring student may find further information with respect to this work in The Checklist of United States Public Documents, 1789-1909, Third Edition, published by the United States Government Printing Office (1911).

In the study of the Bill of Rights, this work is particularly valuable, because it relieves the student of the necessity of the examination of the Journal of the Senate and the Journal of the House of Representatives, as well as the reports of Thomas Lloyd, all of which are carried forward therein.

More than thirty-five hundred commentaries have been written upon the Bill of Rights. It is strange that there has never been a popular priced edition of the reprint of the most authentic materials relating to the history and ultimate submission of the Bill of Rights by the Congress of the United States.

The author has found this work indispensable in the study of the history of the Ninth Amendment to the Constitution of the United States. We realize that very little of this reprint relates to the Ninth Amendment, but we are confident in our belief that it will prove helpful to others in the course of their study and examination of the Bill of Rights.

THE LIBRARY OF CONGRESS
Washington 25, D. C.

March 27, 1951

Dear Mr. Patterson:

Your letter of February 25, 1951 has been referred to this Division for attention and reply.

So far as we have been able to ascertain there has been no book published on the Ninth Amendment to the Constitution of the United States; nor have we been able to identify much substantial literature on this Amendment by examining bibliographical sources and periodical indexes. Only the two items described below seem to merit investigation.

> Black, William H. Our Unknown Constitution. New York, College Entrance Book Co., Inc., 1938. 334 p. Ch. XVI. The Ninth and Tenth Amendments.

> Kelsey, Knowlton H. The Ninth Amendment of the Federal Constitution. Indiana Law Journal (Bloomington) April, 1936, v. 11: 309-323.

You may also wish to examine the following authoritative study which is well documented:

> Matteson, David M. The Organization of the Government Under the Constitution. *In* U. S. *Constitution Sesquicentennial Commission.* History of the Formation of the Union Under the Constitution. Washington, U. S. Govt. Print. Off., 1941. 885 p. Bill of Rights: p. 280-328.

The confusion concerning the publication of two sets of the *Annals of Congress* is explained by Laurence F. Schmeckebier in *Government Publications and Their Use* (Washington, The Brookings Institute, 1939) p. 102 as follows:

> Volumes 1 and 2 for the 1st Congress are duplicated by another compilation with the same title page (as regards wording, but not topography) and imprint date (1834), but with the running page head "Gales and Seaton's History of Debates in Congress." The text in the two sets is apparently the same, but they are not printed from the same type, and after the first few pages the text breaks differently at the end of each page. In the books with the running head "History of Congress," Volume 1 includes the proceedings from March 4, 1789 to February 10, 1790, pages 1-1169:lxx, and includes proceedings from February 10, 1790 to March 3, 1791, pages 1171-2353:lxx. In the books with the running head "History of Debates," Vol-

ume 1 includes the proceedings from March 4, 1789 to February 18, 1790, pages 1-1322:xxx, and Volume 2 includes the proceedings from February 18, 1790 to March 3, 1791, pages 1323-2418:xxx. Why two sets with different make-up should have been published in the same year is somewhat of a mystery.

Our examination of the *Annals* indicates also that all debates and resolutions relating to the first ten Amendments to the Constitution were included in Volumes 1 and 2. Volumes 11 and 12 include proceedings on later Amendments.

We hope that our delay in replying to your inquiry, owing to the heavy demands on our services, has not caused you inconvenience.

Very truly yours,

Henry J. Dubester
Acting Chief
General Reference and
Bibliography Division

Mr. Bennett B. Patterson
Cole, Patterson, Cole & McDaniel
Citizens State Bank Building
Houston 2, Texas

PROCEEDINGS IN THE HOUSE
OF REPRESENTATIVES

Monday, May 4, 1789.

Before the House adjourned, Mr. Madison gave notice, that he intended to bring on the subject of amendments to the constitution, on the 4th Monday of this month.

Monday, June 8, 1789.

AMENDMENTS TO THE CONSTITUTION

MR. MADISON rose, and reminded the House that this was the day that he had heretofore named for bringing forward amendments to the constitution, as contemplated in the fifth article of the constitution, addressing the Speaker as follows: This day, Mr. Speaker, is the day assigned for taking into consideration the subject of amendments to the constitution. As I considered myself bound in honor and in duty to do what I have done on this subject, I shall proceed to bring the amendments before you as soon as possible, and advocate them until they shall be finally adopted or rejected by a constitutional majority of this House. With a view of drawing your attention to this important object, I shall move that this House do now resolve itself into a Committee of the whole on the state of the Union; by which an opportunity will be given, to bring forward some propositions, which I have strong hopes will meet with the unanimous approbation of this House, after the fullest discussion and most serious regard. I therefore move you, that the House now go into a committee on this business.

MR. SMITH was not inclined to interrupt the measures which the public were so anxiously expecting, by going into a Committee of the whole at this time. He observed there were two modes of introducing this business to the House. One by appointing a select committee to take into consideration the several amendments proposed by the State conventions; this he thought the most likely way to shorten the business. The other was, that the gentleman should lay his propositions on the table, for the consideration of the members; that they should be printed, and taken up for discussion at a future day. Either of these modes would enable the House to enter upon business better prepared than could be the case by a sudden transition from other important concerns to which their minds were strongly bent. He therefore hoped that the honorable gentleman would consent to bring the subject forward in one of those ways, in preference to going into a Committee of the whole. For, said he, it must appear extremely impolitic to go into the consideration of amending the Government, before it is organized, before it has begun to operate. Certainly, upon reflection, it must appear to be premature. I wish, therefore, gentlemen would consent to the delay: for the business which lies in an unfinished state—I mean particularly the collection bill—is necessary to be passed; else all we have hitherto done is of no effect. If we go into the discussion of this subject, it will take us three weeks or a month; and during all this time, every other business must be suspended, because we cannot proceed with either accuracy or despatch when the mind is perpetually shifted from one subject to another.

MR. JACKSON.—I am of opinion we ought not to be in a hurry with respect to altering the constitution. For my part, I have no idea of speculating in this serious manner on theory. If I agree to alterations in the mode of administering this Government, I shall like to stand on the sure ground of experience, and not be treading air. What experience have we had of the good or bad qualities of this constitution? Can any gentleman affirm to me one proposition that is a certain and absolute amendment? I deny that he can. Our constitution, sir, is like a vessel just launched, and lying at the wharf; she is untried, you can hardly discover any one of her properties. It is not known how she will answer her helm, or lay her course; whether she will bear with safety the precious freight to be deposited in her hold. But, in this state, will the prudent merchant attempt alterations? Will he employ workmen to tear off the planking and take asunder the frame? He certainly will not. Let us, gentlemen, fit out our vessel, set up her masts, and expand her sails, and be guided by the experiment in our alterations. If she sails upon an uneven keel, let us right her by adding weight where it is wanting. In this way, we may remedy her defects to the satisfaction of all concerned; but if we proceed now to make alterations, we may deface a beauty, or deform a well proportioned piece of workmanship. In short, Mr. Speaker, I am not for amendments at this time; but if gentlemen should think it a subject deserving of attention, they will surely not neglect the more important business which is now unfinished before them. Unless we pass the collection bill we can get no revenue, and without revenue the wheels of Government cannot move. I am against taking up the subject at present, and shall therefore be totally against the amendments, if the Government is not organized, that I may see whether it is grievous or not.

When the propriety of making amendments shall be obvious from experience, I trust there will be virtue enough in my country to make them. Much has been said by the opponents to this constitution, respecting the insecurity of jury trials, that great bulwark of personal safety. All their objections may be done away, by proper regulations on this point, and I do not fear but such regulations will take place. The bill is now before the Senate, and a proper attention is shown to this business. Indeed, I cannot conceive how it could be opposed; I think an almost omnipotent Emperor would not be hardy enough to set himself against it. Then why should we fear a power which cannot be improperly exercised?

We have proceeded to make some regulations under the constitution; but have met with no inaccuracy, unless it may be said that the clause respecting vessels bound to or from one State be obliged to enter, clear, or pay duties in another, is somewhat obscure; yet that is not sufficient, I trust, in any gentleman's opinion to induce an amendment. But let me ask what will be the consequence of taking up this subject? Are we going to finish it in an hour? I believe not; it will take us more than a day, a week, a month—it will take a year to complete it! And will it be doing our duty to our country, to neglect or delay putting the Government in motion, when every thing depends upon its being speedily done?

Let the constitution have a fair trial; let it be examined by experience, discover by that test what its errors are, and then talk of amending; but to attempt it now is doing it at a risk, which is certainly imprudent. I have the honor of coming from a State that ratified the constitution by the unanimous vote of a numerous convention: the people of Georgia have manifested their attachment to it, by adopting a State constitution framed upon the same plan as this. But although they are thus satisfied, I shall not be against such amendments as will gratify the inhabitants of other States, provided they are judged of by experience and not merely on theory. For this reason, I wish the consideration of the subject postponed until the 1st of March, 1790.

MR. GOODHUE.—I believe it would be perfectly right in the gentleman who spoke last, to move a postponement to the time he has mentioned; because he is opposed to the consideration of amendments altogether. But I believe it will be proper to attend to the subject earlier; because it is the wish of many of our constituents, that something should be added to the constitution, to secure in a stronger manner their liberties from the inroads of power. Yet I think the present time premature; inasmuch as we have other business before us, which is incomplete, but essential to the public interest. When that is finished, I shall concur in taking up the subject of amendments.

MR. BURKE thought amendments to the constitution necessary, but this was not the proper time to bring them forward. He wished the Government completely organized before they entered upon this ground. The law for collecting the revenue is immediately necessary; the Treasury Department must be established; till this, and other important subjects are determined, he was against taking this up. He said it might interrupt the harmony of the House, which was necessary to be preserved in order to despatch the great objects of legislation. He hoped it would be postponed for the present, and pledged himself to bring it forward hereafter, if nobody else would.

Mr. Madison.—The gentleman from Georgia (Mr. Jackson) is certainly right in his opposition to my motion for going into a Committee of the whole, because he is unfriendly to the object I have in contemplation; but I cannot see that the gentlemen who wish for amendments to be proposed at the present session, stand on good ground when they object to the House going into committee on this business.

When I first hinted to the House my intention of calling their deliberations to this object, I mentioned the pressure of other important subjects, and submitted the propriety of postponing this till the more urgent business was despatched; but finding that business not despatched, when the order of the day for considering amendments arrived, I thought it a good reason for a farther delay; I moved the postponement accordingly. I am sorry the same reason still exists in some degree, but operates with less force, when it is considered that it is not now proposed to enter into a full and minute discussion of every part of the subject, but merely to bring it before the House, that our constituents may see we pay a proper attention to a subject they have much at heart; and if it does not give that full gratification which is to be wished, they will discover that it proceeds from the urgency of business of a very important nature. But if we continue to postpone from time to time, and refuse to let the subject come into view, it may occasion suspicions, which, though not well founded, may tend to inflame or prejudice the public mind against our decisions. They may think we are not sincere in our desire to incorporate such amendments in the constitution as will secure those rights, which they consider as not sufficiently guarded. The applications for amendments come from a very respectable number of our constituents, and it is certainly proper for Congress to consider the subject, in order to quiet that anxiety which prevails in the public mind. Indeed, I think it would have been of advantage to the Government, if it had been practicable to have made some propositions for amendments the first business we entered upon; it would have stifled the voice of complaint, and made friends of many who doubted the merits of the constitution. Our future measures would then have been more generally agreeably supported; but the justifiable anxiety to put the Government into operation prevented that; it therefore remains for us to take it up as soon as possible. I wish then to commence the consideration at the present moment; I hold it to be my duty to unfold my ideas, and explain myself to the House in some form or other without delay. I only wish to introduce the great work, and, as I said before, I do not expect it will be decided immediately; but if some step is taken in the business, it will give reason to believe that we may come to a final result. This will inspire a reasonable hope in the advocates for amendments, that full justice will be done to the important subject; and I have reason to believe their expectation will not be defeated. I hope the House will not decline my motion for going into a committee.

MR. SHERMAN.—I am willing that this matter should be brought before the House at a proper time. I suppose a number of gentlemen think it their duty to bring it forward; so that there is no apprehension it will be passed over in silence. Other gentlemen may be disposed to let the subject rest until the more important objects of Government are attended to; and I should conclude, from the nature of the case, that the people expect the latter from us in preference to altering the constitution; because they have ratified that instrument, in order that the Government may begin to operate. If this was not their wish, they might as well have rejected the constitution, as North Carolina has done, until the amendments took place. The State I have the honor to come from adopted this system by a very great majority, because they wished for the Government; but they desired no amendments. I suppose this was the case in other States; it will therefore be imprudent to neglect much more important concerns for this. The executive part of the Government wants organization; the business of the revenue is incomplete, to say nothing of the judiciary business. Now, will gentlemen give up these points to go into a discussion of amendments, when no advantage can arise from them? For my part, I question if any alteration which can be now proposed would be an amendment, in the true sense of the word; but nevertheless, I am willing to let the subject be introduced. If the gentleman only desires to go into committee for the purpose of receiving his propositions, I shall consent; but I have strong objections to being interrupted in completing the more important business; because I am well satisfied it will alarm the fears of twenty of our constituents where it will please one.

MR. WHITE.—I hope the House will not spend much time on this subject, till the more pressing business is despatched; but, at the same time, I hope we shall not dismiss it altogether, because I think a majority of the people who have ratified the constitution, did it under the expectation that Congress would, at some convenient time, examine its texture and point out where it was defective, in order that it might be judiciously amended. Whether, while we are without experience, amendments can be digested in such a manner as to give satisfaction to a constitutional majority of this House, I will not pretend to say; but I hope the subject may be considered with all convenient speed. I think it would tend to tranquilize the public mind; therefore, I shall vote in favor of going into a Committee of the whole, and, after receiving the subject, shall be content to refer it to a special committee to arrange and report. I fear, if we refuse to take up the subject, it will irritate many of our constituents, which I do not wish to do. If we cannot, after mature consideration, gratify their wishes, the cause of complaint will be lessened, if not removed. But a doubt on this head will not be a good reason why we should refuse to inquire. I do not say this as it affects my immediate constituents, because I believe a majority of the district which elected me do not require alterations; but I know there are people in other parts who will not be satisfied unless some amendments are proposed.

MR. SMITH, of South Carolina, thought the gentleman who brought forward the subject had done his duty; he had supported his motion with ability and candor, and if he did not succeed, he was not to blame. On considering what had been urged for going into a committee, he was induced to join the gentleman; but it would be merely to receive his propositions, after which he would move something to the effect: That, however desirous this House may be to go into the consideration of amendments to the constitution, in order to establish the liberties of the people of America on the securist foundation, yet the important and pressing business of the Government prevents their entering upon that subject at present.

MR. PAGE.—My colleague tells you he is ready to submit to the Committee of the whole his ideas on this subject. If no objection had been made to his motion, the whole business might have been finished before this. He has done me the honor of showing me certain propositions which he has drawn up; they are very important, and I sincerely wish the House may receive them. After they are published, I think the people will wait with patience till we are at leisure to resume them. But it must be very disagreeable to them to have it postponed from time to time, in the manner it has been for six weeks past; they will be tired out by a fruitless expectation. Putting myself into the place of those who favor amendments, I should suspect Congress did not mean seriously to enter upon the subject; that it was vain to expect redress from them. I should begin to turn my attention to the alternative contained in the fifth article, and think of joining the Legislatures of those States which have applied for calling a new convention. How dangerous such an expedient would be I need not mention; but I venture to affirm, that unless you take early notice of this subject, you will not have power to deliberate. The people will clamor for a new convention; they will not trust the House any longer. Those, therefore, who dread the assembling of a convention, will do well to acquiesce in the present motion, and lay the foundation of a most important work. I do not think we need consume more than half an hour in the Committee of the whole; this is not so much time but we may conveniently spare it, considering the nature of the business. I do not wish to divert the attention of Congress from the organization of the Government, nor do I think it need be done, if we comply with the present motion.

MR. VINING.—I hope the House will not go into a Committee of the whole. It strikes me that the great amendment which the Government wants is expedition in the despatch of business. The wheels of the national machine cannot turn, until the impost and collection bill are perfected; these are the desiderata which the public mind is anxiously expecting. It is well known, that all we have hitherto done amounts to nothing, if we leave the business in its present state. True; but, say gentlemen, let us go into committee; it will take up but a short time; yet it may take a considerable proportion of our time? May it not be procrastinated into days, weeks, nay, months? It is not the most facile subject that can come before the Legislature of the Union. Gentlemen's opinions do not run in a parallel on this topic; it may take up more time to unite or concentre them than is now imagined. And what object is to be attained by going into a committee? If information is what we seek after, cannot that be obtained by the gentleman's laying his propositions on the table; they can be read, or they can be printed. But I have two other reasons for opposing this motion; the first is, the uncertainty with which we must decide on questions of amendment, founded merely on speculative theory; the second is a previous question, how far it is proper to take the subject of amendments into consideration, without the consent of two-thirds of both Houses? I will submit it to gentlemen, whether the words of the constitution, "the Congress, whenever two-thirds of both Houses shall deem it necessary, shall propose amendments," do not bear my construction, that it is as requisite for two-thirds to sanction the expediency of going into the measure at present, as it will be to determine the necessity of amending at all. I take it that the fifth article admits of this construction, and think that two-thirds of the Senate and House of Representatives must concur in the expediency, as to the time and manner of amendments, before we can proceed to the consideration of the amendments themselves. For my part, I do see the expediency of proposing amendments. I think, sir, the most likely way to quiet the perturbation of the public mind, will be to pass salutary laws; to give permanency and stability to constitutional regulations, founded on principles of equity and adjusted by wisdom. Although hitherto we have done nothing to tranquilize that agitation which the adoption of the constitution threw some people into, yet the storm has abated and a calm succeeds. The people are not afraid of leaving the question of amendments to the discussion of their representatives; but is this the juncture for discussing it? What have Congress done towards completing the business of their appointment? They have passed a law regulating certain oaths; they have passed the impost bill; but are not vessels daily arriving, and the revenue slipping through our fingers? Is it not very strange that we neglect the completion of the revenue system? Is the system of jurisprudence unnecessary? And here let me ask gentlemen how they propose to amend that part of the constitution which embraces the judicial branch of Government, when they do not know the regulations proposed by the Senate, who are forming a bill on this subject?

If the honorable mover of the question before the House does not think he discharges his duty without bringing his propositions forward, let him take the mode I have mentioned, by which there will be little loss of time. He knows, as well as any gentleman, the importance of completing the business on your table, and that it is best to finish one subject before the introduction of another. He will not, therefore, persist in a motion which tends to distract our minds, and incapacitates us from making a proper decision on any subject. Suppose every gentleman who desires alterations to be made in the constitution were to submit his propositions to a Committee of the whole; what would be the consequence? We should have strings of them contradictory to each other, and be necessarily engaged in a discussion that would consume too much of our precious time.

Though the State I represent had the honor of taking the lead in the adoption of the constitution, and did it by a unanimous vote; and although I have the strongest predilection for the present form of Government, yet I am open to information, and willing to be convinced of its imperfections. If this be done, I shall cheerfully assist in correcting them. But I cannot think this a proper time to enter upon the subject, because more important business is suspended; and, for want of experience, we are as likely to do injury by our prescriptions as good. I wish to see every proposition which comes from that worthy gentleman on the science of Government; but I think it can be presented better by staying where we are, than by going into committee, and therefore shall vote against his motion.

MR. MADISON.—I am sorry to be accessory to the loss of a single moment of time by the House. If I had been indulged in my motion, and we had gone into a Committee of the whole, I think we might have rose and resumed the consideration of other business before this time; that is, so far as it depended upon what I proposed to bring forward. As that mode seems not to give satisfaction, I will withdraw the motion, and move you, sir, that a select committee be appointed to consider and report such amendments as are proper for Congress to propose to the Legislatures of the several States, conformably to the fifth article of the constitution.

I will state my reasons why I think it proper to propose amendments, and state, the amendments themselves, so far as I think they ought to be proposed. If I thought I could fulfil the duty which I owe to myself and my constituents, to let the subject pass over in silence, I most certainly should not trespass upon the indulgence of this House. But I cannot do this, and am therefore compelled to beg a patient hearing to what I have to lay before you. And I do most sincerely believe, that if Congress will devote but one day to this subject, so far as to satisfy the public that we do not disregard their wishes, it will have a salutary influence on the public councils, and prepare the way for a favorable reception of our future measures. It appears to me that this House is bound by every motive of prudence, not to let the first session pass over without proposing to the State Legislatures some things to be incorporated into the constitution, that will render it as acceptable to the whole people of the United States, as it has been found acceptable to a majority of them. I wish, among other reasons why something should be done, that those who have been friendly to the adoption of this constitution may have the opportunity of proving to those who were opposed to it that they were as sincerely devoted to liberty and a Republican Government, as those who charged them with wishing the adoption of this constitution in order to lay the foundation of an aristocracy or despotism. It will be a desirable thing to extinguish from the bosom of every member of the community, any apprehensions that there are those among his countrymen who wish to deprive them of the liberty for which they valiantly fought and honorably bled. And if there are amendments desired of such a nature as will not injure the constitution, and they can be ingrafted so as to give satisfaction to the doubting part of our fellow-citizens, the friends of the Federal Government will evince that spirit of deference and concession for which they have hitherto been distinguished.

It cannot be a secret to the gentlemen in this House, that, notwithstanding the ratification of this system of Government by eleven of the thirteen United States, in some cases unanimously, in others by large majorities; yet still there is a great number of our constituents who are dissatisfied with it; among whom are many respectable for their talents and patriotism, and respectable for the jealousy they have for their liberty, which, though mistaken in its object, is laudable in its motive. There is a great body of the people falling under this description, who at present feel much inclined to join their support to the cause of Federalism, if they were satisfied on this one point. We ought not to disregard their inclination, but, on principles of amity and moderation, conform to their wishes, and expressly declare the great rights of mankind secured under this constitution. The acquiescence which our fellow-citizens show under the Government, calls upon us for a like return of moderation. But perhaps there is a stronger motive than this for our going into a consideration of the subject. It is to provide those securities for liberty which are required by a part of the community; I allude in a particular manner to those two States that have not thought fit to throw themselves into the bosom of the Confederacy. It is a desirable thing, on our part as well as theirs, that a re-union should take place as soon as possible.

I have no doubt, if we proceed to take those steps which would be prudent and requisite at this juncture, that in a short time we should see that disposition prevailing in those States which have not come in, that we have seen prevailing in those States which have embraced the constitution.

But I will candidly acknowledge, that, over and above all these considerations, I do conceive that the constitution may be amended; that is to say, if all power is subject to abuse, that then it is possible the abuse of the powers of the General Government may be guarded against in a more secure manner than is now done, while no one advantage arising from the exercise of that power shall be damaged or endangered by it. We have in this way something to gain, and, if we proceed with caution, nothing to lose. And in this case it is necessary to proceed with caution; for while we feel all these inducements to go into a revisal of the constitution, we must feel for the constitution itself, and make that revisal a moderate one. I should be unwilling to see a door opened for a reconsideration of the whole structure of the Government—for a reconsideration of the principles and the substance of the powers given; because I doubt, if such a door were opened, we should be very likely to stop at that point which would be safe to the Government itself. But I do wish to see a door opened to consider, so far as to incorporate those provisions for the security of rights, against which I believe no serious objection has been made by any class of our constituents; such as would be likely to meet with the concurrence of two-thirds of both Houses, and the approbation of three-fourths of the State Legislatures. I will not propose a single alteration which I do not wish to see take place, as intrinsically proper in itself, or proper because it is wished for by a respectable number of my fellow-citizens; and therefore I shall not propose a single alteration but is likely to meet the concurrence required by the constitution. There have been objections of various kinds made against the constitution. Some were levelled against its structure because the President was without a council; because the Senate, which is a legislative body, had judicial powers in trials on impeachments; and because the powers of that body were compounded in other respects, in a manner that did not correspond with a particular theory; because it grants more power than is supposed to be necessary for every good purpose, and controls the ordinary powers of the State Governments. I know some respectable characters who opposed this Government on these grounds; but I believe that the great mass of the people who opposed it, disliked it because it did not contain effectual provisions against encroachments on particular rights, and those safeguards which they have been long accustomed to have interposed between them and the magistrate who exercises the sovereign power; nor ought we to consider them safe, while a great number of our fellow-citizens think these securities necessary.

It is a fortunate thing that the objection to the Government has been made on the ground I stated; because it will be practicable, on that ground, to obviate the objection, so far as to satisfy the public mind that their liberties will be perpetual, and this without endangering any part of the constitution, which is considered as essential to the existence of the Government by those who promoted its adoption.

The amendments which have occurred to me, proper to be recommended by Congress to the State Legislatures, are these:

First. That there be prefixed to the constitution a declaration, that all power is originally vested in, and consequently derived from, the people.

That Government is instituted and ought to be exercised for the benefit of the people; which consists in the enjoyment of life and liberty, with the right of acquiring and using property, and generally of pursuing and obtaining happiness and safety.

That the people have an indubitable, unalienable, and indefeasible right to reform or change their Government, whenever it be found adverse or inadequate to the purposes of its institution.

Secondly. That in article 1st, section 2, clause 3, these words be struck out, to-wit: "The number of Representatives shall not exceed one for every thirty thousand, but each State shall have at least one Representative, and until such enumeration shall be made;" and that in place thereof be inserted these words, to-wit: "After the first actual enumeration, there shall be one Representative for every thirty thousand, until the number amounts to ——————, after which the proportion shall be so regulated by Congress, that the number shall never be less than ——————, nor more than ——————, but each State shall, after the first enumeration, have at least two Representatives; and prior thereto."

Thirdly. That in article 1st, section 6, clause 1, there be added to the end of the first sentence, these words, to-wit: "But no law varying the compensation last ascertained shall operate before the next ensuing election of Representatives."

Fourthly. That in article 1st, section 9, between clauses 3 and 4, be inserted these clauses, to-wit: The civil rights of none shall be abridged on account of religious belief or worship, nor shall any national religion be established, nor shall the full and equal rights of conscience be in any manner, or on any pretext, infringed.

The people shall not be deprived or abridged of their right to speak, to write, or to publish their sentiments; and the freedom of the press, as one of the great bulwarks of liberty, shall be inviolable.

The people shall not be restrained from peaceably assembling and consulting for their common good; nor from applying to the Legislature by petitions, or remonstrances, for redress of their grievances.

The right of the people to keep and bear arms shall not be infringed; a well armed and well regulated militia being the best security of a free country: but no person religiously scrupulous of bearing arms shall be compelled to render military service in person.

No soldier shall in time of peace be quartered in any house without the consent of the owner; nor at any time, but in a manner warranted by law.

No person shall be subject, except in cases of impeachment, to more than one punishment or one trial for the same offense; nor shall be compelled to be a witness against himself; nor be deprived of life, liberty, or property, without due process of law; nor be obliged to relinquish his property, where it may be necessary for public use, without a just compensation.

Excessive bail shall not be required, nor excessive fines imposed, nor cruel and unusual punishments inflicted.

The rights of the people to be secured in their persons; their houses, their papers, and their other property, from all unreasonable searches and seizures, shall not be violated by warrants issued without probable cause, supported by oath or affirmation, or not particularly describing the places to be searched, or the persons or things to be seized.

In all criminal prosecutions, the accused shall enjoy the right to a speedy and public trial, to be informed of the cause and nature of the accusation, to be confronted with his accusers, and the witnesses against him; to have a compulsory process for obtaining witnesses in his favor; and to have the assistance of counsel for his defense.

The exceptions here or elsewhere in the constitution, made in favor of particular rights, shall not be so construed as to diminish the just importance of other rights retained by the people, or as to enlarge the powers delegated by the constitution; but either as actual limitations of such powers, or as inserted merely for greater caution.

Fifthly. That in article 1st, section 10, between clauses 1 and 2, be inserted this clause, to-wit:

No State shall violate the equal rights of conscience, or the freedom of the press, or the trial by jury in criminal cases.

Sixthly. That, in article 3d, section 2, be annexed to the end of clause 2d, these words, to-wit:

But no appeal to such court shall be allowed where the value in controversy shall not amount to ———— dollars; nor shall any fact triable by jury, according to the course of common law, be otherwise re-examinable than may consist with the principles of common law.

Seventhly. That in article 3d, section 2, the third clause be struck out, and in its place be inserted the clauses following, to-wit:

The trial of all crimes (except in cases of impeachments, and cases arising in the land or naval forces, or the militia when on actual service, in time of war or public danger) shall be by an impartial jury of freeholders of the vicinage, with the requisite of unanimity for conviction, of the right of challenge, and other accustomed requisites; and in all crimes punishable with loss of life or member, presentment or indictment by a grand jury shall be an essential preliminary, provided that in cases of crimes committed within any county which may be in possession of an enemy, or in which a general insurrection may prevail, the trial may by law be authorized in some other county of the same State, as near as may be to the seat of the offence.

In cases of crimes committed not within any county, the trial may by law be in such county as the laws shall have prescribed. In suits at common law, between man and man, the trial by jury, as one of the best securities to the rights of the people, ought to remain inviolate.

Eighthly.   That immediately after article 6th, be inserted, as article 7th, the clauses following, to-wit:

The powers delegated by this constitution are appropriated to the departments to which they are respectively distributed: so that the legislative department shall never exercise the powers vested in the executive or judicial nor the executive exercise the powers vested in the legislative or judicial, nor the judicial exercise the powers vested in the legislative or executive departments.

The powers not delegated by this constitution, nor prohibited by it to the States, are reserved to the States respectively.

Ninthly.   That article 7th be numbered as article 8th.

The first of these amendments relates to what may be called a bill of rights. I will own that I never considered this provision so essential to the federal constitution, as to make it improper to ratify it, until such an amendment was added; at the same time, I always conceived, that in a certain form, and to a certain extent, such a provision was neither improper nor altogether useless. I am aware, that a great number of the most respectable friends to the Government, and champions for republican liberty, have thought such a provision, not only unnecessary, but even improper; nay, I believe some have gone so far as to think it even dangerous. Some policy has been made use of, perhaps, by gentlemen on both sides of the question: I acknowledge the ingenuity of those arguments which were drawn against the constitution, by a comparison with the policy of Great Britain, in establishing a declaration of rights; but there is too great a difference in the case to warrant the comparison: therefore, the arguments drawn from that source were in a great measure inapplicable. In the declaration of rights which that country has established, the truth is, they have gone no farther than to raise a barrier against the power of the Crown; the power of the Legislature is left altogether indefinite. Although I know whenever the great rights, the trial by jury, freedom of the press, or liberty of conscience, come in question in that body, the invasion of them is resisted by able advocates, yet their Magna Charta does not contain any one provision for the security of those rights, respecting which the people of America are most alarmed. The freedom of the press and rights of conscience, those choicest privileges of the people, are unguarded in the British constitution.

But although the case may be widely different, and it may not be thought necessary to provide limits for the legislative power in that country, yet a different opinion prevails in the United States. The people of many States have thought it necessary to raise barriers against power in all forms and departments of Government, and I am inclined to believe, if once bills of rights are established in all the States, as well as the federal constitution, we shall find that although some of them are rather unimportant, yet, upon the whole, they will have a salutary tendency.

It may be said, in some instances, they do no more than state the perfect equality of mankind. This, to be sure, is an absolute truth, yet it is not absolutely necessary to be inserted at the head of a constitution.

In some instances they assert those rights which are exercised by the people in forming and establishing a plan of Government. In other instances, they specify those rights which are retained when particular powers are given up to be exercised by the Legislature. In other instances, they specify positive rights, which may seem to result from the nature of the compact. Trial by jury cannot be considered as a natural right, but a right resulting from a social compact which regulates the action of the community, but is as essential to secure the liberty of the people as any one of the pre-existent rights of nature. In other instances, they lay down dogmatic maxims with respect to the construction of the Government; declaring that the legislative, executive, and judicial branches shall be kept separate and distinct. Perhaps the best way of securing this in practice is, to provide such checks as will prevent the encroachment of the one upon the other.

But whatever may be the form which the several States have adopted in making declarations in favor of particular rights, the great object in view is to limit and qualify the powers of Government, by excepting out of the grant of power those cases in which the Government ought not to act, or to act only in a particular mode. They point these exceptions sometimes against the abuse of the executive power, sometimes against the legislative, and, in some cases, against the community itself; or, in other words, against the majority in favor of the minority.

In our Government it is, perhaps, less necessary to guard against the abuse in the executive department than any other; because it is not the stronger branch of the system, but the weaker. It therefore must be levelled against the legislative, for it is the most powerful, and most likely to be abused, because it is under the least control. Hence, so far as a declaration of rights can tend to prevent the exercise of undue power, it cannot be doubted but such declaration is proper. But I confess that I do conceive, that in a Government modified like this of the United States, the great danger lies rather in the abuse of the community than in the legislative body. The prescriptions in favor of liberty ought to be levelled against that quarter where the greatest danger lies, namely, that which possesses the highest prerogative of power. But this is not found in either the executive or legislative departments of Government, but in the body of the people, operating by the majority against the minority.

It may be thought that all paper barriers against the power of the community are too weak to be worthy of attention. I am sensible they are not so strong as to satisfy gentlemen of every description who have seen and examined thoroughly the texture of such a defence; yet, as they have a tendency to impress some degree of respect for them, to establish the public opinion in their favor, and rouse the attention of the whole community, it may be one means to control the majority from those acts to which they might be otherwise inclined.

It has been said, by way of objection to a bill of rights, by many respectable gentlemen out of doors, and I find opposition on the same principles likely to be made by gentlemen on this floor, that they are unnecessary articles of a Republican Government, upon the presumption that the people have those rights in their own hands, and that is the proper place for them to rest. It would be a sufficient answer to say, that this objection lies against such provisions under the State Government, as well as under the General Government; and there are, I believe, but few gentlemen who are inclined to push their theory so far as to say that a declaration of rights in those cases is either ineffectual or improper. It has been said, that in the Federal Government they are unnecessary, because the powers are enumerated, and it follows, that all that are not granted by the constitution are retained; that the constitution is a bill of powers, the great residuum being the rights of the people; and, therefore, a bill of rights cannot be so necessary as if the residuum was thrown into the hands of the Government. I admit that these arguments are not entirely without foundation; but they are not conclusive to the extent which has been supposed. It is true, the powers of the General Government are circumscribed, they are directed to particular objects; but even if Government keeps within those limits, it has certain discretionary powers with respect to the means, which may admit of abuse to a certain extent, in the same manner as the powers of the State Governments under their constitutions may to an indefinite extent; because in the constitution of the United States, there is a clause granting to Congress the power to make all laws which shall be necessary and proper for carrying into execution all the powers vested in the Government of the United States, or in any department or officer thereof; this enables them to fulfil every purpose for which the Government was established. Now, may not laws be considered necessary and proper by Congress, for it is for them to judge of the necessity and propriety to accomplish those special purposes which they may have in contemplation, which laws in themselves are neither necessary nor proper; as well as improper laws could be enacted by the State Legislatures, for fulfilling the more extended objects of those Governments. I will state an instance, which I think in point, and proves that this might be the case. The General Government has a right to pass all laws which shall be necessary to collect its revenue; the means for enforcing the collection are within the direction of the Legislature: may not general warrants be considered necessary for the purpose, as well as for some purposes which it was supposed at the framing of their constitutions the State Governments had in view? If there was reason for restraining the State Governments from exercising this power, there is like reason for restraining the Federal Government.

It may be said, indeed it has been said, that a bill of rights is not necessary, because the establishment of this Government has not repealed those declarations of rights which are added to the several State constitutions; that those rights of the people, which had been established by the most solemn act, could not be annihilated by a subsequent act of that people, who meant, and declared at the head of the instrument, that they ordained and established a new system, for the express purpose of securing to themselves and posterity the liberties they had gained by an arduous conflict.

I admit the force of this observation, but I do not look upon it to be conclusive. In the first place, it is too uncertain ground to leave this provision upon, if a provision is at all necessary to secure rights so important as many of those I have mentioned are conceived to be, by the public in general, as well as those in particular who opposed the adoption of this constitution. Besides, some States have no bills of rights, there are others provided with very defective ones, and there are others whose bills of rights are not only defective, but absolutely improper; instead of securing some in the full extent which republican principles would require, they limit them too much to agree with the common ideas of liberty.

It has been objected also against a bill of rights, that, by enumerating particular exceptions to the grant of power, it would disparage those rights which were not placed in that enumeration; and it might follow, by implication, that those rights which were not singled out, were intended to be assigned into the hands of the General Government, and were consequently insecure. This is one of the most plausible arguments I have ever heard urged against the admission of a bill of rights into this system; but, I conceive, that it may be guarded against. I have attempted it, as gentlemen may see by turning to the last clause of the fourth resolution.

It has been said, that it is unnecessary to load the constitution with this provision, because it was not found effectual in the constitution of the particular States. It is true, there are a few particular States in which some of the most valuable articles have not, at one time or other, been violated; but it does not follow but they may have, to a certain degree, a salutary effect against the abuse of power. If they are incorporated into the constitution, independent tribunals of justice will consider themselves in a peculiar manner the guardians of those rights; they will be an impenetrable bulwark against every assumption of power in the legislative or executive; they will be naturally led to resist every encroachment upon rights expressly stipulated for in the constitution by the declaration of rights. Besides this security, there is a great probability that such a declaration in the federal system would be enforced; because the State Legislatures will jealously and closely watch the operations of this Government, and be able to resist with more effect every assumption of power, than any other power on earth can do; and the greatest opponents to a Federal Government admit the State Legislatures to be sure guardians of the people's liberty. I conclude, from this view of the subject, that it will be proper in itself, and highly politic, for the tranquility of the public mind, and the stability of the Government, that we should offer something, in the form I have proposed, to be incorporated in the system of Government, as a declaration of the rights of the people.

In the next place, I wish to see that part of the constitution revised which declares that the number of Representatives shall not exceed the proportion of one for every thirty thousand persons, and allows one Representative to every State which rates below that proportion. If we attend to the discussion of this subject, which has taken place in the State conventions, and even in the opinion of the friends to the constitution, an alteration here is proper. It is the sense of the people of America, that the number of Representatives ought to be increased, but particularly that it should not be left in the discretion of the Government to diminish them, below that proportion which certainly is in the power of the Legislature as the constitution now stands; and they may, as the population of the country increases, increase the House of Representatives to a very unwieldly degree. I confess I always thought this part of the constitution defective, though not dangerous; and that it ought to be particularly attended to whenever Congress should go into the consideration of amendments.

There are several minor cases enumerated in my proposition, in which I wish also to see some alteration take place. That article which leaves it in the power of the Legislature to ascertain its own emolument, is one to which I allude. I do not believe this is a power which, in the ordinary course of Government, is likely to be abused. Perhaps of all the powers granted, it is least likely to abuse; but there is a seeming impropriety in leaving any set of men without control to put their hand into the public coffers, to take out money to put in their pockets; there is a seeming indecorum in such power, which leads me to propose a change. We have a guide to this alteration in several of the amendments which the different conventions have proposed. I have gone, therefore, so far as to fix it, that no law, varying the compensation, shall operate until there is a change in the Legislature; in which case it cannot be for the particular benefit of those who are concerned in determining the value of the service.

I wish also, in revising the constitution, we may throw into that section, which interdicts the abuse of certain powers in the State Legislatures, some other provisions of equal, if not greater importance than those already made. The words, "No State shall pass any bill of attainder, *ex post facto* law," etc. were wise and proper restrictions in the constitution. I think there is more danger of those powers being abused by the State Governments than by the Government of the United States. The same may be said of other powers which they possess, if not controlled by the general principle, that laws are unconstitutional which infringe the rights of the community. I should therefore wish to extend this interdiction, and add, as I have stated in the 5th resolution, that no State shall violate the equal right of conscience, freedom of the press, or trial by jury in criminal cases; because it is proper that every Government should be disarmed of powers which trench upon those particular rights. I know, in some of the State constitutions, the power of the Government is controlled by such a declaration; but others are not. I cannot see any reason against obtaining even a double security on those points; and nothing can give a more sincere proof of the attachment of those who oppose this constitution to these great and important rights, than to see them join in obtaining the security I have now proposed; because it must be admitted, on all hands, that the State Governments are as liable to attack these invaluable privileges as the General Government is, and therefore ought to be as cautiously guarded against.

I think it will be proper, with respect to the judiciary powers, to satisfy the public mind on those points which I have mentioned. Great inconvenience has been apprehended to suitors from the distance they would be dragged to obtain justice in the Supreme Court of the United States, upon an appeal on an action for a small debt. To remedy this, declare that no appeal shall be made unless the matter in controversy amounts to a particular sum; this, with the regulations respecting jury trials in criminal cases, and suits at common law, it is to be hoped, will quiet and reconcile the minds of the people to that part of the constitution.

I find, from looking into the amendments proposed by the State conventions, that several are particularly anxious that it should be declared in the constitution, that the powers not therein delegated should be reserved to the several States. Perhaps words which may define this more precisely than the whole of the instrument now does, may be considered as superfluous. I admit they may be deemed unnecessary; but there can be no harm in making such a declaration, if gentlemen will allow that the fact is as stated. I am sure I understand it so, and do therefore propose it.

These are the points on which I wish to see a revision of the constitution take place. How far they will accord with the sense of this body, I cannot take upon me absolutely to determine; but I believe every gentleman will readily admit that nothing is in contemplation, so far as I have mentioned, that can endanger the beauty of the Government in any one important feature, even in the eyes of its most sanguine admirers. I have proposed nothing that does not appear to me as proper in itself, or eligible as patronized by a respectable number of our fellow-citizens; and if we can make the constitution better in the opinion of those who are opposed to it, without weakening its frame, or abridging its usefulness, in the judgment of those who are attached to it, we act the part of wise and liberal men to make such alterations as shall produce that effect.

Having done what I conceived was my duty, in bringing before this House the subject of amendments, and also stated such as I wish for and approve, and offered the reasons which occurred to me in their support, I shall content myself, for the present, with moving "that a committee be appointed to consider of and report such amendments as ought to be proposed by Congress to the Legislatures of the States, to become, if ratified by three-fourths thereof, part of the constitution of the United States." By agreeing to this motion, the subject may be going on in the committee, while other important business is proceeding to a conclusion in the House. I should advocate greater despatch in the business of amendments, if I were not convinced of the absolute necessity there is of pursuing the organization of the Government; because I think we should obtain the confidence of our fellow-citizens, in proportion as we fortify the rights of the people against the encroachments of the Government.

MR. JACKSON.—The more I consider the subject of amendments, the more I am convinced it is improper. I revere the rights of my constituents as much as any gentleman in Congress, yet I am against inserting a declaration of rights in the constitution, and that for some of the reasons referred to by the gentleman last up. If such an addition is not dangerous or improper, it is at least unnecessary:

that is a sufficient reason for not entering into the subject at a time when there are urgent calls for our attention to important business. Let me ask gentlemen, what reason there is for the suspicions which are to be removed by this measure? Who are Congress, that such apprehensions should be entertained of them? Do we not belong to the mass of the people? Is there a single right that, if infringed, will not affect us and our connections as much as any other person? Do we not return at the expiration of two years into private life? and is not this a security against encroachments? Are we not sent here to guard those rights which might be endangered, if the Government was an aristocracy or a despotism? View for a moment the situation of Rhode Island, and say whether the people's rights are more safe under State Legislatures than under a Government of limited powers? Their liberty is changed to licentiousness. But do gentlemen suppose bills of rights necessary to secure liberty? If they do, let them look at New York, New Jersey, Virginia, South Carolina, and Georgia. Those States have no bills of rights, and is the liberty of the citizens less safe in those States, than in the other of the United States? I believe it is not.

There is a maxim in law, and it will apply to bills of rights, that when you enumerate exceptions, the exceptions operate to the exclusion of all circumstances that are omitted; consequently, unless you except every right from the grant of power, those omitted are inferred to be resigned to the discretion of the Government.

The gentleman endeavors to secure the liberty of the press; pray how is this in danger? There is no power given to Congress to regulate this subject as they can commerce, or peace, or war. Has any transaction taken place to make us suppose such an amendment necessary? An honorable gentleman, a member of this House, has been attacked in the public newspapers on account of sentiments delivered on this floor. Have Congress taken any notice of it? Have they ordered the writer before them, even for a breach of privilege, although the constitution provides that a member shall not be questioned in any place for any speech or debate in the House? No, these things are offered to the public view, and held up to the inspection of the world. These are principles which will always prevail. I am not afraid, nor are other members I believe, our conduct should meet the severest scrutiny. Where, then, is the necessity of taking measures to secure what neither is nor can be in danger?

I hold, Mr. Speaker, that the present is not a proper time for considering of amendments. The States of Rhode Island and North Carolina are not in the Union. As to the latter, we have every presumption that she will come in. But in Rhode Island I think the anti-federal interest yet prevails. I am sorry for it, particularly on account of the firm friends of the Union, who are kept without the embrace of the confederacy by their countrymen. These persons are worthy of our patronage; and I wish they would apply to us for protection; they should have my consent to be taken into the Union upon such application. I understand there are some important mercantile and manufacturing towns in that State, who ardently wish to live under the laws of the General Government; if they were to come forward and request us to take measures for this purpose, I would give my sanction to any which would be likely to bring about such an event.

But to return to my argument. It being the case that those States are not yet come into the Union, when they join us, we shall have another list of amendments to consider, and another bill of rights to frame. Now, in my judgment, it is better to make but one work of it whenever we set about the business.

But in what a situation shall we be with respect to those foreign Powers with whom we desire to be in treaty? They look upon us as a nation emerging into figure and importance. But what will be their opinion, if they see us unable to retain the national advantages we have just gained? They will smile at our infantine efforts to obtain consequence, and treat us with the contempt we have hitherto borne by reason of the imbecility of our Government. Can we expect to enter into a commercial competition with any of them, while our system is incomplete? And how long it will remain in such a situation, if we enter upon amendments, God only knows. Our instability will make us objects of scorn. We are not content with two revolutions in less than fourteen years; we must enter upon a third, without necessity or propriety. Our faith will be like the *punica fides* of Carthage; and we shall have none that will repose confidence in us. Why will gentlemen press us to propose amendments, while we are without experience? Can they assure themselves that the amendments, as they call them, will not want amendments, as soon as they are adopted? I will not tax gentlemen with a desire of amusing the people; I believe they venerate their country too much for this; but what more can amendments lead to? That part of the constitution which is proposed to be altered, may be the most valuable part of the whole; and perhaps those who now clamor for alterations may, ere long, discover that they have marred a good Government, and rendered their own liberties insecure. I again repeat it, this is not the time for bringing forward amendments; and, notwithstanding the honorable gentleman's ingenious arguments on that point, I am now more strongly persuaded it is wrong.

If we actually find the constitution bad upon experience, or the rights and privileges of the people in danger, I here pledge myself to step forward among the first friends of liberty to prevent the evil; and if nothing else will avail, I will draw my sword in the defence of freedom, and cheerfully immolate at that shrine my property and my life. But how are we now proceeding? Why, on nothing more than theoretical speculation, pursuing a mere *ignis fatuus,* which may lead us into serious embarrassments. The imperfections of the Government are now unknown; let it have a fair trial, and I will be bound they show themselves; then we can tell where to apply the remedy, so as to secure the great object we are aiming at.

There are, Mr. Speaker, a number of important bills on the table which require despatch; but I am afraid, if we enter on this business, we shall not be able to attend to them for a long time. Look, sir, over the long list of amendments proposed by some of the adopting States, and say, when the House could get through the discussion; and I believe, sir, every one of those amendments will come before us. Gentlemen may feel themselves called by duty or inclination to oppose them. How are we then to extricate ourselves from this labyrinth of business? Certainly we shall lose much of our valuable time, without any advantage whatsoever. I hope, therefore, the gentleman will press us no further; he has done his duty, and acquitted himself of the obligation under which he lay. He may now accede to what I take to be the sense of the House, and let the business of amendments lie over until next Spring; that will be soon enough to take it up to any good purpose.

MR. GERRY.—I do not rise to go into the merits or demerits of the subject of amendments; nor shall I make any other observations on the motion for going into a committee of the whole on the State of the Union, which is now withdrawn, than merely to say, that, referring the subject to that committee is treating it with the dignity its importance requires. But I consider it improper to take up this business, when our attention is occupied by other important objects. We should despatch the subjects now on the table, and let this lie over until a period of more leisure for discussion and attention. The gentleman from Virginia says it is necessary to go into a consideration of this subject, in order to satisfy the people. For my part, I cannot be of his opinion. The people know we are employed in the organization of the Government, and cannot expect that we should forego this business for any other. But I would not have it understood, that I am against entering upon amendments when the proper time arrives. I should be glad to set about it as soon as possible, but I would not stay the operation of the Government on this account. I think with the gentleman from Delaware (MR. VINING), that the great wheels of the political machine should first be set in motion; and with the gentleman from Georgia (MR. JACKSON), that the vessel ought to be got under way, lest she lie by the wharf till she beats off her rudder, and runs herself a wreck on shore.

I say I wish as early a day as possible may be assigned for taking up this business, in order to prevent the necessity which the States may think themselves under of calling a new convention. For I am not, sir, one of those blind admirers of this system, who think it all perfection; nor am I so blind as not to see its beauties. The truth is, it partakes of humanity; in it is blended virtue and vice, errors and excellence. But I think, if it is referred to a new convention, we run the risk of losing some of its best properties; this is a case I never wish to see. Whatever might have been my sentiments of the ratification of the constitution without amendments, my sense now is, that the salvation of America depends upon the establishment of this Government, whether amended or not. If the constitution which is now ratified should not be supported, I despair of ever having a Government of these United States.

I wish the subject to be considered early for another reason. There are two States not in the Union; it would be a very desirable circumstance to gain them. I should therefore be in favor of such amendments as might tend to invite them and gain their confidence; good policy will dictate to us to expedite that event. Gentlemen say, that we shall not obtain the consent of two-thirds of both Houses to amendments. Are gentlemen willing then to throw Rhode Island and North Carolina into the situation of foreign nations? They have told you that they cannot accede to the Union, unless certain amendments are made to the constitution; if you deny a compliance with their request in that particular, you refuse an accommodation to bring about that desirable event, and leave them detached from the Union.

I have another reason for going early into this business. It is necessary to establish an energetic Government. My idea of such a Government is, that due deliberation be had in making laws, and efficiency in the execution. I hope, in this country, the latter may obtain without the dread of despotism. I would wish to see the execution of good laws irresistible. But from the view which we have already had of the disposition of the Government, we seem really to be afraid to administer the powers with which we are invested, lest we give offence. We appear afraid to exercise the constitutional powers of the Government, which the welfare of the State requires, lest a jealousy of our powers be the consequence. What is the reason of this timidity? Why, because we see a great body of our constituents opposed to the constitution as it now stands, who are apprehensive of the enormous powers of Government. But if this business is taken up, and it is thought proper to make amendments, it will remove this difficulty. Let us deal fairly and candidly with our constituents, and give the subject a full discussion; after that, I have no doubt but the decision will be such as, upon examination, we shall discover to be right. If it shall then appear proper and wise to reject the amendments, I dare to say the reasons for so doing will bring conviction to the people out of doors, as well as it will to the members of this House; and they will acquiesce in the decision, though they may regret the disappointment of their fondest hopes for the security of the liberties of themselves and their posterity. Thus, and thus only, the Government will have its due energy, and accomplish the end for which it was instituted.

I am against referring the subject to a select committee, because I conceive it would be disrespectful to those States which have proposed amendments. The conventions of the States consisted of the most wise and virtuous men of the community; they have ratified this constitution, in full confidence that their objections would at least be considered; and shall we, sir, preclude them by the appointment of a special committee, to consider of a few propositions brought forward by an individual gentleman? Is it in contemplation that the committee should have the subject at large before them, or that they should report upon the particular amendments just mentioned, as they think proper? And are we to be precluded from the consideration of any other amendments but those the committee may report? A select committee must be considered improper, because it is putting their judgments against that of the conventions which have proposed amendments; but if the committee are to consider the matter at large, they will be liable to this objection, that their report will only be waste of time. For if they do not bring forward the whole of the amendments recommended, individual members will consider themselves bound to bring them forward for the decision of the House. I would therefore submit, if gentlemen are determined to proceed in the business at this time, whether it is not better that it should go, in the first instance, to a Committee of the whole, as first proposed by the gentleman from Virginia?

Some gentlemen consider it necessary to do this to satisfy our constituents. I think referring the business to a special committee will be attempting to amuse them with trifles. Our fellow-citizens are possessed of too much discernment not to be able to discover the intention of Congress by such procedure. It will be the duty of their representatives to tell them, if they were not able to discover it of themselves, they require the subject to be fairly considered; and if it be found to be improper to comply with their reasonable expectations, to tell them so. I hope there is no analogy between federal and punic faith; but unless Congress shall candidly consider the amendments which have been proposed in confidence by the State conventions, federal faith will not be considered very different from the *punica fides* of Carthage. The ratification of the constitution in several States would never have taken place, had they not been assured that the objections would have been duly attended to by Congress. And I believe many members of these conventions would never have voted for it, if they had not been persuaded that Congress would notice them with that candor and attention which their importance requires. I will say nothing respecting the amendments themselves; they ought to stand or fall on their own merits. If any of them are eligible, they will be adopted; if not, they will be rejected.

MR. LIVERMORE was against this motion; not that he was against amendments at a proper time. It is enjoined on him to act a rational part in procuring certain amendments, and he meant to do so; but he could not say what amendments were requisite, until the Government was organized. He supposed the judiciary law would contain certain regulations that would remove the anxiety of the people respecting such amendments as related thereto; because he thought much of the minutiae respecting suits between citizens of different States, etc. might be provided for by law. He could not agree to make jury trials necessary on every occasion; they were not practiced even at this time, and there were some cases in which a cause could be better decided without a jury than with one.

In addition to the judiciary business, there is that which relates to the revenue. Gentlemen had let an opportunity go through their hands of getting a considerable supply from the impost on the Spring importations. He reminded them of this; and would tell them now was the time to finish that business; for if they did not sow in seed-time, they would be beggars in harvest. He was well satisfied in his own mind, that the people of America did not look for amendments at present; they never could imagine it to be the first work of Congress.

He wished the concurrence of the Senate upon entering on this business, because if they opposed the measure, all the House did would be mere waste of time; and there was some little difficulty on this point, because it required the consent of two-thirds of both Houses to agree to what was proper on this occasion. He said, moreover, it would be better to refer the subject generally, if referred to them at all, than to take up the propositions of individual members.

MR. SHERMAN.—I do not suppose the constitution to be perfect, nor do I imagine if Congress and all the Legislatures on the continent were to revise it, that their united labors would make it perfect. I do not expect any perfection on this side of the grave in the works of man; but my opinion is, that we are not at present in circumstances to make it better. It is at wonder that there has been such unanimity in adopting it, considering the ordeal it had to undergo; and the unanimity which prevailed at its formation is equally astonishing; amidst all the members from the twelve States present at the federal convention, there were only three who did not sign the instrument to attest their opinion of its goodness. Of the eleven States who have received it, the majority have ratified it without proposing a single amendment. This circumstance leads me to suppose that we shall not be able to propose any alterations that are likely to be adopted by nine States; and gentlemen know, before the alterations take effect, they must be agreed to by the Legislatures of three-fourths of the States in the

Union. Those States which have not recommended alterations, will hardly adopt them, unless it is clear that they tend to make the constitution better. Now how this can be made out to their satisfaction I am yet to learn; they know of no defect from experience. It seems to be the opinion of gentlemen generally, that this is not the time for entering upon the discussion of amendments: our only question therefore is, how to get rid of the subject. Now, for my own part, I would prefer to have it referred to a Committee of the whole, rather than a special committee, and therefore shall not agree to the motion now before the House.

MR. GERRY moved, that the business lie over until the 1st day of July next, and that it be the order for that day.

MR. SUMTER.—I consider the subject of amendments of such great importance to the Union, that I shall be glad to see it undertaken in any manner. I am not, Mr. Speaker, disposed to sacrifice substance to form; therefore, whether the business shall originate in a Committee of the whole, or in the House, is a matter of indifference to me, so that it be put in train. Although I am seriously inclined to give this subject a full discussion, yet I do not wish it to be fully entered into at present, but am willing it should be postponed to a future day, when we shall have more leisure. With respect to referring to a select committee, I am rather against it; because I consider it as treating the applications of the State conventions rather slightly; and I presume it is the intention of the House to take those applications into consideration as well as any other. If it is not, I think it will give fresh cause for jealousy; it will rouse the alarm which is now suspended, and the people will become clamorous for amendments. They will decline any further application to Congress, and resort to the other alternative pointed out in the constitution. I hope, therefore, this House, when they do go into the business, will receive those propositions generally. This I apprehend will tend to tranquilize the public mind, and promote that harmony which ought to be kept up between those in the exercise of the powers of Government, and those who have clothed them with the authority, or, in other words, between Congress and the people. Without a harmony and confidence subsist between them, the measures of Government will prove abortive, and we shall have still to lament that imbecility and weakness which have long marked our public councils.

MR. VINING found himself in a delicate situation respecting the subject of amendments. He came from a small State, and therefore his sentiments would not be considered of so much weight as the sentiments of those gentlemen who spoke the sense of much larger States. Besides, his constituents had prejudged the question, by a unanimous adoption of the constitution, without suggesting any amendments thereto. His sense accorded with the declared sense of the State of Delaware, and he was doubly bound to object to amendments which were either improper or unnecessary. But he had good reasons for opposing the consideration of even proper alterations at this time. He would ask the gentleman who pressed them whether he would be responsible for the risk the Government would run of being injured by an *interregnum?* Proposing amendments at this time, is suspending the operations of Government, and may be productive of its ruin.

He would not follow the gentleman in his arguments, though he supposed them all answerable, because he would not take up the time of the House; he contented himself with saying, that a bill of rights was unnecessary in a Government deriving all its powers from the people; and the constitution enforced the principle in the strongest manner by the practical declaration prefixed to that instrument; he alluded to the words, "We the people do ordain and establish."

There were many things mentioned by some of the State conventions which he would never agree to, on any conditions whatsoever; they changed the principles of the Government, and were therefore obnoxious to its friends. The honorable gentleman from Virginia had not touched upon any of them; he was glad of it, because he could by no means bear the idea of an alteration respecting them; he referred to the mode of obtaining direct taxes, judging of elections, etc.

He found he was not speaking to the question; he would therefore return to it, and declare he was against committing the subject to a select committee; if it was to be committed at all, he preferred a Committee of the whole, but hoped the subject would be postponed.

MR. MADISON found himself unfortunate in not satisfying gentlemen with respect to the mode of introducing the business; he thought, from the dignity and peculiarity of the subject, that it ought to be referred to a Committee of the whole. He accordingly made that motion first, but finding himself not likely to succeed in that way, he had changed his ground. Fearing again to be discomfited, he would change his mode, and move the propositions he had stated before, and the House might do what they thought proper with them. He accordingly moved the propositions by way of resolutions to be adopted by the House.

MR. LIVERMORE objected to these propositions, because they did not take up the amendments of the several States.

MR. PAGE was much obliged to his colleague for bringing the subject forward in the manner he had done. He conceived it to be just and fair. What was to be done when the House would not refer it to a committee of any sort, but bring the question at once before them? He hoped it would be the means of bringing about a decision.

Mr. Lawrence moved to refer Mr. Madison's motion to the Committee of the whole on the state of the Union.

Mr. Lee thought it ought to be taken up in that committee; and hoped his colleague would bring the propositions before the committee, when on the state of the Union, as he had originally intended.

Mr. Boudinot wished the appointment of a select committee, but afterwards withdrew his motion.

At length Mr. Lawrence's motion was agreed to, and Mr. Madison's propositions were ordered to be referred to a Committee of the whole. Adjourned.

. . .

Tuesday, July 21, 1789.

AMENDMENTS TO THE CONSTITUTION

Mr. Madison begged the House to indulge him in the further consideration of amendments to the constitution, and as there appeared, in some degree, a moment of leisure, he would move to go into a Committee of the whole on the subject, conformably to the order of the 8th of last month.

Mr. Ames hoped that the House would be induced, on mature reflection, to rescind their vote of going into a committee on the business, and refer it to a select committee. It would certainly tend to facilitate the business. If they had the subject at large before a Committee of the whole, he could not see where the business was likely to end. The amendments proposed were so various, that their discussion must inevitably occupy many days, and that at a time when they can be ill spared; whereas a select committee could go through and cull out those of the most material kind, without interrupting the principal business of the House. He therefore moved, that the Committee of the whole be discharged, and the subject referred to a select committee.

Mr. Sedgwick opposed the motion, for the reasons given by his colleague, observingly that the members from the several States proposing amendments would no doubt drag the House through the consideration of every one, whatever their fate might be after they were discussed; now gentlemen had only to reflect on this, and conceive the length of time the business would take up, if managed in this way.

Mr. White thought no time would be saved by appointing a select committee. Every member would like to be satisfied with the reasons upon which the amendments offered by the select committee are grounded, consequently the train of argument which gentlemen have in contemplation to avoid, must be brought forward.

He did not presume to say the constitution was perfect, but it was such as had met with the approbation of wise and good men in the different States. Some of the proposed amendments were also of high value; but he did not expect they would be supported by two-thirds of both Houses, without undergoing a thorough investigation. He did not like to refer any business to a select committee, until the sense of the House had been expressed upon it, because it rather tended to retard than despatch it; witness the collection bill, which had cost them much time, but after all had to be deserted.

MR. SHERMAN.—The provision for amendments made in the fifth article of the constitution, was intended to facilitate the adoption of those which experience should point out to be necessary. This constitution has been adopted by eleven States, a majority of those eleven have received it without expressing a wish for amendments; now, is it improbable that three-fourths of the eleven States will agree to amendments offered on mere speculative points, when the constitution has had no kind of trial whatever? It is hardly to be expected that they will. Consequently we shall lose our labor, and had better decline having anything further to do with it for the present.

But if the House are to go into a consideration, it had better be done in such a way as not to interfere much with the organization of the Government.

MR. PAGE hoped the business would proceed as heretofore directed. He thought it would be very agreeable to the majority of the Union, he knew it would be to his constituents, to find that the Government meant to give every security to the rights and liberties of the people, and to examine carefully into the grounds of the apprehensions expressed by several of the State conventions; he thought they would be satisfied with the amendments brought forward by his colleague, when the subject was last before the House.

MR. PARTRIDGE knew the subject must be taken up in some way or other, and preferred, for the sake of expedition, doing it by a select committee.

MR. JACKSON was sorry to see the House was to be troubled any further on the subject; he looked upon it as a mere waste of time; but as he always chose the least of two evils, he acquiesced in the motion for referring it to a special committee.

MR. GERRY asked, whether the House had cognizance of the amendments proposed by the State conventions? If they had not, he would make a motion to bring them forward.

MR. PAGE replied, that such motion would be out of order, until the present question was determined.

A desultory conversation ensued, and it was questioned whether the subject generally was to be before the Committee of the whole, or those specific propositions only which had already been introduced.

Mr. Gerry said, that it was a matter of indifference how this question was understood, because no gentleman could pretend to deny another the privilege of bringing forward propositions conformably to his sentiments. If gentlemen, then, might bring forward resolutions to be added, or motions of amendment, there would be no time saved by referring the subject to a special committee. But such procedure might tend to prejudice the House against an amendment neglected by the committee, and thereby induce them not to show that attention to the State which proposed it that would be delicate and proper.

He wished gentlemen to consider the situation of the States; seven out of thirteen had thought the constitution very defective, yet five of them have adopted it with a perfect reliance on Congress for its improvement. Now, what will these States feel if the subject is discussed in a select committee, and their recommendations totally neglected? The indelicacy of treating the application of five States in a manner different from other important subjects, will give no small occasion for disgust, which is a circumstance that this Government ought carefully to avoid. If, then, the House could gain nothing by this manner of proceeding, he hoped they would not hesitate to adhere to their former vote for going into a Committee of the whole. That they would gain nothing was pretty certain, for gentlemen must necessarily come forward with their amendments to the report when it was brought in. The members from Massachusetts were particularly instructed to press the amendments recommended by the convention of that State at all times, until they had been maturely considered by Congress; the same duties were made incumbent on the members from some other States; consequently, any attempt to smother the business, or prevent a full investigation, must be nugatory, while the House paid a proper deference to their own rules and orders. He did not contend for going into a Committee of the whole at the present moment; he would prefer a time of greater leisure than the present, from the business of organizing the Government.

Mr. Ames declared to the House, that he was no enemy to the consideration of amendments; but he had moved to rescind their former vote, in order to save time, which he was confident would be the consequence of referring it to a select committee.

He was sorry to hear an intention avowed by his colleague of considering every part of the frame of this constitution. It was the same as forming themselves into a convention of the United States. He did not stand for words, the thing would be the same in fact. He could not but express a degree of anxiety at seeing the system of Government encounter another ordeal when it ought to be extending itself to furnish security to others. He apprehended, if the zeal of some gentlemen broke out on this occasion that there would be no limits to the time necessary to discuss the subject; he was certain the session would not be long enough; perhaps they might be bounded by the period of their appointment, but he questioned it.

When gentlemen suppose themselves called upon to vent their ardor in some favorite pursuit, in securing to themselves and their posterity the inestimable rights and liberties they have just snatched from the hand of despotism, they are apt to carry their exertions to an extreme; but he hoped the subject itself would be limited; not that he objected to the consideration of the amendments proposed, indeed he should move himself for the consideration, by the committee, of those recommended by Massachusetts, if his colleagues omitted to do it; but he hoped gentlemen would not think of bringing in new amendments, such as were not recommended, but went to tear the frame of Government into pieces.

He had considered a select committee much better calculated to consider and arrange a complex business, than a Committee of the whole; he thought they were like the senses to the soul, and on an occasion like the present, could be made equally useful.

If he recollected rightly the decision made by the House on the 8th of June, it was that certain specific amendments be referred to the Committee of the whole; not that the subject generally be referred, and that amendments be made in the committee that were not contemplated, before. This public discussion would be like a dissection of the constitution, it would be defacing its symmetry, laying bare its sinews and tendons, ripping up the whole form, and tearing out its vitals; but is it presumable that such conduct would be attended with success? Two-thirds of both Houses must agree in all these operations, before they can have effect. His opposition to going into a Committee of the whole, did not arise from any fear that the constitution would suffer by a fair discussion in this, or any other House; but while such business was going on, the Government was laid prostrate, and every artery ceased to beat. The unfair advantages that might be taken in such a situation, were easier apprehended than resisted. Wherefore, he wished to avoid the danger, by a more prudent line of conduct.

Mr. TUCKER would not say whether the discussion alluded to by the gentleman last up would do good or harm, but he was certain it ought to take place no where but in a Committee of the whole; the subject is of too much importance for a select committee. Now, suppose such a committee to be appointed, and that the amendments proposed by the several States, together with those brought forward by the gentleman from Virginia, are referred to them; after some consideration they report, but not one of the amendments proposed by either State; what is the inference? They have considered them, and as they were better capable than the House of considering them, the House ought to reject every proposition coming from the State conventions. Will this give satisfaction to the States who have required amendments? Very far from it. They will expect that their propositions would be fully brought before the House, and regularly and fully considered; if indeed then they are rejected, it may be some satisfaction to them, to know that their applications have been treated with respect.

What I have said with respect to the propositions of the several States, may apply in some degree to the propositions brought forward by the gentleman (MR. MADISON) from Virginia; the select committee may single out one or two, and reject the remainder, notwithstanding the vote of the House for considering them. The gentleman would have a right to complain, and every State would be justly disgusted.

Will it tend to reconcile the Government to that great body of the people who are dissatisfied, who think themselves and all they hold most dear, unsafe under it, without certain amendments are made? Will it answer any one good purpose to slur over this business, and reject the propositions without giving them a fair chance of a full discussion? I think not, Mr. Speaker. Both the Senate and this House ought to treat the present subject with delicacy and impartiality.

The select committee will have it in their power so to keep this business back, that it may never again come before the House; this is an imprudent step for us to take; not that I would insinuate it is an event likely to take place, or which any gentleman has in contemplation. I give every gentleman credit for his declaration, and believe the honorable mover means to save time by this arrangement; but do not let us differ on this point. I would rather the business should lie over for a month, nay, for a whole session, than have it put into other hands, and passed over without investigation.

MR. GERRY inquired of his colleague, how it was possible that the House could be a federal convention without the Senate, and when two-thirds of both Houses are to agree to the amendments? He would also be glad to find out how a committee was the same to the House as the senses to the soul? What, said he, can we neither see, hear, smell, or feel, without we employ a committee for the purpose? My colleague further tells us, that if we proceed in this way, we shall lay bare the sinews and tendons of the constitution; that we shall butcher it, and put it to death.

Now, what does this argument tend to prove? Why, sir, to my mind, nothing more nor less than this, that we ought to adopt the report of the committee, whatever the report may be; for we are to judge by the knowledge derived through our senses, and not to proceed on to commit murder. If these are the arguments to induce the House to refer the subject to a select committee, they are arguments to engage to go further, and give into the hands of select committees the whole legislative power. But what was said respecting a public discussion? Are gentlemen afraid to meet the public ear on this topic? Do they wish to shut the gallery doors? Perhaps nothing would be attended with more dangerous consequences. No, sir, let us not be afraid of full and public investigation. Let our means, like our conclusions, be justified; let our constituents see, hear, and judge for themselves.

The question on discharging the Committee of the whole on the state of the Union from proceeding on the subject of amendments, as referred to them, was put, and carried in the affirmative—the House divided, 34 for it, and 15 against it.

It was then ordered that MR. MADISON's motion, stating certain specific amendments, proper to be proposed by Congress to the Legislatures of the States, to become, if ratified by three-fourths thereof, part of the constitution of the United States, together with the amendments to the said constitution, as proposed by the several States, be referred to a committee, to consist of a member from each State, with instruction to take the subject of amendments to the constitution of the United States generally into their consideration, and to report thereupon to the House.

The committee appointed were, MESSRS. VINING, MADISON, BALDWIN, SHERMAN, BURKE, GILMAN, CLYMER, BENSON, GOODHUE, BOUDINOT, and GALE.

Then the House adjourned.

. . .

Tuesday, July 28, 1789.

MR. VINING, from the committee to whom it was referred to take the subject of amendments to the constitution generally into their consideration, and to report thereon, made a report, which was ordered to lie on the table.

Thursday, August 13, 1789.

AMENDMENTS TO THE CONSTITUTION

MR. LEE moved that the House now resolve itself into a Committee of the whole, on the report of the committee of eleven, to whom it had been referred to take the subject of amendments to the constitution of the United States generally into their consideration.

MR. PAGE hoped the House would agree to the motion of his colleague without hesitation, because he conceived it essentially necessary to proceed and finish the business as speedily as possible; for whatever might be the fact with respect to the security which the citizens of America had for their rights and liberties under the new constitution, yet unless they saw it in that light, they would be uneasy, not to say dissatisfied.

He thought, likewise, that the business would be expedited by the simplicity and self-evidence which the propositions reported possessed, as it was impossible that much debate could take place.

MR. SEDGWICK was sorry that the motion was made, because he looked upon this as a very improper time to enter upon the consideration of a subject which would undoubtedly consume many days; and when they had so much other and more important business requiring immediate attention, he begged gentlemen to recollect that all they had hitherto done was of little or no effect; their impost and tonnage laws were but a dead letter.

MR. MADISON did not think it was an improper time to proceed in this business; the House had already gone through with subjects of a less interesting nature; now if the Judiciary bill was of such vast importance, its consideration ought not to have been postponed for those purposes.

He would remind gentlemen that there were many who conceived amendments of some kind necessary and proper in themselves; while others who are not so well satisfied of the necessity and propriety, may think they are rendered expedient from some other consideration. Is it desirable to keep up a division among the people of the United States on a point in which they consider their most essential rights are concerned? If this is an object worthy the attention of such a numerous part of our constituents, why should we decline taking it into our consideration, and thereby promote that spirit of urbanity and unanimity which the Government itself stands in need of for its more full support?

Already has the subject been delayed much longer than could have been wished. If after having fixed a day for taking it into consideration, we should put it off again, a spirit of jealousy may be excited, and not allayed without great inconvenience.

MR. VINING, impressed by the anxiety which the honorable gentleman from Virginia had discovered for having the subject of amendments considered, had agreed, in his own mind, to waive, for the present, the call he was well authorized to make, for the House to take into consideration the bill for establishing a Land Office for the disposal of the vacant lands in the Western Territory. In point of time, his motion had the priority; in point of importance, every candid mind would acknowledge its preference; and he conceived the House was bound to pay attention to it as early as possible; as they had given leave for a bill to be brought in, they ought not to neglect proceeding onwards with it.

Mr. Sedgwick hoped the House would not consume their time in a lengthy discussion upon what business should be done first. He was of opinion that there were several matters before them of more importance than the present; and he believed the people abroad were neither anxious nor jealous about it; but if they were, they would be satisfied at the delay, when they were informed of the cause. He begged, therefore, that the question proposed by the gentleman from Virginia (Mr. Lee) might be put without further debate.

Mr. Smith said that the judicial bill was entitled to the preference in point of order, and in point of propriety it deserved the first attention of the House. For his part, he could not conceive the necessity of going into any alterations of the Government until the Government itself was perfected. The constitution establishes three branches to constitute a whole; the legislative and executive are now in existence, but the judicial is uncreated. While we remain in this state, not a single part of the revenue system can operate; no breach of your laws can be punished; illicit trade cannot be prevented. Greater harm will arise from delaying the establishment of the judicial system, than can possibly grow from a delay of the other subject. If gentlemen are willing to let it lie over to a period of greater leisure, I shall join them cheerfully and candidly, said he, in a full discussion of that business.

An honorable gentleman from Virginia observed to us that these propositions were self-evident, that little or no debate could grow out of them. That may be his opinion, but truly, sir, it is not mine; for I think some of them are not self-evident, and some of them will admit of lengthy discussion; and some others, I hope, may be rejected, while their place may be better supplied by others hereafter to be brought forward. Some members are pledged to support amendments, and will, no doubt, support them with all the arguments their fancy or ingenuity can suggest. Viewing it in this light, it is not to be expected that the discussion will be ended in less than a fortnight or three weeks; and let gentlemen consult their own feelings whether they have so much time now to spare.

Mr. Hartley thought the judicial system ought to be finished before any other business was entered upon, and was willing to consider of amendments to the constitution when the House was more disengaged; because he wished very much that the constitution was so modified as to give satisfaction to honest and candid minds. Such would be satisfied with securing to themselves and their posterity all those blessings of freedom which they are now possessed of. As to the artful and designing, who had clamored against the whole work, he had not the smallest desire to gratify them: he hoped and trusted their numbers were but few.

MR. GERRY thought the discussion would take up more time than the House could now spare; he was, therefore, in favor of postponing the consideration of the subject, until the Judicial bill, and the bill for registering and clearing vessels, and some other bills relating to the revenue business, were gone through. He asked the gentleman from Virginia, if he conceived that the amendments in the report were all that were to be taken into consideration. He thought the community would be little more pleased with them than if they had omitted the subject altogether. Besides, it was absurd to suppose that the members were obliged to confine their deliberations solely to those objects, when it was very well known that the members from Massachusetts and New Hampshire were bound to bring forward and support others. The members from other States may be inclined to do the same with respect to the amendments of their own conventions; this will inevitably produce a more copious debate than the gentleman contemplates. From these considerations it might be hoped that honorable gentlemen would no longer press the motion.

MR. LAWRENCE had no objection to consider amendments at a proper time, but did not think that the present was a proper time to enter upon them, nor did he suppose that gentlemen would be precluded from a full discussion of the whole subject whenever it was taken up. Gentlemen would find him ready to acquiesce in every thing that was proper, but he could not consent to let the great business of legislation stand still, and thereby incur an absolute evil in order to rid themselves of an imaginary one; for whether the subject of amendments was considered now or at a more distant period, appeared to his mind a matter of mere indifference. It may further be observed, that few, if any, of the State Assemblies are now in session; consequently the business could not be completed even if Congress had already done their part; but certainly the people in general are more anxious to see the Government in operation, than speculative amendments upon an untried constitution.

MR. MADISON.—I beg leave to make one or two remarks more, in consequence of the observations which have fallen from the different sides of the House. Some gentlemen seem to think that additional propositions will be brought forward; whether they will or not, I cannot pretend to say; but if they are, I presume they will be no impediment to our deciding upon those contained in the report. But gentlemen who introduce these propositions will see, that if they are to produce more copious debate than has hitherto taken place, they will consume a great part of the remainder of the session. I wish the subject well considered, but I do not wish to see any unnecessary waste of time; and gentlemen will please to remember that this subject has yet to go before the Senate.

I admit, with the worthy gentleman who preceded me, that a great number of the community are solicitous to see the Government carried into operation; but I believe that there is a considerable part also anxious to secure those rights which they are apprehensive are endangered by the present constitution. Now, considering the full confidence they reposed at the time of its adoption in their future representatives, I think we ought to pursue the subject to effect. I confess it has already appeared to me, in point of candor and good faith, as well as policy, to be incumbent on the first Legislature of the United States, at their first session, to make such alterations in the constitution as will give satisfaction, without injuring or destroying any of its vital principles.

I should not press the subject at this time, because I am well aware of the importance of the other business enumerated by the gentlemen who are adverse to the present motion, but from an apprehension that, if it is delayed until the other is gone through, gentlemen's patience and application will be so harassed and fatigued, as to oblige them to leave it in an unfinished state until the next session; besides, were the Judicial bill to pass now, it could not take effect until others were enacted, which probably at this time are not drawn up.

Mr. Smith.—The honorable gentleman has concluded his remarks by assigning the best reason in the world why we should go into a consideration of the Judicial bill. He says, that even if it were now passed, it would take some time before it could get into operation; he must admit it to be an essential part of the Government, and, as such, ought not to remain a single instant in a state of torpidity.

Mr. Fitzsimons wished gentlemen would suffer the question to be put, and not consume the time in arguing about what should be done. If a majority was not in favor of considering amendments, they might proceed to some other business.

Mr. Page was positive the people would never support the Government unless their anxiety was removed. They, in some instances, adopted it, in confidence of its being speedily amended; they will complain of being deceived unless their expectations are fulfilled. So much time has elapsed since the subject was first brought forward, said he, that people will not think us serious, unless we now set about and complete it.

He begged gentlemen to consider the importance of the number of citizens, who were anxious for amendments; if these had been added to those who openly opposed the constitution, it possibly might have met a different fate. Can the Government, under these circumstances, possess energy, as some gentlemen suppose? Is not the confidence of the people absolutely necessary to support it?

The question was now put, and carried in the affirmative.

The House then resolved itself into a Committee of the whole, MR. BOUDINOT in the chair, and took the amendments under consideration. The first article ran thus: "In the introductory paragraph of the constitution, before the words 'We the people,' add 'Government being intended for the benefit of the people, and the rightful establishment thereof being derived from their authority alone.' "

MR. SHERMAN.—I believe, Mr. Chairman, this is not the proper mode of amending the constitution. We ought not to interweave our propositions into the work itself, because it will be destructive of the whole fabric. We might as well endeavor to mix brass, iron, and clay, as to incorporate such heterogeneous articles; the one contradictory to the other. Its absurdity will be discovered by comparing it with a law. Would any Legislature endeavor to introduce into a former act a subsequent amendment, and let them stand so connected? When an alteration is made in an act, it is done by way of supplement; the latter act always repealing the former in every specified case of difference.

Besides this, sir, it is questionable whether we have the right to propose amendments in this way. The constitution is the act of the people, and ought to remain entire. But the amendments will be the act of the State Governments. Again, all the authority we possess is derived from that instrument; if we mean to destroy the whole, and establish a new constitution, we remove the basis on which we mean to build. For these reasons, I will move to strike out that paragraph and substitute another.

The paragraph proposed was to the following effect:

Resolved by the Senate and House of Representatives of the United States in Congress assembled, That the following articles be proposed as amendments to the constitution, and when ratified by three-fourths of the State Legislatures shall become valid to all intents and purposes, as part of the same.

Under this title, the amendments might come in nearly as stated in the report, only varying the phraseology so as to accommodate them to a supplementary form.

MR. MADISON.—Form, sir, is always of less importance than the substance; but on this occasion, I admit that form is of some consequence, and it will be well for the House to pursue that which, upon reflection, shall appear to be the most eligible. Now it appears to me, that there is a neatness and propriety in incorporating the amendments into the constitution itself; in that case the system will remain uniform and entire; it will certainly be more simple, when the amendments are interwoven into those parts to which they naturally belong, than it will if they consist of separate and distinct parts. We shall then be able to determine its meaning without references or comparison; whereas, if they are supplementary, its meaning can only be ascertained by a comparison of the two instruments, which will be a very considerable embarrassment. It will be difficult to ascertain to what parts of the instrument the amendments particularly refer; they will create unfavorable comparisons; whereas, if they are placed upon the footing here proposed, they will stand upon as good foundation as the original work.

Nor is it so uncommon a thing as gentlemen suppose; systematic men frequently take up the whole law, and, with its amendments and alterations, reduce it into one act. I am not, however, very solicitous about the form, provided the business is but well completed.

MR. SMITH did not think the amendment proposed by the honorable gentlemen from Connecticut was compatible with the constitution, which declared, that the amendments recommended by Congress, and ratified by the Legislatures of three-fourths of the several States, should be part of this constitution; in which case it would form one complete system; but according to the idea of the amendment, the instrument is to have five or six suits of improvements. Such a mode seems more calculated to embarrass the people than anything else, while nothing in his opinion was a juster cause of complaint than the difficulties of knowing the law, arising from legislative obscurities that might easily be avoided. He said, that it had certainly been the custom in several of the State Governments, to amend their laws by way of supplement. But South Carolina had been an instance of the contrary practice, in revising the old code; instead of making acts in addition to acts, which is always attended with perplexity, she has incorporated them, and brought them forward as a complete system, repealing the old. This is what he understood was intended to be done by the committee; the present copy of the constitution was to be done away, and a new one substituted in its stead.

MR. TUCKER wished to know whether the deliberations of the committee were intended to be confined to the propositions on the table. If they were not, he should beg leave to bring before them the amendments proposed by South Carolina. He considered himself as instructed to bring them forward, and he meant to perform his duty by an early and prompt obedience. He wished to have the sense of the House on this point, whether he was in order to bring them forward.

MR. LIVERMORE was clearly of opinion, that whatever amendments were made to the constitution, they ought to stand separate from the original instrument. We have no right, said he, to alter a clause, any otherwise than by a new proposition. We have well-established precedents for such a mode of procedure in the practice of the British Parliament and the State Legislatures throughout America. I do not mean, however, to assert that there has been no instance of a repeal of the whole law on enacting another; but this has generally taken place on account of the complexity of the original, with its supplements. Were we a mere Legislative body, no doubt it might be warrantable in us to pursue a similar method; but it is questionable whether it is possible for us, consistent with the oath we have taken, to attempt a repeal of the constitution of the United States, by making a new one to substitute in its place; the reason of this is grounded on a very simple consideration. It is by virtue of the present constitution, I presume, that we attempt to make another; now, if we proceed to the repeal of this, I cannot see upon what authority we shall erect another; if we destroy the base, the superstructure falls of course. At some future day it may be asked upon what authority we proceeded to raise and appropriate public moneys. We suppose we do it in virtue of the present constitution; but it may be doubted whether we have right to exercise any of its authorities while it is suspended, as it will certainly be from the time that two-thirds of both Houses have agreed to submit it to the State Legislatures; so that, unless we mean to destroy the whole constitution, we ought to be careful how we attempt to amend it in the way proposed by the committee. From hence, I presume it will be more prudent to adopt the mode proposed by the gentleman from Connecticut, than it will be to risk the destruction of the whole by proposing amendments in the manner recommended by the committee.

MR. VINING disliked a supplementary form, and said it was a bad reason to urge the practice of former ages, when there was a more convenient method of doing the business at hand. He had seen an act entitled an act to amend a supplement to an act entitled an act for altering part of an act entitled an act for certain purposes therein mentioned. If gentlemen were disposed to run into such jargon in amending and altering the constitution, he could not help it; but he trusted they would adopt a plainness and simplicity of style on this and every other occasion, which should be easily understood. If the mode proposed by the gentleman from Connecticut was adopted, the system would be distorted, and, like a careless written letter, have more attached to it in a postscript than was contained in the original composition.

The constitution being a great and important work, ought all to be brought into one view, and made as intelligible as possible.

MR. CLYMER was of opinion with the gentleman from Connecticut, that the amendments ought not to be incorporated in the body of the work, which he hoped would remain a monument to justify those who made it; by a comparison, the world would discover the perfection of the original, and the superfluity of the amendments. He made this distinction, because he did not conceive any of the amendments essential, but as they were solicited by his fellow-citizens, and for that reason they were acquiesced in by others; he therefore wished the motion for throwing them into a supplementary form might be carried.

Mr. Stone.—It is not a matter of much consequence, with respect to the preservation of the original instrument, whether the amendments are incorporated or made distinct; because the records will always show the original form in which it stood. But in my opinion, we ought to mark its progress with truth in every step we take. If the amendments are incorporated in the body of the work, it will appear, unless we refer to the archives of Congress, that GEORGE WASHINGTON, and the other worthy characters who composed the convention, signed an instrument which they never had in contemplation. The one to which he affixed his signature purports to be adopted by the unanimous consent of the delegates from every State there assembled. Now if we incorporate these amendments, we must undoubtedly go further, and say that the constitution so formed was defective, and had need of alteration; we therefore purpose to repeal the old and substitute a new one in its place. From this consideration alone, I think we ought not to pursue the line of conduct drawn for us by the committee. This perhaps is not the last amendment the constitution may receive; we ought therefore to be careful how we set a precedent which, in dangerous and turbulent times, may unhinge the whole.

With respect to the observations of the gentleman from South Carolina, I shall just remark, that we have no authority to repeal the whole constitution. The words referred to in that instrument only authorized us to propose amendments to it, which, when properly ratified, are to become valid as a part of the same; but these can never be construed to empower us to make a new constitution.

For these reasons, I would wish our expressions might be so guarded, as to purport nothing but what we really have in view.

Mr. Livermore.—The mode adopted by the committee might be very proper, provided Congress had the forming of a constitution in contemplation; then they, or an individual member, might propose to strike out a clause and insert another, as is done with respect to article 3, section 2. But certainly no gentleman acquainted with legislative business would pretend to alter and amend, in this manner, a law already passed. He was convinced it could not be done properly in any other way than by the one proposed by the gentleman from Connecticut.

Mr. Gerry asked, if the mode could make any possible difference, provided the sanction was the same; or whether it would operate differently in any one instance? If it will not, we are disputing about form, and the question will turn on the expediency. Now one gentleman tells you, that he is so attached to this instrument, that he is unwilling to lose any part of it; therefore, to gratify him, we may throw it into a supplementary form. But let me ask, will not this as effectually destroy some parts, as if the correction had been made by way of incorporation? or will posterity have a more favorable opinion of the original, because it has been amended by distinct acts? For my part, I cannot see what advantage can accrue from adopting the motion of the honorable gentleman from Connecticut, unless it be to give every one the trouble of erasing out of his copy of the constitution certain words and sentences, and inserting others. But, perhaps, in our great veneration for the original composition, we may go further, and pass an act to prohibit these interpolations, as it may injure the text.

All this, sir, I take to be trifling about matters of little consequence. The constitution has undoubtedly provided that the amendments shall be incorporated if I understand the import of the words, "and shall be valid to all intents and purposes, as part of the constitution." If it had said that the present form should be preserved, then it would be proper to propose the alterations by way of a supplement. One gentleman has said we shall lose the names that are now annexed to the instrument. They are names, sir, I admit, of high respect; but I would ask that gentleman, if they would give validity to the constitution if it were not ratified by the several States? or if their names were struck out, whether it would be of less force than it is at present? If he answers these questions in the negative, I shall consider it of no consequence whether the names are appended to it or not. But it will be time enough to discuss this point, when a motion is made for striking them out.

If we proceed in the way proposed by the honorable gentleman from Connecticut, I presume the title of our first amendment will be, a supplement to the constitution of the United States; the next a supplement to the supplement, and so on, until we have supplements annexed five times in five years, wrapping up the constitution in a maze of perplexity; and as great an adept as that honorable gentleman is at finding out the truth, it will take him, I apprehend, a week or a fortnight's study to ascertain the true meaning of the constitution.

It is said, if the amendments are incorporated, it will be a virtual repeal of the constitution. I say the effect will be the same in a supplementary way; consequently the objection goes for nothing, or it goes against making any amendments whatever.

It is said that the present form of the amendments is contrary to the 5th article. I will not undertake to define the extent of the word amendment, as it stands in the fifth article; but I suppose if we propose to change the division of the powers given to the three branches of the Government, and that proposition is accepted and ratified by three-fourths of the State Legislatures, it will become as valid, to all intents and purposes, as any part of the constitution; but if it is the opinion of gentlemen that the original is to be kept sacred, amendments will be of no use, and had better be omitted; whereas, on the other hand, if they are to be received as equal in authority, we shall have five or six constitutions, perhaps differing in material points from each other, but all equally valid; so that they may require a man of science to determine what is or is not the constitution. This will certainly be attended with great inconvenience, as the several States are bound not to make laws contradictory thereto, and all officers are sworn to support it, without knowing precisely what it is.

MR. STONE asked the gentleman last up, how he meant to have the amendments incorporated? Was it intended to have the constitution republished, and the alterations inserted in their proper places? He did not see how it was practicable to propose amendments, without making out a new constitution, in the manner brought forward by the committee.

MR. LAWRENCE could not conceive how gentlemen meant to engraft the amendments into the constitution. The original one, executed by the convention at Philadelphia, was lodged in the archives of the late Congress, it was impossible for this House to take, and correct, and interpolate that without making it speak a different language: this would be supposing several things which never were contemplated. But what would become of the acts of Congress? They will certainly be vitiated, unless they are provided for by an additional clause in the constitution.

What shall we say with respect to the ratification of the several States? They adopted the original constitution, but they have not thereby enabled us to change the one form of Government for another. It is true, amendments were proposed by some of them; but it does not follow, of necessity, that we should alter the form of the original which they have ratified. Amendments in this way are only proper in legislative business, while the bill is on its passage, as was justly observed before.

MR. BENSON said, that this question had been agitated in the select committee, and determined in favor of the form in which it was reported; he believed this decision was founded in a great degree upon the recommendation of the State conventions, which had proposed amendments in the very form. This pointed out the mode most agreeable to the people of America, and therefore the one most eligible for Congress to pursue; it will likewise be the most convenient way. Suppose the amendments ratified by the several States; Congress may order a number of copies to be printed, into which the alterations will be inserted, and the work stand perfect and entire.

I believe it never was contemplated by any gentleman to alter the original constitution deposited in the archives of the Union, that will remain there with the names of those who formed it, while the Government has a being. But certainly there is convenience and propriety in completing the work in a way provided for in itself. The records of Congress and the several States will mark the progress of the business, and nothing will appear to be done but what is actually performed.

Mr. MADISON.—The gentleman last up has left me but one remark to add, and that is, if we adopt the amendment, we shall so far unhinge the business, as to occasion alterations in every article and clause of the report.

Mr. HARTLEY hoped the committee would not agree to the alteration, because it would perplex the business. He wished the propositions to be simple and entire, that the State Legislatures might decide without hesitation, and every man know what was the ground on which he rested his political welfare. Besides, the consequent changes which the motion would induce, were such as, he feared, would take up some days, if not weeks; and the time of the House was too precious to be squandered away in discussing mere matter of form.

Mr. PAGE was sorry to find the gentlemen stop at the preamble; he hoped they would proceed as soon as the obstruction was removed, and that would be when the motion was negatived.

He thought the best way to view this subject, was to look at the constitution as a bill on its passage through the House, and to consider and amend its defects, article by article; for which reason he was for entering at once upon the main business. After that was gone through, it would be time enough to arrange the materials with which the House intended to form the preamble.

Mr. LIVERMORE insisted, that neither this Legislature, nor all the Legislatures in America, were authorized to repeal a constitution; and that must be an inevitable consequence of an attempt to amend it in a way proposed by the committee. He then submitted to gentlemen the propriety of the alteration.

As to the difficulty which had been supposed in understanding supplemental laws, he thought but little of it; he imagined there were things in the constitution more difficult to comprehend than any thing he had yet seen in the amendments.

Mr. JACKSON.—I do not like to differ with gentlemen about form; but as so much has been said, I wish to give my opinion; it is this: that the original constitution ought to remain inviolate, and not be patched up, from time to time, with various stuffs resembling Joseph's coat of many colors.

Some gentlemen talk of repealing the present constitution, and adopting an improved one. If we have this power, we may go on from year to year, making new ones; and in this way, we shall render the basis of the superstructure the most fluctuating thing imaginable, and the people will never know what the constitution is. As for the alteration proposed by the committee to prefix before "We the people," certain dogmas, I cannot agree to it; the words, as they now stand, speak as much as it is possible to speak; it is a practical recognition of the right of the people to ordain and establish Governments, and is more expressive than any other mere paper declaration.

But why will gentlemen contend for incorporating amendments into the constitution? They say, that it is necessary for the people to have the whole before them in one view. Have they precedent for this assertion? Look at the constitution of Great Britain; is that all contained in one instrument? It is well known, that *magna charta* was extorted by the barons from King John some centuries ago. Has that been altered since by the incorporation of amendments? Or does it speak the same language now, as it did at the time it was obtained? Sir, it is not altered a little from its original form. Yet there have been many amendments and improvements in the constitution of Britain since that period. In the subsequent reign of his son, the great charters were confirmed with some supplemental acts. Is the *habeas corpus* act, or the statute *De Tollagio non concedendo* incorporated in *magna charta*? And yet there is not an Englishman but would spill the last drop of his blood in their defence; it is these, with some other acts of Parliament and *magna charta*, that form the basis of English liberty. We have seen amendments to their constitution during the present reign, by establishing the independence of the judges, who are hereafter to be appointed during good behavior; formerly they were at the pleasure of the crown. But was this done by striking out and inserting other words in the great charter? No, sir, the constitution is composed of many distinct acts; but an Englishman would be ashamed to own that, on this account, he could not ascertain his own privileges or the authority of the Government.

The constitution of the Union has been ratified and established by the people; let their act remain inviolable; if any thing we can do has a tendency to improve it, let it be done, but without mutilating and defacing the original.

Mr. Sherman.—If I had looked upon this question as mere matter of form, I should not have brought it forward or troubled the committee with such a lengthy discussion. But, sir, I contend that amendments made in the way proposed by the committee are void. No gentleman ever knew an addition and alteration introduced into an existing law, and that any part of such law was left in force; but if it was improved or altered by a supplemental act, the original retained all its validity and importance, in every case where the two were not incompatible. But if these observations alone should be thought insufficient to support my motion, I would desire gentlemen to consider the authorities upon which the two constitutions are to stand. The original was established by the people at large, by conventions chosen by them for the express purpose. The preamble to the constitution declares the act: but will it be a truth in ratifying the next constitution, which is to be done perhaps by the State Legislatures, and not conventions chosen for the purpose? Will gentlemen say it is "We the people" in this case? Certainly they cannot; for, by the present constitution, we, nor all the Legislatures in the Union together, do not possess the power of repealing it. All that is granted us by the 5th article is, that whenever we shall think it necessary, we may propose amendments to the constitution; not that we may propose to repeal the old, and substitute a new one.

Gentlemen say, it would be convenient to have it in one instrument, that people might see the whole at once; for my part, I view no difficulty on this point. The amendments reported are a declaration of rights; the people are secure in them, whether we declare them or not; the last amendment but one provides that the three branches of Government shall each exercise its own rights. This is well secured already; and, in short, I do not see that they lessen the force of any article in the constitution; if so, there can be little more difficulty in comprehending them whether they are combined in one, or stand distinct instruments.

Mr. SMITH read extracts from the amendments proposed by several of the State conventions at the time they ratified the constitution, from which, he said, it appeared that they were generally of opinion that the phraseology of the constitution ought to be altered; nor would this mode of proceeding repeal any part of the constitution but such as it touched, the remainder will be in force during the time of considering it and ever after.

As to the observations made by the honorable gentleman from Georgia, respecting the amendments made to the constitution of Great Britain, they did not apply; the cases were nothing like similar, and consequently, could not be drawn into precedent. The constitution of Britain is neither the *magna charta* of John, nor the *habeas corpus* act, nor all the charters put together; it is what the Parliament wills. It is true, there are rights granted to the subject that cannot be resumed; but the constitution, or form of Government may be altered by the authority of Parliament, whose power is absolute without control.

Mr. SENEY was afraid the House would consume more time than was at first apprehended in discussing the subject of amendments, if he was to infer any thing from what had now taken place. He hoped the question would soon be put and decided.

Mr. VINING was an enemy to unnecessary debate, but he conceived the question to be an important one, and was not displeased with the discussion that had taken place; he should, however, vote in favor of the most simple mode.

Mr. Gerry.—The honorable gentleman from Connecticut, if I understand him right, says that the words "We the people" cannot be retained, if Congress should propose amendments, and they be ratified by the State Legislatures. Now, if this is a fact, we ought most undoubtedly to adopt his motion; because if we do not, we cannot obtain any amendments whatever. But upon what ground does the gentleman's position stand? The constitution of the United States was proposed by a convention met at Philadelphia; but, with all its importance, it did not possess as high authority as the President, Senate, and House of Representatives of the Union. For that convention was not convened in consequence of any express will of the people, but an implied one, through their members in the State Legislatures. The constitution derived no authority from the first convention; it was concurred in by conventions of the people, and that concurrence armed it with power and invested it with dignity. Now the Congress of the United States are expressly authorized by the sovereign and uncontrollable voice of the people, to propose amendments whenever two-thirds of both Houses shall think fit. Now, if this is the fact, the propositions of amendment will be found to originate with a higher authority than the original system. The conventions of the States, respectively, have agreed for the people, that the State Legislatures shall be authorized to decide upon these amendments in the manner of a convention. If these acts of the State Legislatures are not good, because they are not specifically instructed by their constituents, neither were the acts calling the first and subsequent conventions.

Does he mean to put amendments on this ground, that after they have been ratified by the State Legislatures, they are not to have the same authority as the original instrument? If this is his meaning, let him avow it; and if it is well founded, we may save ourselves the trouble of proceeding in the business. But, for my part, I have no doubt but a ratification of the amendments, in any form, would be as valid as any part of the constitution. The Legislatures are elected by the people. I know no difference between them and conventions, unless it be that the former will generally be composed of men of higher characters than may be expected in conventions; and in this case, the ratification by the Legislatures would have the preference.

Now, if it is clear that the effect will be the same in either mode, will gentlemen hesitate to approve the most simple and clear? It will undoubtedly be more agreeable to have it all brought into one instrument, than have to refer to five or six different acts.

Mr. Sherman.—The gentlemen who oppose the motion say we contend for matter of form; they think it nothing more. Now we say we contend for substance, and therefore cannot agree to amendments in this way. If they are so desirous of having the business completed, they had better sacrifice what they consider but a matter of indifference to gentlemen, to go more unanimously along with them in altering the constitution.

The question on MR. SHERMAN's motion was now put and lost.

MR. LIVERMORE wished to know whether it was necessary, in order to carry a motion in committee, that two-thirds should agree.

MR. HARTLEY mentioned, that in Pennsylvania, they had a council of censors who were authorized to call a convention to amend the constitution when it was thought necessary, but two-thirds were required for that purpose. He had been a member of that body, when they had examined the business in a committee of council; the majority made a report, which was lost for want of two-thirds to carry it through the council.

Some desultory conversation took place on this subject, when it was decided by the chairman of the committee that a majority of the committee were sufficient to form a report.

An appeal being made from the opinion of the chair, it was, after some observations, confirmed by the committee. After which the committee rose and reported progress.

Adjourned.

Friday, August 14, 1789.

ABIEL FOSTER, from New Hampshire, appeared and took his seat.

AMENDMENTS TO THE CONSTITUTION

The House then again resolved itself into a Committee of the whole, on the amendments to the constitution, MR. TRUMBULL in the chair; when,

MR. SMITH wished to transpose the words of the first amendment, as they did not satisfy his mind in the manner they stood.

MR. GERRY said, they were not well expressed; we have it here "government being intended for the benefit of the people;" this holds up an idea that all the Governments of the earth are intended for the benefit of the people. Now, I am so far from being of this opinion, that I do not believe that one out of fifty is intended for any such purpose. I believe the establishment of most Governments is to gratify the ambition of an individual, who, by fraud, force, or accident, had made himself master of the people. If we contemplate the history of nations, ancient or modern, we shall find they originated either in fraud or force, or both. If this is demonstrable, how can we pretend to say that Governments are intended for the benefit of those who are most oppressed by them. This maxim does not appear to me to be strictly true in fact, therefore I think we ought not to insert it in the constitution. I shall therefore propose to amend the clause, by inserting "of right," then it will stand as it ought. I do not object to the principle, sir; it is a good one, but it does not generally hold in practice.

The question of inserting the words "of right" was put, and determined in the negative.

MR. TUCKER.—I presume these propositions are brought forward under the idea of being amendments to the constitution; but can this be esteemed an amendment of the constitution? If I understand what is meant by the introductory paragraph, it is the preamble to the constitution; but a preamble is no part of the constitution. It is, to say the best, a useless amendment. For my part, I should as soon think of amending the concluding part, consisting of General Washington's letter to the President of Congress, as the preamble; but if the principle is of importance, it may be introduced into a bill of rights.

MR. SMITH read the amendments on this head, proposed by the conventions of New York, Virginia, and North Carolina, from which it appeared that these States had expressed a desire to have an amendment of this kind.

MR. TUCKER replied, that the words "We the people do ordain and establish this constitution for the United States of America," were a declaration of their action; this being performed, Congress have nothing to do with it. But if it was necessary to retain the principle, it might come in at some other place.

MR. SUMTER thought this was not a proper place to introduce any general principle; perhaps, in going through with the amendments, something might be proposed subversive of what was there declared; wherefore he wished the committee would pass over the preamble until they had gone through all the amendments, and then, if alterations were necessary, they could be accommodated to what had taken place in the body of the constitution.

MR. LIVERMORE was not concerned about the preamble; he did not care what kind it was agreed to form in the committee; because, when it got before the House, it would be undone if one member more than one-third of the whole opposed it.

MR. PAGE thought the preamble no part of the constitution; but if it was, it stood in no need of amendment; the words "We the people," had the neatness and simplicity, while its expression was the most forcible of any he had ever seen prefixed to any constitution. He did not doubt the truth of the proposition brought forward by the committee, but he doubted its necessity in this place.

MR. MADISON.—If it be a truth, and so self-evident that it cannot be denied; if it be recognized, as is the fact in many of the

State constitutions; and if it be desired by three important States, to be added to this, I think they must collectively offer a strong inducement to the mind desirous of promoting harmony, to acquiesce with the report; at least, some strong arguments should be brought forward to show the reason why it is improper.

My worthy colleague says, the original expression is neat and simple; that loading it with more words may destroy the beauty of the sentence; and others say it is unnecessary, as the paragraph is complete without it. Be it so, in their opinion; yet, still it appears important in the estimation of three States, that this solemn truth should be inserted in the constitution. For my part, sir, I do not think the association of ideas anywise unnatural; it reads very well in this place; so much so, that I think gentlemen, who admit it should come in somewhere, will be puzzled to find a better place.

MR. SHERMAN thought they ought not to come in in this place. The people of the United States have given their reasons for doing a certain act. Here we propose to come in and give them a right to do what they did on motives which appeared to them sufficient to warrant their determination; to let them know that they had a right to exercise a natural and inherent privilege, which they have asserted in the solemn ordination and establishment of the constitution. Now, if this right is indefeasible, and the people have recognized it in practice, the truth is better asserted than it can be by any words whatever. The words "We the people" in the original constitution, are as copious and expressive as possible; any addition will only drag out the sentence without illuminating it; for these reasons, it may be hoped the committee will reject the proposed amendment.

The question on the first paragraph of the report was put and carried in the affirmative, twenty-seven to twenty-three.

The second paragraph in the report was read as follows:

Article I. Section 2. Paragraph 3. Strike out all between the words "direct" and "and until such." and instead thereof, insert "after the first enumeration, there shall be one representative for every thirty thousand, until the number shall amount to one hundred. After which the proportion shall be so regulated by Congress, that the number of representatives shall never be less than one hundred, nor more than one hundred and seventy-five; but each State shall always have at least one representative."

MR. VINING.—The duty, sir, which I owe to my constituents, and my desire to establish the constitution on a policy, dictated by justice and liberality, which will ever secure domestic tranquility and promote the general welfare, induces me to come forward with a motion, which I rest upon its own merits. Gentlemen who have a magnanimous policy in view, I trust, will give it their support, and concede to what is proper in itself, and likely to procure a greater degree of harmony. I therefore move you, sir, to insert after the words "one hundred and seventy-five," these words: "That where the number of inhabitants of any particular State amounts to forty-five thousand, they shall be entitled to two representatives."

This motion was negatived without a division.

MR. AMES moved to strike out "thirty thousand," and insert "forty thousand." I am induced to this, said he, because I think my fellow citizens will be dissatisfied with too numerous a representation. The present, I believe, is in proportion to one for forty thousand, the number I move to insert. I believe we have hitherto experienced no difficulty on account of the smallness of our number; if we are embarrassed, I apprehend the embarrassment will arise from our want of knowing the general interest of the nation at large; or for want of local information. If the present number is found sufficient for the purpose of legislation, without any such embarrassment, it ought to be preferred, inasmuch as it is most adequate to its object.

But before we proceed in the discussion, let us consider the effect which a representation, founded on one member for 30,000 citizens, will produce. In the first place, it will give four members for every three now entitled to a seat in this House, which will be an additional burthen to the Union, in point of expense, in the same ratio. Add to this another consideration, that probably before the first census is taken, the number of inhabitants will be considerably increased from what it was when the convention which formed this constitution obtained their information. This will probably increase the expenses of Government to 450,000 dollars annually. Now those who have attended particularly to economy; who, upon the most careful calculation, find that our revenue is likely to fall infinitely short of our expenses, will consider this saving as a considerable object, and deserving their most serious regard.

It may become dissatisfactory to the people as an intolerable burthen. Again, it must be abundantly clear to every gentleman, that, in proportion as you increase the number of Representatives, the body degenerates; you diminish the individual usefulness; gentlemen will not make equal exertions to despatch public business, when they can lean upon others for the arrangement.

By enlarging the representation, we lessen the chance of selecting men of the greatest wisdom and abilities; because small district elections may be conducted by intrigue, but in large districts nothing but real dignity of character can secure an election. Gentlemen ought to consider how essential it is to the security and welfare of their constituents, that this branch of the Government should support its independence and consequence.

Another effect of it, will be an excitement or fermentation in the representative body. Numerous assemblies are supposed to be less under the guidance of reason than smaller ones; their deliberations are confused; they will fall the prey of party spirit; they will cabal to carry measures which they would be unable to get through by fair and open argument. All these circumstances tend to retard the public business, and increase the expense; making Government, in the eyes of some, so odious, as to induce them to think it rather a curse than a blessing.

It lessens that responsibility which is annexed to the representative of a more numerous body of people. For I believe it will be found true, that the representative of 40,000 citizens will have more at risk than the man who represents a part of them. He has more dignity of character to support, and must use the most unremitting industry in their service to preserve it unsullied; he will be more sensible of the importance of his charge, and more indefatigable in his duty.

It is said, that these amendments are introduced with a view to conciliate the affections of the people to the Government. I am persuaded the people are not anxious to have a large representation, or a representation of one for every 30,000; they are satisfied with the representation they now enjoy. The great object which the convention of Massachusetts had in view by proposing this amendment, was to obtain a security that Congress should never reduce the representation below what they conceived to be a point of security. Their object was not augmentation, it was certainty alone they wished for; at the next census, the number of representatives will be seventy or eighty, and in twenty years it will be equal to the desires of any gentleman. We shall have to guard against its growth in less than half a century. The number of proper characters to serve in the Legislature of any country is small; and of those, many are inclined to pursue other objects. If the representation is greatly enlarged, men of inferior abilities will undoubtedly creep in, for although America has as great a proportion of men of sense and judgment as any nation on earth, yet she may not have sufficient to fill a legislative body unduly enlarged. Now if it has been questioned whether this country can remain united under a Government administered by men of the most consummate abilities, the sons of wisdom, and the friends of virtue, how much more doubtful will it be, if the administration is thrown into different hands; and different hands must inevitably be employed, if the representation is too large.

Mr. Madison.—I cannot concur in sentiment with the gentleman last up, that one representative for forty thousand inhabitants will conciliate the minds of those to the Government, who are desirous of amendments; because they have rather wished for an increase, than confined themselves to a limitation.

I believe, by this motion, we shall avoid no inconvenience that can be considered of much consequence, for one member for either thirty thousand or forty thousand inhabitants, will, in a few years, give the number beyond which it is proposed Congress shall not go.

Now, if good policy requires that we accommodate the constitution to the wishes of that part of the community who are anxious for amendments, we shall agree to something like what is proposed in the report, for the States of New Hampshire, Massachusetts, New York, Virginia, and North Carolina, have desired an alteration on this head; some have required an increase as far as two hundred at least. This does not look as if certainty was their sole object.

I do not consider it necessary, on this occasion, to go into a lengthy discussion of the advantages of a less or greater representation. I agree that after going beyond a certain point, the number may become inconvenient; that is proposed to be guarded against; but it is necessary to go to a certain number, in order to secure the great objects of representation. Numerous bodies are undoubtedly liable to some objections, but they have their advantages also; if they are more exposed to passion and fermentation, they are less subject to venality and corruption; and in a Government like this, where the House of Representatives is connected with a smaller body, it might be good policy to guard them in a particular manner against such abuse.

But for what shall we sacrifice the wishes of the people? Not for a momentary advantage. Yet the amendments proposed by the gentleman from Massachusetts will lose its efficacy after the second census. I think, with respect to futurity, it makes little or no difference; and as it regards the present time, thirty thousand is the most proper, because it is the number agreed upon in the original constitution, and what is required by several States.

MR. SEDGWICK observed, that the amendment proposed by the convention of Massachusetts was carried there, after a full discussion; since then, the whole of the amendments proposed by the convention had been recommended by the Legislature of that State to the attention of their delegates in Congress. From these two circumstances he was led to believe, that his and his colleague's constituents were generally in favor of the amendment as stated in the report.

He did not expect any advantage would arise from enlarging the number of representatives beyond a certain point; but he thought one hundred and seventy-five rather too few.

MR. GERRY.—My colleague (MR. AMES) has said, that we experience no inconvenience for want of either general or local knowledge. Sir, I may dispute the fact, from the difficulties we encountered in carrying through the collection bill, and on some other occasions, where we seemed much at a loss to know what are the dispositions of our constituents. But admitting this to be the fact, is information the only principle upon which we are to stand? Will that gentleman pretend to say we have as much security in a few representatives as in many? Certainly he will not. Not that I would insist upon a burthensome representation, but upon an adequate one. He supposes the expenses of the Government will be increased in a very great proportion; but if he calculates with accuracy, he will find the difference of the pay of the additional members not to exceed a fourth. The civil list was stated to cost three hundred thousand dollars, but the House of Representatives does not cost more than a ninth of that sum; consequently the additional members, at the ratio of four for three, could not amount to more than a thirtieth part, which would fall far short of what he seemed to apprehend. Is this such an object as to induce the people to risk every security which they ought to have in a more numerous representation?

One observation which I understand fell from him, was, that multiplying the number of representatives diminished the dignity and importance of the individuals who compose the House. Now I wish to know, whether he means that we should establish our own importance at the risk of the liberties of America; if so, it has been of little avail that we successfully opposed the lordly importance of a British Parliament. We shall now, I presume, be advised to keep the representation where it is, in order to secure our dignity; but I hope it will be ineffectual, and that gentlemen will be inclined to give up some part of their consequence to secure the rights of their constituents.

My honorable colleague has said, that large bodies are subject to fermentations; true, sir, but so are small ones also, when they are composed of aspiring and ambitious individuals. Large bodies in this country are likely to be composed, in a great measure, of gentlemen who represent the landed interest of the country; these are generally more temperate in debate than in others, consequently, by increasing the representation we shall have less of this fermentation than on the present establishment. As to the other objections, they are not of sufficient weight to induce the House to refuse adopting an amendment recommended by so large a body of our constituents.

MR. LIVERMORE was against the alteration, because he was certain his constituents were opposed to it. He never heard a single person but supposed that one member was little enough to represent the interest of thirty thousand inhabitants; many had thought the proposition ought to be one for twenty or twenty-five thousand. It would be useless to propose amendments which there was no probability of getting ratified, and he feared this would be the fate of the one under consideration, if the honorable gentleman's alteration took place.

MR. AMES begged to know the reasons upon which amendments were founded. He hoped it was not purely to gratify an indigested opinion; but in every part where they retouched the edifice it was with an intention of improving the structure; they certainly could not think of making alterations for the worse. Now that his motion would be an improvement was clearly demonstrable from the advantage in favor of deliberating by a less numerous body, and various other reasons already mentioned; but to those, the honorable gentleman from Virginia (MR. MADISON) replied, by saying we ought to pay attention to the amendments recommended by the States. If this position is true, we have nothing more to do than read over their amendments, and propose them without exercising our judgment upon them. But he would undertake to say, that the object of the people was rather to procure certainty than increase; if so, it was the duty of Congress rather to carry the spirit of the amendment into operation than the letter of it.

The House of Representatives will furnish a better check upon the Senate, if filled with men of independent principles, integrity, and eminent abilities, than if consisting of a numerous body of inferior characters; in this opinion, said he, my colleague cannot but agree with me. Now if you diminish the consequence of the whole you diminish the consequence of each individual; it was in this view that he contended for the importance of the amendment.

He said it could not be the wish of Massachusetts to have the representation numerous, because they were convinced of its impropriety in their own Legislature, which might justly be supposed to require a greater number, as the objects of their deliberation extended to minute and local regulations. But that kind of information was not so much required in Congress, whose power embraced national objects alone. He contended, that all the local information necessary in this House, was to be found as fully among the ten members from Massachusetts, as if there had been one from every town in the State.

It is not necessary to increase the representation, in order to guard against corruption, because no one will presume to think that a body composed like this, and increased in a ratio of four to three, will be much less exposed to sale than we are. Nor is a greater number necessary to secure the rights and liberties of the people for the representative of a great body of people, is likely to be more watchful of its interests than the representative of a lesser body.

MR. JACKSON.—I have always been afraid of letting this subject come before the House, for I was apprehensive that something would be offered striking at the very foundation of the constitution, by lessening it in the good opinion of the people. I conceive that the proposition for increasing the ratio of representation will have this tendency; but I am not opposed to the motion only on the principle of expediency, but because I think it grounded on wrong principles. The honorable gentleman's arguments were as much in favor of intrusting the business of legislation to one, two, or three men, as to a body of sixty or a hundred, they would dispatch business with greater facility and be an immense saving to the public; but will the people of America be gratified with giving the power of managing their concerns into the hands of one man? Can this take place upon the democratic principle of the constitution, I mean the doctrine of representation? Can one man, however consummate his abilities, however unimpeachable his integrity, and however superior his wisdom, be supposed capable of understanding, combining and managing interests so diversified as those of the people of America? It has been complained of, that the representation is too small at one for thirty thousand; we ought not therefore attempt to reduce it.

In a republic, the laws should be founded upon the sense of the community; if every man's opinion could be obtained, it would be the better; it is only in aristocracies, where the few are supposed to understand the general interests of the community better than the many. I hope I shall never live to see that doctrine established in this country.

Mr. STONE supposed the United States to contain three millions of people; these, at one representative for every thirty thousand, would give a hundred members, of which fifty-one were a quorum to do business; twenty-six men would be a majority, and give law to the United States, together with seven in the Senate. If this was not a number sufficiently small to administer the Government, he did not know what was. He was satisfied that gentlemen, upon mature reflection, would deem it inexpedient to reduce that number one-fourth.

Mr. SENEY said, it had been observed by the gentleman from Massachusetts, that it would tend to diminish the expense; but he considered this object as very inconsiderable when compared with that of having a fair and full representation of the people of the United States.

Mr. AMES's motion was now put, and lost by a large majority.

Mr. SEDGWICK.—When he reflected on the country, and the increase of population which was likely to take place, he was led to believe that one hundred and seventy-five members would be a body rather too small to represent such extensive concerns; for this reason he would move to strike out a hundred and seventy-five and insert two hundred.

Mr. SHERMAN said, if they were now forming a constitution, he should be in favor of one representative for forty thousand, rather than thirty thousand. The proportion by which the several States are now represented in this House was founded on the former calculation. In the convention that framed the constitution, there was a majority in favor of forty thousand, and though there were some in favor of thirty thousand, yet that proposition did not obtain until after the constitution was agreed to, when the President had expressed a wish that thirty thousand should be inserted, as more favorable to the public interest; during the contest between thirty and forty thousand, he believed there were not more than nine States who voted in favor of the former.

The objects of the Federal Government were fewer than those of the State Government; they did not require an equal degree of local knowledge; the only case, perhaps, where local knowledge would be advantageous, was in laying direct taxes; but here they were freed from an embarrassment, because the arrangements of the several States might serve as a pretty good rule on which to found their measures.

So far was he from thinking a hundred and seventy-five insufficient, that he was about to move for a reduction, because he always considered that a small body deliberated to better purpose than a greater one.

Mr. Madison hoped gentlemen would not be influenced by what had been related to have passed in the convention; he expected the committee would determine upon their own sense of propriety; though as several States had proposed the number of two hundred, he thought some substantial reason should be offered to induce the House to reject it.

Mr. Livermore said, he did not like the amendment as it was reported; he approved of the ratio being one for thirty thousand, but he wished the number of representatives might be increased in proportion as the population of the country increased, until the number of representatives amounted to two hundred.

Mr. Tucker said, the honorable gentleman who spoke last had anticipated what he was going to remark. It appeared to him that the committee had looked but a very little way forward when they agreed to fix the representation at one hundred members, on a ratio of one to every thirty thousand upon the first enumeration. He apprehended the United States would be found to comprehend nearly three millions of people, consequently they would give a hundred members. Now, by the amendment, it will be in the power of Congress to prevent any addition to that number; if it should be a prevalent opinion among the members of the House that a small body was better calculated to perform the public business than a larger one, they will never suffer their members to increase to a hundred and seventy-five, the number to which the amendment extended.

Mr. Gerry expressed himself in favor of extending the number to two hundred, and wished that the amendment might be so modified as to insure an increase in proportion to the increase of population.

MR. SHERMAN was against any increase. He thought if a future House should be convinced of the impropriety of increasing this number to about one hundred, they ought to have it at their discretion to prevent it; and if that was likely to be the case, it was an argument why the present House should not decide. He did not consider that all that had been said with respect to the advantages of a large representation was founded upon experience; it had been intimated, that a large body was more incorruptible than a smaller one; this doctrine was not authenticated by any proof; he could invalidate it by an example notorious to every gentleman in this House; he alluded to the British House of Commons, which although it consisted of upwards of five hundred members, the minister always contrived to procure votes enough to answer his purpose.

MR. LAWRENCE said, that it was a matter of opinion upon which gentlemen held different sentiments, whether a greater or less number than a certain point was best for a deliberate body. But he apprehended that whatever number was now fixed would be continued by a future Congress, if it were left to their discretion. He formed this opinion from the influence of the Senate, in which the small States were represented in an equal proportion with the larger ones. He supposed that the Senators from New Hampshire, Rhode Island, Connecticut, Jersey, and Delaware, would ever oppose an augmentation of the number of representatives; because their influence in the House would be proportionably abated. These States were incapable of extending their population beyond a certain point, inasmuch as they were confined with respect to territory. If, therefore, they could never have more than one representative, they would hardly consent to double that of others, by which their own importance would be diminished. If such a measure was carried by the large States through this House, it might be successfully opposed in the Senate; he would, therefore, be in favor of increasing the number to two hundred, and making its increase gradual till it arrived at that height.

MR. GERRY.—The presumption is, that if provision is not made for the increase of the House of Representatives, by the present Congress, the increase never will be made. Gentlemen ought to consider the difference between the Government in its infancy and when well established. The people suppose their liberties somewhat endangered; they have expressed their wishes to have them secured, and instructed their representatives to endeavor to obtain for them certain amendments, which they imagine will be adequate to the object they have in view. Besides this, there are two States not in the Union; but which we hope to annex to it by the amendments now under deliberation. These are inducements for us to proceed and adopt this amendment, independent of the propriety of the amendment itself, and such inducements as no future Congress will have, the principle of self-interest and self-importance will always operate on them to prevent any addition to the number of representatives. Cannot gentlemen contemplate a difference in situation between this and a future Congress on other accounts. We have neither money nor force to administer the constitution; but this will not be the case hereafter. In the progress of this Government its revenues will increase, and an army will be established; a future Legislature will find other means to influence the people than now exist.

This circumstance proves that we ought to leave as little as possible to the discretion of the future Government; but it by no means proves that the present Congress ought not to adopt the amendment moved by my colleague, MR. SEDGWICK.

MR. AMES.—It has been observed that there will be an indisposition in future Legislatures to increase the number of representatives. I am by no means satisfied that this observation is true. I think there are motives which will influence Legislatures of the best kind to increase the number of its members. There is a constant tendency in a republican Government to multiply what it thinks to be the popular branch. If we consider that men are often more attached to their places than they are to their principles, we shall not be surprised to see men of the most refined judgment advocating a measure which will increase their chance of continuing in office.

My honorable colleague has intimated that a future Legislature will be against extending the number of this branch; and that if the people are displeased, they will have it in their power, by force, to compel their acquiescence. I do not see, sir, how the Legislature is strengthened by the increase of an Army. I have generally understood that it gave power to the executive arm, but not to the deliberative head; the example of every nation is against him. Nor can I conceive upon what foundation he rests his reasoning. If there is a natural inclination in the Government to increase the number of administrators, it will be prudent in us to endeavor to counteract its baneful influence.

MR. LIVERMORE now proposed to strike out the words "one hundred," and insert "two hundred."

MR. SEDGWICK suspended his motion until this question was determined; whereupon it was put and lost, there being twenty-two in favor of, and twenty-seven against it.

MR. SEDGWICK's motion was then put, and carried in the affirmative.

MR. LIVERMORE wished to amend the clause of the report in such a manner as to prevent the power of Congress from deciding the rate of increase. He thought the constitution had better fix it, and let it be gradual until it arrived at two hundred. After which, if it was the sense of the committee, it might be stationary, and liable to no other variation than that of being apportioned among the members of the Union.

Mr. Ames suggested to the consideration of gentlemen, whether it would not be better to arrange the subject in such a way as to let the representation be proportioned to a ratio of one for thirty thousand at the first census, and one for forty thousand at the second, so as to prevent a too rapid increase of the number of members. He did not make a motion of this nature, because he conceived it to be out of order, after the late decision of the committee; but it might be brought forward in the House, and he hoped would accommodate both sides.

Mr. Gerry wished that the gentleman last up would pen down the idea he had just thrown out; he thought it very proper for the consideration of the House.

The question on the second proposition of the report, as amended, was now put and carried, being twenty-seven for, and twenty-two against it.

The next proposition in the report was as follows:

Article 1. Section 6. Between the words "United States," and "shall in all cases," strike out "they," and insert "but no law varying the compensation shall take effect, until an election of representatives shall have intervened. The members."

Mr. Sedgwick thought much inconvenience and but very little good would result from this amendment; it might serve as a tool for designing men; they might reduce the wages very low, much lower than it was possible for any gentleman to serve without injury to his private affairs, in order to procure popularity at home, provided a diminution of pay was looked upon as a desirable thing. It might also be done in order to prevent men of shining and disinterested abilities, but of indigent circumstances, from rendering their fellow-citizens those services they are well able to perform, and render a seat in this House less eligible than it ought to be.

Mr. Vining thought every future Legislature would feel a degree of gratitude to the preceding one, which had performed so disagreeable a task for them. The committee who had made this a part of their report, had been guided by a single reason, but which appeared to them a sufficient one. There was, to say the least of it, a disagreeable sensation, occasioned by leaving it in the breast of any man to set a value on his own work; it is true it is unavoidable in the present House, but it might, and ought to be avoided in future; he therefore hoped it would obtain without any difficulty.

Mr. Gerry would be in favor of this clause, if they could find means to secure an adequate representation; but he apprehended that it would be considerably endangered; he should therefore be against it.

Mr. Madison thought the representation would be as well secured under this clause as it would be if it was omitted; and as it was desired by a great number of the people of America, he would consent to it, though he was not convinced it was absolutely necessary.

Mr. Sedgwick remarked once more, that the proposition had two aspects which made it disagreeable to him; the one was to render a man popular to his constituents, the other to render the place ineligible to his competitor.

He thought there was very little danger of an abuse of the power of laying their own wages: gentlemen were generally more inclined to make them moderate than excessive.

The question being put on the proposition, it was carried in the affirmative, twenty-seven for, and twenty against it.

The committee then rose and reported progress, and the House adjourned.

Saturday, August 15, 1789.

Amendments to the Constitution

The House again went into a Committee of the whole on the proposed amendments to the constitution, Mr. Boudinot in the chair.

The fourth proposition being under consideration, as follows:

Article 1. Section 9. Between paragraphs two and three insert "no religion shall be established by law, nor shall the equal rights of conscience be infringed."

Mr. Sylvester had some doubts of the propriety of the mode of expression used in this paragraph. He apprehended that it was liable to a construction different from what had been made by the committee. He feared it might be thought to have a tendency to abolish religion altogether.

Mr. Vining suggested the propriety of transposing the two members of the sentence.

Mr. Gerry said it would read better if it was, that no religious doctrine shall be established by law.

Mr. Sherman thought the amendment altogether unnecessary, inasmuch as Congress had no authority whatever delegated to them by the constitution to make religious establishments; he would, therefore, move to have it struck out.

Mr. Carroll.—As the rights of conscience are, in their nature, of peculiar delicacy, and will little bear the gentlest touch of governmental hand; and as many sects have concurred in opinion that they are not well secured under the present constitution, he said he was much in favor of adopting the words. He thought it would tend more towards conciliating the minds of the people to the Government than almost any other amendment he had heard proposed. He would not contend with gentlemen about the phraseology, his object was to secure the substance in such a manner as to satisfy the wishes of the honest part of the community.

MR. MADISON said, he apprehended the amending of the words to be, that Congress should not establish a religion, and enforce the legal observation of it by law, nor compel men to worship God in any manner contrary to their conscience. Whether the words are necessary or not, he did not mean to say, but they had been required by some of the State Conventions, who seemed to entertain an opinion that under the clause of the constitution, which gave power to Congress to make all laws necessary and proper to carry into execution the constitution, and the laws made under it, enabled them to make such laws of such a nature as might infringe the rights of conscience, and establish a national religion; to prevent these effects he presumed the amendment was intended, and he thought it as well expressed as the nature of the language would admit.

MR. HUNTINGTON said that he feared, with the gentleman first up on this subject, that the words might be taken in such latitude as to be extremely hurtful to the cause of religion. He understood the amendment to mean what had been expressed by the gentleman from Virginia; but others might find it convenient to put another construction upon it. The ministers of their congregations to the Eastward were maintained by the contributions of those who belonged to their society; the expense of building meeting-houses was contributed in the same manner. These things were regulated by by-laws. If an action was brought before a Federal Court on any of these cases, the person who had neglected to perform his engagements could not be compelled to do it; for a support of ministers, or building of places of worship might be construed into a religious establishment.

By the charter of Rhode Island, no religion could be established by law; he could give a history of the effects of such a regulation; indeed the people were now enjoying the blessed fruits of it. He hoped, therefore, the amendment would be made in such a way as to secure the rights of conscience, and a free exercise of the rights of religion, but not to patronize those who professed no religion at all.

MR. MADISON thought, if the word national was inserted before religion, it would satisfy the minds of honorable gentlemen. He believed that the people feared one sect might obtain a pre-eminence, or two combine together, and establish a religion to which they would compel others to conform. He thought if the word national was introduced, it would point the amendment directly to the object it was intended to prevent.

MR. LIVERMORE was not satisfied with that amendment; but he did not wish them to dwell long on the subject. He thought it would be better if it was altered, and made to read in this manner, that Congress shall make no laws touching religion, or infringing the rights of conscience.

MR. GERRY did not like the term national, proposed by the gentleman from Virginia, and he hoped it would not be adopted by the House. It brought to his mind some observations that had taken place in the conventions at the time they were considering the present constitution. It had been insisted upon by those who were called antifederalists, that this form of Government consolidated the Union; the honorable gentleman's motion shows that he considers it in the same light. Those who were called antifederalists at that time complained that they had injustice done them by the title, because they were in favor of a Federal Government, and the others were in favor of a national one; the federalists were for ratifying the constitution as it stood, and the others not until amendments were made. Their names then ought not to have been distinguished by federalists and antifederalists, but rats and antirats.

MR. MADISON withdrew his motion, but observed that the words "no national religion shall be established by law," did not imply that the Government was a national one; the question was then taken on MR. LIVERMORE's motion, and passed in the affirmative, thirty-one for, and twenty against it.

The next clause of the fourth proposition was taken into consideration, and was as follows: "The freedom of speech and of the press, and the right of the people peaceably to assemble and consult for their common good, and to apply to the Government for redress of grievances, shall not be infringed."

MR. SEDGWICK submitted to those gentlemen who had contemplated the subject, what effect such an amendment as this would have; he feared it would tend to make them appear trifling in the eyes of their constituents; what, said he, shall we secure the freedom of speech, and think it necessary, at the same time, to allow the right of assembling? If people freely converse together, they must assemble for that purpose; it is a self-evident, unalienable right which the people possess; it is certainly a thing that never would be called in question; it is derogatory to the dignity of the House to descend to such minutiae; he therefore moved to strike out "assemble and."

MR. BENSON.—The committee who framed this report proceeded on the principle that these rights belonged to the people; they conceived them to be inherent; and all that they meant to provide against was their being infringed by the Government.

MR. SEDGWICK replied, that if the committee were governed by that general principle, they might have gone into a very lengthy enumeration of rights; they might have declared that a man should have a right to wear his hat if he pleased; that he might get up when he pleased, and go to bed when he thought proper; but he would ask the gentleman whether he thought it necessary to enter these trifles in a declaration of rights, in a Government where none of them were intended to be infringed.

Mr. Tucker hoped the words would not be struck out, for he considered them of importance; besides, they were recommended by the States of Virginia and North Carolina, though he noticed that the most material part proposed by those States was omitted, which was, a declaration that the people should have a right to instruct their representatives. He would move to have those words inserted as soon as the motion for striking out was decided.

Mr. Gerry was also against the words being struck out, because he conceived it to be an essential right; it was inserted in the constitutions of several States; and though it had been abused in the year 1786 in Massachusetts, yet that abuse ought not to operate as an argument against the use of it. The people ought to be secure in the peaceable enjoyment of this privilege, and that can only be done by making a declaration to that effect in the constitution.

Mr. Page.—The gentleman from Massachusetts, (Mr. Sedgwick,) who made this motion, objects to the clause, because the right is of so trivial a nature. He supposes it no more essential than whether a man has a right to wear his hat or not; but let me observe to him that such rights have been opposed, and a man has been obliged to pull off his hat when he appeared before the face of authority; people have also been prevented from assembling together on their lawful occasions, therefore it is well to guard against such stretches of authority, by inserting the privilege in the declaration of rights. If the people could be deprived of the power of assembling under any pretext whatsoever, they might be deprived of every other privilege contained in the clause.

Mr. Vining said, if the thing was harmless, and it would tend to gratify the States that had proposed amendments, he should agree to it.

Mr. Hartley observed, that it had been asserted in the convention of Pennsylvania, by the friends of the constitution, that all the rights and powers that were not given to the Government were retained by the States and the people thereof. This was also his own opinion; but as four or five States had required to be secured in those rights by an express declaration in the constitution, he was disposed to gratify them; he thought every thing that was not incompatible with the general good ought to be granted, if it would tend to obtain the confidence of the people in the Government; and, upon the whole, he thought these words were as necessary to be inserted in the declaration of rights as most in the clause.

Mr. Gerry said, that his colleague contended for nothing, if he supposed that the people had a right to consult for the common good, because they could not consult unless they met, for the purpose.

Mr. Sedgwick replied that if they were understood or implied in the word consult, they were utterly unnecessary, and upon that ground he moved to have them struck out.

The question was now put upon Mr. Sedgwick's motion, and lost by a considerable majority.

Mr. Tucker then moved to insert these words, "to instruct their Representatives."

Mr. Hartley wished the motion had not been made, for gentlemen acquainted with the circumstances of this country, and the history of the country from which we separated, differed exceedingly on this point. The members of the House of Representatives, said he, are chosen for two years, the members of the Senate for six.

According to the principles laid down in the Constitution, it is presumable that the persons elected know the interests and the circumstances of their constituents, and being checked in their determinations by a division of the Legislative power into two branches, there is little danger of error. At least it ought to be supposed that they have the confidence of the people during the period for which they are elected; and if, by misconduct, they forfeit it, their constituents have the power of leaving them out at the expiration of that time—thus they are answerable for the part they have taken in measures that may be contrary to the general wish.

Representation is the principle of our Government; the people ought to have confidence in the honor and integrity of those they send forward to transact their business; their right to instruct them is a problematical subject. We have seen it attended with bad consequences, both in England and America. When the passions of the people are excited, instructions have been resorted to and obtained, to answer party purposes; and although the public opinion is generally respectable, yet at such moments it has been known to be often wrong; and happy is that Government composed of men of firmness and wisdom to discover, and resist popular error.

If, in a small community, where the interests, habits, and manners are neither so numerous or diversified, instructions bind not, what shall we say of instructions to this body? Can it be supposed that the inhabitants of a single district in a State, are better informed with respect to the general interests of the Union, than a select body assembled from every part? Can it be supposed that a part will be more desirous of promoting the good of the whole than the whole will of the part? I apprehend, sir, that Congress will be the best judges of proper measures, and that instructions will never be resorted to but for party purposes, when they will generally contain the prejudices and acrimony of the party, rather than the dictates of honest reason and sound policy.

In England this question has been considerably agitated. The representatives of some towns in Parliament have acknowledged, and submitted to the binding force of instructions, while the majority have thrown off the shackles with disdain. I would not have this precedent influence our decision; but let the doctrine be tried upon its own merits, and stand or fall as it shall be found to deserve.

It appears to my mind, that the principle of representation is distinct from an agency, which may require written instructions. The great end of meeting is to consult for the common good; but can the common good be discerned without the object is reflected and shown in every light. A local or partial view does not necessarily enable any man to comprehend it clearly; this can only result from an inspection into the aggregate. Instructions viewed in this light will be found to embarrass the best and wisest men. And were all the members to take their seats in order to obey instructions, and those instructions were as various as it is probable they would be, what possibility would there exist of so accommodating each to the other as to produce any act whatsoever? Perhaps a majority of the whole might not be instructed to agree to any one point, and is it thus the people of the United States propose to form a more perfect union, provide for the common defense, and promote the general welfare?

Sir, I have known within my own time so many inconveniences and real evils arise from adopting the popular opinions on the moment, that although I respect them as much as any man, I hope this Government will particularly guard against them, at least that they will not bind themselves by a constitutional act, and by oath, to submit to their influence; if they do, the great object which this Government has been established to attain, will inevitably elude our grasp on the uncertain and veering winds of popular commotion.

MR. PAGE.—The gentleman from Pennsylvania tells you, that in England this principle is doubted; how far this is consonant with the nature of the Government I will not pretend to say; but I am not astonished to find that the administrators of a monarchial Government are unassailable by the weak voice of the people; but under a democracy, whose great end is to form a code of laws congenial with the public sentiment, the popular opinion ought to be collected and attended to. Our present object is, I presume, to secure to our constituents and to posterity these inestimable rights.

Our Government is derived from the people, of consequence the people have a right to consult for the common good; but to what end will this be done, if they have not the power of instructing their representatives? Instruction and representation in a republic appear to me to be inseparably connected; but were I the subject of a monarch, I should doubt whether the public good did not depend more upon the prince's will than the will of the people. I should dread a popular assembly consulting for the public good, because, under its influence, commotions and tumults might arise that would shake the foundation of the monarch's throne, and make the empire tremble in expectation. The people of England have submitted the crown to the Hanover family, and have rejected the Stuarts. If instructions upon such a revolution were considered binding, it is difficult to know what would have been the effects. It might be well, therefore, to have the doctrine exploded from that kingdom; but it will not be advanced as a substantial reason in favor of our treading in the same steps.

The honorable gentleman has said, that when once the people have chosen a representative, they must rely on his integrity and judgment during the period for which he is elected. I think, sir, to doubt the authority of the people to instruct their representatives, will give them just cause to be alarmed for their fate. I look upon it as a dangerous doctrine, subversive of the great end for which the United States have confederated. Every friend of mankind, every well-wisher of this country, will be desirous of obtaining the sense of the people on every occasion of magnitude; but how can this be so well expressed as in instructions to their representatives? I hope, therefore, that gentlemen will not oppose the insertion of it in this part of the report.

Mr. Clymer.—I hope the amendment will not be adopted; but if our constituents choose to instruct us, that they may be left at liberty to do so. Do gentlemen foresee the extent of these words? If they have a constitutional right to instruct us, it infers that we are bound by those instructions; and as we ought not to decide constitutional questions by implication, I presume we shall be called upon to go further, and expressly declare the members of the Legislature bound by the instruction of their constituents. This is a most dangerous principle, utterly destructive of all ideas of an independent and deliberative body, which are essential requisites in the Legislatures of free Governments; they prevent men of abilities and experience from rendering those services to the community that are in their power, destroying the object contemplated by establishing an efficient General Government, and rendering Congress a mere passive machine.

Mr. Sherman.—It appears to me, that the words are calculated to mislead the people, by conveying an idea that they have a right to control the debates of the Legislature. This cannot be admitted to be just, because it would destroy the object of their meeting. I think, when the people have chosen a representative, it is his duty to meet others from the different parts of the Union, and consult, and agree with them to such acts as are for the general benefit of the whole community. If they were to be guided by instructions, there would be no use in deliberation; all that a man would have to do, would be to produce his instructions, and lay them on the table, and let them speak for him. From hence I think it may be fairly inferred, that the right of the people to consult for the common good can go no further than to petition the Legislature, or apply for a redress of grievances. It is the duty of a good representative to inquire what measures are most likely to promote the general welfare, and, after he has discovered them, to give them his support. Should his instructions, therefore, coincide with his ideas on any measure, they would be unnecessary; if they were contrary to the conviction of his own mind, he must be bound by every principle of justice to disregard them.

Mr. Jackson was in favor of the right of the people to assemble and consult for the common good; it had been used in this country as one of the best checks on the British Legislature in their unjustifiable attempts to tax the colonies without their consent. America had no representatives in the British Parliament, therefore they could instruct none, yet they exercised the power of consultation to a good effect. He begged gentlemen to consider the dangerous tendency of establishing such a doctrine; it would necessarily drive the house into a number of factions. There might be different instructions from every State, and the representation from each State would be a faction to support its own measures.

If we establish this as a right, we shall be bound by those instructions; now, I am willing to leave both the people and representatives to their own discretion on this subject. Let the people consult and give their opinion; let the representative judge of it; and if it is just, let him govern himself by it as a good member ought to do; but if it is otherwise, let him have it in his power to reject their advice.

What may be the consequence of binding a man to vote in all cases according to the will of others? He is to decide upon a constitutional point, and on this question his conscience is bound by the obligation of a solemn oath; you now involve him in a serious dilemma. If he votes according to his conscience, he decides against his instructions; but in deciding against his instructions, he commits a breach of the constitution, by infringing the prerogative of the people, secured to them by this declaration. In short, it will give rise to such a variety of absurdities and inconsistencies, as no prudent Legislature would wish to involve themselves in.

Mr. Gerry.—By the checks provided in the constitution, we have good grounds to believe that the very framers of it conceived that the Government would be liable to mal-administration, and I presume that the gentlemen of this House do not mean to arrogate to themselves more perfection than human nature has as yet been found to be capable of; if they do not, they will admit an additional check against abuses which this, like every other government, is subject to. Instruction from the people will furnish this in a considerable degree.

It has been said that the amendment proposed by the honorable gentleman from South Carolina (MR. TUCKER) determines this point, "that the people can bind their representatives to follow their instructions." I do not conceive that this necessarily follows. I think the representative, notwithstanding the insertion of these words, would be at liberty to act as he pleased; if he declined to pursue such measures as he was directed to attain, the people would have a right to refuse him their suffrages at a future election.

Now, though I do not believe the amendment would bind the representatives to obey the instructions, yet I think the people have a right both to instruct and bind them. Do gentlemen conceive that on any occasion instructions would be so general as to proceed from all our constituents? If they do, it is the sovereign will; for gentlemen will not contend that the sovereign will presides in the Legislature. The friends and patrons of this constitution have always declared that the sovereignty vests in the people, and that they have not a right to instruct and control their representatives, is absurd to the last degree. They must either give up their principle, or grant that the people have a right to exercise their sovereignty to control the whole government, as well as this branch of it. But the amendment does not carry the principle to such an extent, it only declares the right of the people to send instructions; the representative will, if he thinks proper, communicate his instructions to the House, but how far they shall operate on his conduct, he will judge for himself.

The honorable gentleman from Georgia (MR. JACKSON) supposes that instructions will tend to generate factions in this House; but he did not see how it could have that effect, any more than the freedom of debate had. If the representative entertains the same opinion with his constituents, he will decide with them in favor of the measure; if other gentlemen, who are not instructed on this point, are convinced by argument that the measure is proper, they will also vote with them; consequently, the influence of debate and of instruction is the same.

The gentleman says further, that the people have the right of instructing their representatives; if so, why not declare it? Does he mean that it shall lie dormant and never be exercised? If so, it will be a right of no utility. But much good may result from a declaration in the constitution that they possess this privilege; the people will be encouraged to come forward with their instructions, which will form a fund of useful information for the Legislature. We cannot, I apprehend, be too well informed of the true state, condition, and sentiment of our constituents, and perhaps this is the best mode in our power of obtaining information. I hope we shall never shut our ears against that information which is to be derived from the petitions and instructions of our constituents. I hope we shall never presume to think that all the wisdom of this country is concentrated within the walls of this House. Men, unambitious of distinctions from their fellow-citizens, remain within their own domestic walk, unheard of and unseen, possession all the advantages resulting from a watchful observance of public men and public measures, whose voice, if we would descend to listen to it, would give us knowledge superior to what could be acquired amidst the cares and bustles of a public life; let us then adopt the amendment, and encourage the diffident to enrich our stock of knowledge with the treasure of their remarks and observations.

MR. MADISON.—I think the committee acted prudently in omitting to insert these words in the report they have brought forward; if, unfortunately, the attempt of proposing amendments should prove abortive, it will not arise from the want of a disposition in the friends of the constitution to do what is right with respect to securing the rights and privileges of the people of America, but from the difficulties arising from discussing and proposing abstract propositions, of which the judgment may not be convinced. I venture to say, that if we confine ourselves to an enumeration of simple, acknowledged principles, the ratification will meet with but little difficulty. Amendments of a doubtful nature will have a tendency to prejudge the whole system; the proposition now suggested partakes highly of this nature. It is doubted by many gentlemen here; it has been objected to in intelligent publications throughout the Union; it is doubted by many members of the State Legislatures. In one sense this declaration is true, in many others it is certainly not true; in the sense in which it is true we have asserted the right sufficiently in what we have done; if we mean nothing more than this, that the people have a right to express and communicate their sentiments and wishes, we have provided for it already. The right of freedom of speech is secured; the liberty of the press is expressly declared to be beyond the reach of this Government; the people may therefore publicly address their representatives, may privately advise them, or declare their sentiments by petition to the whole body; in all these ways they may communicate their will. If gentlemen mean to go further, and to say that the people have a right to instruct their representatives in such a sense as that the delegates are obliged to conform to those instructions, the declaration is not true. Suppose they instruct a representative, by his vote, to violate the constitution; is he at liberty to obey such instructions? Suppose he is instructed to patronize certain measures, and from circumstances known to him, but not to his constituents, he is convinced that they will endanger the public good; is he obliged to sacrifice his own judgment to them? Is he absolutely bound to perform what he is instructed to do? Suppose he refuses, will his vote be the less valid, or the community be disengaged from that obedience which is due to the laws of the Union? If his vote must inevitably have the same effect, what sort of a right is this in the constitution, to instruct a representative who has a right to disregard the order, if he pleases? In this sense, the right does not exist; in the other sense it does exist, and is provided largely for.

The honorable gentleman from Massachusetts asks if the sovereignty is not with the people at large. Does he infer that the people can, in detached bodies, contravene an act established by the whole people? My idea of the sovereignty of the people is, that the people can change the constitution if they please; but while the constitution exists, they must conform themselves to its dictates. But I do not believe that the inhabitants of any district can speak the voice of the people; so far from it, their ideas may contradict the sense of the whole people; hence the consequence that instructions are binding on the representative is of a doubtful, if not of a dangerous nature. I do not conceive, therefore, that it is necessary to agree to the proposition now made; so far as any real good is to arise from it, so far that real good is provided for; so far as it is of a doubtful nature, so far as it obliges us to run the risk of losing the whole system.

Mr. Smith, of South Carolina.—I am opposed to this motion, because I conceive it will operate as a partial inconvenience to the more distant States. If every member is to be bound by instructions how to vote, what are gentlemen from the extremities of the continent to do? Members from the neighboring States can obtain their instructions earlier than those from the Southern ones, and I presume that particular instructions will be necessary for particular measures; of consequence, we vote perhaps against instructions on their way to us, or we must decline voting at all. But what is the necessity of having a numerous representation? One member from a State can receive the instructions, and by his vote answer all the purposes of many, provided his vote is allowed to count for the proportion the State ought to send; in this way the business might be done at a less expense than having one or two hundred members in the House, which had been strongly contended for yesterday.

Mr. Stone.—I think the clause would change the Government entirely; instead of being a Government founded upon representation, it would be a democracy of singular properties.

I differ from the gentleman from Virginia, (MR. MADISON,) if he thinks this clause would not bind the representatives; in my opinion, it would bind him effectually, and I venture to assert, without diffidence, that any law passed by the Legislature would be of no force, if a majority of the members of this House were instructed to the contrary, provided the amendment became part of the constitution. What would follow from this? Instead of looking in the code of laws passed by Congress, your Judiciary would have to collect and examine the instructions from the various parts of the Union. It follows very clearly from hence, that the Government would be altered from a representative one to a democracy, wherein all laws are made immediately by the voice of the people.

This is a power not to be found in any part of the earth except among the Swiss cantons; there the body of the people vote upon the laws, and give instructions to their delegates. But here we have a different form of Government; the people at large are not authorized under it to vote upon the law, nor did I ever hear that any man required it. Why, then, are we called upon to propose amendments subversive of the principles of the constitution, which were never desired?

Several members now called for the question, and the Chairman being about to put the same:

MR. GERRY.—Gentlemen seem in a great hurry to get this business through. I think, Mr. Chairman, it requires a further discussion; for my part, I had rather do less business and do it well, than precipitate measures before they are fully understood.

The honorable gentleman from Virginia (MR. MADISON) stated, that if the proposed amendments are defeated, it will be by the delay attending the discussion of doubtful propositions; and he declares this to partake of that quality. It is natural, sir, for us to be fond of our own work. We do not like to see it disfigured by other hands. That honorable gentleman brought forward a string of propositions; among them was the clause now proposed to be amended; he is no doubt ready for the question, and determined not to admit what we think an improvement. The gentlemen who were on the committee, and brought in the report, have considered the subject, and are also ripe for a decision. But other gentlemen may crave a like indulgence. Is not the report before us for deliberation and discussion, and to obtain the sense of the House upon it; and will not gentlemen allow us a day or two for these purposes, after they have forced us to proceed upon them at this time? I appeal to their candor and good sense on the occasion, and am sure not to be refused; and I must inform them now, that they may not be surprised hereafter, that I wish all the amendments proposed by the respective States to be considered. Gentlemen say it is necessary to finish the subject, in order to reconcile a number of our fellow-citizens to the Government. If this is their principle, they ought to consider the wishes and intentions which the convention has expressed for them; if they do this, they will find that they expect and wish for the declaration proposed by the honorable gentleman over the way, (Mr. Tucker,) and, of consequence, they ought to agree to it; and why it, with others recommended in the same way, were not reported, I cannot pretend to say; the committee know this best themselves.

The honorable gentleman near me (Mr. Stone) says, that the laws passed contrary to instruction will be nugatory. And other gentlemen ask, if their constituents instruct them to violate the constitution, whether they must do it. Sir, does not the constitution declare that all laws passed by Congress are paramount to the laws and constitutions of the several States; if our decrees are of such force as to set aside the State laws and constitutions, certainly they may be repugnant to any instructions whatever, without being injured thereby. But can we conceive that our constituents would be so absurd as to instruct us to violate our oath, and act directly contrary to the principles of a Government ordained by themselves? We must look upon them to be absolutely abandoned and false to their own interests, to suppose them capable of giving such instructions.

If this amendment is introduced into the constitution, I do not think we shall be much troubled with instructions; a knowledge of the right will operate to check a spirit that would render instruction necessary.

The honorable gentleman from Virginia asked, will not the affirmative of a member who votes repugnant to his instructions bind the community as much as the votes of those who conform? There is no doubt, sir, but it will; but does this tend to show that the constituent has no right to instruct? Surely not. I admit, sir, that instructions contrary to the constitution ought not to bind, though the sovereignty resides in the people. The honorable gentleman acknowledges that the sovereignty vests there; if so, it may exercise its will in any case not inconsistent with a previous contract. The same gentleman asks if we are to give the power to the people in detached bodies to contravene the Government while it exists. Certainly not; nor does the proposed proposition extend to that point; it is only intended to open for them a convenient mode in which they may convey their sense to their agents. The gentleman therefore takes for granted what is inadmissible, that Congress will always be doing illegal things, and make it necessary for the sovereign to declare its pleasure.

He says the people have a right to alter the constitution, but they have no right to oppose the Government. If, while the Government exists, they have no right to control it, it appears that they have divested themselves of the sovereignty over the constitution. Therefore, our language, with our principles, must change, and we ought to say that the sovereignty existed in the people previous to the establishment of this Government. This will be ground for alarm indeed, if it is true; but I trust, sir, too much to the good sense of my fellow-citizens ever to believe that the doctrine will generally obtain in this country of freedom.

MR. VINING.—If, Mr. Chairman, there appears on one side too great an urgency to despatch this business, there appears on the other an unnecessary delay and procrastination equally improper and unpardonable. I think this business has been already well considered by the House, and every gentleman in it; however, I am not for an unseemingly expedition.

The gentleman last up has insinuated a reflection upon the committee for not reporting all the amendments proposed by some of the State conventions. I can assign a reason for this. The committee conceived some of them superfluous or dangerous, and found many of them so contradictory that it was impossible to make any thing of them; and this is a circumstance the gentleman cannot pretend ignorance of.

Is it not inconsistent in that honorable member to complain of hurry, when he comes day after day reiterating the same train of arguments, and demanding the attention of this body by rising six or seven times on a question? I wish, sir, this subject discussed coolly and dispassionately, but hope we shall have no more re-iterations or tedious discussions; let gentlemen try to expedite public business, and their arguments will be conducted in a laconic and consistent manner. As to the business of instruction, I look upon it inconsistent with the general good. Suppose our constituents were to instruct us to make paper money; no gentleman pretends to say it would be unconstitutional, yet every honest mind must shudder at the thought. How can we then assert that instructions ought to bind us in all cases not contrary to the constitution?

MR. LIVERMORE was not very anxious whether the words were inserted or not, but he had a great deal of doubt on the meaning of this whole amendment; it provides that the people may meet and consult for the common good. Does this mean a part of the people in a township or district, or does it mean the representatives in the State Legislatures? If it means the latter, there is no occasion for a provision that the Legislature may instruct the members of this body.

In some States the representatives are chosen by districts. In such case, perhaps, the instructions may be considered as coming from the district; but in other States, each representative is chosen by the whole people. In New Hampshire it is the case; the instructions of any particular place would have but little weight, but a legislative instruction would have considerable influence upon each representative. If therefore, the words mean that the Legislature may instruct, he presumed it would have considerable effect, though he did not believe it binding. Indeed, he was inclined to pay a deference to any information he might receive from any number of gentlemen, even by a private letter; but as for full binding force, no instructions contained that quality. They could not, nor ought not to have it, because different parties pursue different measures; and it might be expedient, nay, absolutely necessary, to sacrifice them in mutual concessions.

The doctrine of instructions would hold better in England than here, because the boroughs and corporations might have an interest to pursue totally immaterial to the rest of the kingdom; in that case, it would be prudent to instruct their members in Parliament.

Mr. Gerry wished the constitution amended without his having any hand in it; but if he must interfere, he would do his duty. The honorable gentleman from Delaware had given him an example of moderation and laconic and consistent debate that he meant to follow; and he would just observe to the worthy gentleman last up, that several States have proposed the amendment, and among the rest, New Hampshire.

There was one remark which escaped him, when he was up before. The gentleman from Maryland (Mr. Stone) had said that the amendment would change the nature of the Government, and make it a Democracy. Now he had always heard that it was a Democracy; but perhaps he was misled, and the honorable gentleman was right in distinguishing it by some other appellation; perhaps an aristocracy was a term better adapted to it.

Mr. Sedgwick opposed the idea of the gentleman from New Hampshire, that the State Legislature had the power of instructing the members of this House; he looked upon it as a subordination of the rights of the people to admit such an authority. We stand not here, said he, the representatives of the State Legislatures, as under the former Congress, but as the representatives of the great body of the people. The sovereignty, the independence, and the rights of the States are intended to be guarded by the Senate; if we are to be viewed in any other light, the greatest security the people have for their rights and privileges is destroyed.

But with respect to instructions, it is well worthy of consideration how they are to be procured. It is not the opinion of an individual that is to control my conduct; I consider myself as the representative of the whole Union. An individual may give me information, but his sentiments may be in opposition to the sense of the majority of the people. If instructions are to be of any efficacy, they must speak the sense of the majority of the people, at least of a State. In a State so large as Massachusetts it would behoove gentlemen to consider how the sense of the majority of the freemen is to be obtained and communicated. Let us take care to avoid the insertion of crude and indigested propositions, more likely to produce acrimony than that spirit of harmony which we ought to cultivate.

MR. LIVERMORE said that he did not understand the honorable gentleman, or was not understood by him; he did not presume peremptorily to say what degree of influence the legislative instructions would have on a representative. He knew it was not the thing in contemplation here; and what he had said respected only the influence it would have on his private judgment.

MR. AMES said there would be a very great inconvenience attending the establishment of the doctrine contended for by his colleague. Those States which had selected their members by districts would have no right to give them instructions, consequently the members ought to withdraw; in which case the House might be reduced below a majority, and not be able, according to the constitution, to do any business at all.

According to the doctrine of the gentleman from New Hampshire, one part of the Government would be annihilated; for of what avail is it that the people have the appointment of a representative, if he is to pay obedience to the dictates of another body?

Several members now rose, and called for the question.

MR. PAGE was sorry to see gentlemen so impatient; the more so, as he saw there was very little attention paid to any thing that was said; but he would express his sentiments if he was only heard by the Chair. He discovered clearly, notwithstanding what had been observed by the most ingenious supporters of the opposition, that there was an absolute necessity for adopting the amendment. It was strictly compatible with the spirit and the nature of the Government; all power vests in the people of the United States; it is, therefore, a Government of the people, a democracy. If it were consistent with the peace and tranquility of the inhabitants, every freeman would have a right to come and give his vote upon the law; but, inasmuch as this cannot be done, by reason of the extent of territory, and some other causes, the people have agreed that their representatives shall exercise a part of their authority. To pretend to refuse them the power of instructing their agents, appears to me to deny them a right. One gentleman asks how the instructions are to be collected. Many parts of this country have been in the practice of instructing their representatives; they found no difficulty in communicating their sense. Another gentleman asks if they were to instruct us to make paper money, what we would do. I would tell them, said he, it was unconstitutional; alter that, and we will consider on that point. Unless laws are made satisfactory to the people, they will lose their support, they will be abused or done away; this tends to destroy the efficiency of the Government.

It is the sense of several of the conventions that this amendment should take place; I think it my duty to support it, and fear it will spread an alarm among our constituents if we decline to do it.

MR. WADSWORTH.—Instructions have frequently been given to the representatives of the United States; but the people did not claim as a right that they should have any obligation upon the representatives; it is not right that they should. In troublesome times, designing men have drawn the people to instruct the representatives to their harm; the representatives have, on such occasions, refused to comply with their instructions. I have known, myself, that they have been disobeyed, and yet the representative was not brought to account for it; on the contrary, he was caressed and reelected, while those who have obeyed them, contrary to their private sentiments, have ever after been despised for it. Now, if people considered it an inherent right in them to instruct their representatives, they would have undoubtedly punished the violation of them. I have no idea of instructions, unless they are obeyed; a discretional power is incompatible with them.

The honorable gentleman who was up last says, if he were instructed to make paper money, he would tell his constituents it was unconstitutional. I believe that is not the case, for this body would have a right to make paper money; but if my constituents were to instruct me to vote for such a measure, I would disobey them, let the consequence be what it would.

MR. SUMTER.—The honorable gentlemen who are opposed to the motion of my colleague, do not treat it fairly. They suppose that it is meant to bind the representative to conform to his instructions. The mover of this question, I presume to say, has no such thing in idea. That they shall notice them and obey them, as far as is consistent and proper, may be very just; perhaps they ought to produce them to the House, and let them have as much influence as they deserve; nothing further, I believe, is contended for.

I rose on this occasion, not so much to make any observations upon the point immediately under consideration, as to beg the committee to consider the consequences that may result from an undue precipitancy and hurry. Nothing can distress me more than to be obliged to notice what I conceive to be somewhat improper in the conduct of so respectable a body. Gentlemen will reflect how difficult it is to remove error when once the passions are engaged in the discussion; temper and coolness are necessary to complete what must be the work of time. It cannot be denied but that the present constitution is imperfect; we must, therefore, take time to improve it. If gentlemen are pressed for want of time, and are disposed to adjourn the session of Congress at a very early period, we had better drop the subject of amendments, and leave it until we have more leisure to consider and do the business effectually.

For my part, I would rather sit till this day twelvemonth, than have this all-important subject inconsiderately passed over. The people have already complained that the adoption of the constitution was done in too hasty a manner; what will they say of us if we press the amendments with so much haste?

Mr. Burke.—It has been asserted, Mr. Chairman, that the people of America do not require this right. I beg leave to ask the gentleman from Massachusetts, whether the constitution of that State does not recognize that right, and the gentleman from Maryland, whether their declaration of rights does not expressly secure it to the inhabitants of that State? These circumstances, added to what has been proposed by the State conventions as amendments to this constitution, pretty plainly declare the sense of the people to be in favor of securing to themselves and to their posterity a right of this nature.

Mr. Seney said that the declaration of rights prefixed to the constitution of Maryland secured to every man a right of petitioning the Legislature for a redress of grievances, in a peaceable and orderly manner.

Mr. Burke.—I am not positive with respect to the particular expression in the declaration of rights of the people of Maryland, but the constitutions of Massachusetts, Pennsylvania, and North Carolina, all of them recognize in express terms, the right of the people to give instructions to their representatives. I do not mean to insist particularly upon this amendment; but I am very well satisfied that those that are reported and likely to be adopted by this House are very far from giving satisfaction to our constituents; they are not those solid and substantial amendments which the people expect; they are little better than whip-syllabub, frothy and full of wind, formed only to please the palate; or they are like a tub thrown out to a whale, to secure the freight of the ship and its peaceable voyage. In my judgment, the people will not be gratified by the mode we have pursued in bringing them forward. There was a committee of eleven appointed; and out of the number I think there were five who were members of the convention that formed the constitution. Such gentlemen, having already given their opinion with respect to the perfection of the work, may be thought improper agents to bring forward amendments. Upon the whole, I think it will be found that we have done nothing but lose our time, and that it will be better to drop the subject now, and proceed to the organization of the Government.

Mr. Sinnickson inquired of Mr. Chairman what was the question before the committee, for really the debate had become so desultory, as to induce him to think it was lost sight of altogether.

Mr. Lawrence was averse to entering on the business at first; but since they had proceeded so far, he hoped they would finish it. He said, if gentlemen would confine themselves to the question when they were speaking, that the business might be done in a more agreeable manner. He was against the amendment proposed by the gentleman from South Carolina, (MR. TUCKER,) because every member on this floor ought to consider himself the representative of the whole Union, and not of the particular district which had chosen him; as their decisions were to bind every individual of the confederation of States, it was wrong to be guided by the voice of a single district, whose interests might happen to clash with those of the general good; and unless instructions were to be considered as binding, they were altogether superfluous.

MR. MADISON was unwilling to take up any more of the time of the committee; but, on the other hand, he was not willing to be silent after the charges that had been brought against the committee, and the gentleman who introduced the amendments, by the honorable members on each side of him, (MESSRS. SUMTER and BURKE.) Those gentlemen say that we are precipitating the business, and insinuate that we are not acting with candor. I appeal to the gentlemen who have heard the voice of their country, to those who have attended the debates of the State conventions, whether the amendments now proposed are not those most strenuously required by the opponents to the constitution? It was wished that some security should be given for those great and essential rights which they have been taught to believe were in danger. I concurred, in the convention of Virginia, with those gentlemen, so far as to agree to a declaration of those rights which correspond with my own judgment, and the other alterations which I have the honor to bring forward before the present Congress. I appeal to the gentlemen on this floor who are desirous of amending the constitution, whether these proposed are not compatible with what are required by our constituents? Have not the people been told that the rights of conscience, the freedom of speech, the liberty of the press, and trial by jury, were in jeopardy, that they ought not to adopt the constitution until those important rights were secured to them?

But while I approve of these amendments, I should oppose the consideration at this time of such as are likely to change the principles of the Government, or that are of a doubtful nature; because I apprehend there is little prospect of obtaining the consent of two-thirds of both Houses of Congress, and three-fourths of the State Legislatures, to ratify propositions of this kind; therefore, as a friend to what is attainable, I would limit it to the plain, simple, and important security that has been required. If I were inclined to make no alteration in the constitution, I would bring forward such amendments as were of a dubious cast, in order to have the whole adjusted.

MR. BURKE never entertained an idea of charging gentlemen with the want of candor; but he would appeal to any man of sense and candor, whether the amendments contained in the report were anything like the amendments required by the States of New York, Virginia, New Hampshire, and Carolina; and having these amendments in his hands, he turned to them to show the difference, concluding that all the important amendments were omitted from the report.

MR. SMITH, of South Carolina, understood his colleague, who had just sat down, to have asserted that the amendment under consideration was contained in the constitution of the State of South Carolina: this was not the fact.

MR. BURKE said he mentioned the State of North Carolina, and there it was inserted in express terms.

The question was now called for from several parts of the House; but a desultory conversation took place before the question was put. At length the call became general, it was stated from the Chair, and determined in the negative, 10 rising in favor of it and 41 against it.

The question was now taken on the second clause of the fourth proposition, as originally reported and agreed to.

MR. AMES moved the committee to rise and report progress; which being agreed to,

MR. SPEAKER having resumed the chair,

MR. AMES moved to discharge the committee from any further proceeding. He was led to make the motion from two considerations: first, that as the committee were not restrained in their discussions, a great deal of time was consumed in unnecessary debate; and, second, that as the constitution required two-thirds of the House to acquiesce in amendments, the decisions of the committee, by a simple majority, might be set aside for the want of the constitutional number to support them in the House. He further observed, that it might have an evil influence if alterations agreed to in committee were not adopted by the House.

MR. SMITH, of South Carolina, was in favor of the motion.

MR. GERRY thought that the object of the motion was to prevent such a thorough discussion of the business as the nature of it demanded. He called upon gentlemen to recollect the consistency of his honorable colleague, who had proposed to refer the subject to a select committee, lest an open and full examination should lay bare the muscles and sinews of the constitution. He had succeeded on that occasion, and the business was put into the hands of a select committee. He now proposes to curtail the debate, because gentlemen will not swallow the propositions as they stand, when their judgment and their duty require to have them improved. Will this House, said he, agree that an important subject like this shall have less consideration than the most trifling business yet come before us? I hope they will not. If they are tired of it, let it be postponed until another session, when it can be attended to with leisure and good temper. Gentlemen now feel the weather warm, and the subject is warm; no wonder it produces some degree of heat. Perhaps, as our next will be a winter session, we may go through more coolly and dispassionately.

Mr. SEDGWICK seconded Mr. AMES's motion, thinking there was little probability of getting through with the business, if gentlemen were disposed to offer motions, and dwell long upon them in committee, when there was no likelihood they would meet the approbation of two-thirds of both Houses, and three-fourths of the State Legislatures.

Mr. GERRY moved to call the yeas and nays on the motion.

Mr. PAGE begged gentlemen to consider that the motion tended to deprive the members of that freedom of debate which they had heretofore been indulged in, and prevented the Speaker from giving his sentiments. He was sorry to see this hurry, and hoped the subject would be fairly treated, otherwise the people might think they were unjustly dealt with. They would have a right to suppose, with the honorable gentleman from Carolina, (Mr. BURKE,) that we meant nothing more than to throw out a tub to the whale.

Mr. BURKE would oppose the motion, and join in calling the yeas and nays, because its object must be to preclude debate. He was certain the subject was so varigated and at the same time so important, that it could not be thoroughly discussed in any other manner than in a Committee of the whole; and unless it was discussed in a satisfactory manner, he apprehended it would occasion a great deal of mischief. He said the people knew, and were sensible, that in ratifying the present constitution, they parted with their liberties; but it was under a hope that they would get them back again. Whether this was to be the case or not, he left it to time to discover, but the spirit which now seemed to prevail in the House was no favorable omen. He begged gentlemen to treat the subject with fairness and candor, and not depart from their usual mode of doing business.

Mr. SMITH, of South Carolina, had said he would support the motion, under an impression that it was useless to carry a measure through the committee, with a small majority, which was unlikely to meet the approbation of two-thirds of the House; but as gentlemen appeared so desirous of pursuing the common routine of doing business, he would withdraw his support.

Mr. TUCKER was in hopes the honorable mover would have seen the impropriety of his motion, and have withdrawn it; but as he had not, he would presume to ask him upon what principle it was founded? Is it to precipitate the business, and prevent an investigation? or is it because the committee have spent some time on it, and made no progress? He thought the latter was not the case, because the committee had proceeded as far in it as could reasonably be expected for the time. The gentleman says he is apprehensive it may do harm to have propositions agreed to in committee, and rejected by the House. Certainly there is no foundation for this apprehension, or the clause in the constitution requiring the consent of two-thirds of the Legislature to amendments is formed on wrong principles. If the propositions are reasonable in themselves, they ought to be admitted; but if they are improper, they ought to be rejected. We would not presume to prevent our constituents from contemplating the subject in their own mind.

Is this haste produced by desire to adjourn? He was as desirous of adjourning as any member, but he would not sacrifice the duty he owed the public to his own private convenience.

MR. LIVERMORE hoped the gentleman would withdraw his motion, because it would have a disagreeable aspect to leave the business in the unfinished state it now stood. He thought it had better been altogether let alone.

MR. AMES withdrew his motion, and laid another on the table, requiring two-thirds of the committee to carry a question; and, after some desultory conversation,

The House adjourned.

Monday, August 17, 1789.

AMENDMENTS TO THE CONSTITUTION

The House again resolved itself into a committee, MR. BOUDINOT in the Chair, on the proposed amendments to the constitution. The third clause of the fourth proposition in the report was taken into consideration, being as follows: "A well regulated militia, composed of the body of the people, being the best security of a free state, the right of the people to keep and bear arms shall not be infringed; but no person religiously scrupulous shall be compelled to bear arms."

MR. GERRY.—This declaration of rights, I take it, is intended to secure the people against the mal-administration of the Government; if we could suppose that, in all cases, the rights of the people would be attended to, the occasion for guards of this kind would be removed. Now, I am apprehensive, sir, that this clause would give an opportunity to the people in power to destroy the constitution itself. They can declare who are those religiously scrupulous, and prevent them from bearing arms.

What, sir, is the use of militia? It is to prevent the establishment of a standing army, the bane of liberty. Now, it must be evident, that, under this provision, together with their other powers, Congress could take such measures with respect to a militia, as to make a standing army necessary. Whenever Government mean to invade the rights and liberties of the people, they always attempt to destroy the militia, in order to raise an army upon their ruins. This was actually done by Great Britain at the commencement of the late revolution. They used every means in their power to prevent the establishment of an effective militia to the eastward. The Assembly of Massachusetts, seeing the rapid progress that administration were making to divest them of their inherent privileges, endeavored to counteract them by the organization of the militia; but they were always defeated by the influence of the Crown.

Mr. Seney wished to know what question there was before the committee, in order to ascertain the point upon which the gentleman was speaking.

Mr. Gerry replied that he meant to make a motion, as he disapproved of the words as they stood. He then proceeded. No attempts that they made were successful until they engaged in the struggle which emancipated them at once from their thraldom. Now, if we give a discretionary power to exclude those from militia duty who have religious scruples, we may as well make no provisions on this head. For this reason, he wished the words to be altered so as to be confined to persons belonging to a religious sect scrupulous of bearing arms.

Mr. Jackson did not expect that all the people of the United States would turn Quakers or Moravians; consequently, one part would have to defend the other in case of invasion. Now this, in his opinion, was unjust, unless the constitution secured an equivalent: for this reason he moved to amend the clause, by inserting at the end of it, "upon paying an equivalent, to be established by law."

Mr. Smith, of South Carolina, inquired what were the words used by the conventions respecting this amendment. If the gentleman would conform to what was proposed by Virginia and Carolina, he would second him. He thought they were to be excused provided they found a substitute.

Mr. Jackson was willing to accommodate. He thought the expression was, "No one, religiously scrupulous of bearing arms, shall be compelled to render military service, in person, upon paying an equivalent."

Mr. Sherman conceived it difficult to modify the clause and make it better. It is well known that those who are religiously scrupulous of bearing arms, are equally scrupulous of giving substitutes or paying an equivalent. Many of them would rather die than do either one or the other; but he did not see an absolute necessity for a clause of this kind. We do not live under an arbitrary Government, said he, and the States, respectively, will have the government of the militia, unless when called into active service; beside, it would not do to alter it so as to exclude the whole of any sect, because there are men amongst the Quakers who will turn out, notwithstanding the religious principles of the society, and defend the cause of their country. Certainly, it will be improper to prevent the exercise of such favorable dispositions, at least whilst it is the practice of nations to determine their contests by the slaughter of their citizens and subjects.

MR. VINING hoped the clause would be suffered to remain as it stood, because he saw no use in it if it was amended so as to compel a man to find a substitute, which, with respect to the Government, was the same as if the person himself turned out to fight.

MR. STONE inquired what the words "religiously scrupulous" had reference to: was it of bearing arms? If it was, it ought so to be expressed.

MR. BENSON moved to have the words "but no person religiously scrupulous shall be compelled to bear arms," struck out. He would always leave it to the benevolence of the Legislature, for, modify it as you please, it will be impossible to express it in such a manner as to clear it from ambiguity. No man can claim this indulgence of right. It may be a religious persuasion, but it is no natural right, and therefore ought to be left to the discretion of the Government. If this stands part of the constitution, it will be a question before the Judiciary on every regulation you make with respect to the organization of the militia, whether it comports with this declaration or not. It is extremely injudicious to intermix matters of doubt with fundamentals.

I have no reason to believe but the Legislature will always possess humanity enough to indulge this class of citizens in a matter they are so desirous of; but they ought to be left to their discretion.

The motion for striking out the whole clause being seconded, was put, and decided in the negative—22 members voting for it, and 24 against it.

MR. GERRY objected to the first part of the clause, on account of the uncertainty with which it is expressed. A well regulated militia being the best security of a free State, admitted an idea that a standing army was a secondary one. It ought to read, "a well regulated militia, trained to arms;" in which case it would become the duty of the Government to provide this security, and furnish a greater certainty of its being done.

MR. GERRY's motion not being seconded, the question was put on the clause as reported; which being adopted,

MR. BURKE proposed to add to the clause just agreed to, an amendment to the following effect: "A standing army of regular troops in time of peace is dangerous to public liberty, and such shall not be raised or kept up in time of peace but from necessity, and for the security of the people, nor then without the consent of two-thirds of the members present of both Houses; and in all cases the military shall be subordinate to the civil authority." This being seconded,

MR. VINING asked whether this was to be considered as an addition to the last clause, or an amendment by itself. If the former, he would remind the gentleman the clause was decided; if the latter, it was improper to introduce new matter, as the House had referred the report specially to the Committee of the whole.

MR. BURKE feared that, what with being trammelled in rules, and the apparent disposition of the committee, he should not be able to get them to consider any amendment; he submitted to such proceeding because he could not help himself.

MR. HARTLEY thought the amendment in order, and was ready to give his opinion on it. He hoped the people of America would always be satisfied with having a majority to govern. He never wished to see two-thirds or three-fourths required, because it might put it in the power of a small minority to govern the whole Union.

The question on MR. BURKE's motion was put, and lost by a majority of thirteen.

The fourth clause of the fourth proposition was taken up as follows: "No soldier shall, in time of peace, be quartered in any house, without the consent of the owner, nor in time of war, but in a manner to be prescribed by law."

MR. SUMTER hoped soldiers would never be quartered on the inhabitants, either in time of peace or war, without the consent of the owner. It was a burthen, and very oppressive, even in cases where the owner gave his consent; but where this was wanting, it would be a hardship indeed! Their property would lie at the mercy of men irritated by a refusal, and well disposed to destroy the peace of the family.

He moved to strike out all the words from the clause but "no soldier shall be quartered in any house without the consent of the owner."

MR. SHERMAN observed that it was absolutely necessary that marching troops should have quarters, whether in time of peace or war, and that it ought not to be put in the power of an individual to obstruct the public service; if quarters were not to be obtained in public barracks, they must be procured elsewhere. In England, where they paid considerable attention to private rights, they billeted the troops upon the keepers of public houses, and upon private houses also, with the consent of the magistracy.

Mr. Sumter's motion being put, was lost by a majority of sixteen.

Mr. Gerry moved to insert between "but" and, "in a manner" the words "by a civil magistrate," observing that there was no part of the Union but where they could have access to such authority.

Mr. Hartley said those things ought to be entrusted to the Legislature; that cases might arise where the public safety would be endangered by putting it in the power of one person to keep a division of troops standing in the inclemency of the weather for many hours; therefore he was against inserting the words.

Mr. Gerry said either his amendment was essential, or the whole clause was unnecessary.

On putting the question, thirteen rose in favor of the motion, thirty-five against it; and then the clause was carried as reported.

The fifth clause of the fourth proposition was taken up, viz: "No person shall be subject, in case of impeachment, to more than one trial or one punishment for the same offence, nor shall be compelled to be a witness against himself, nor be deprived of life, liberty, or property, without due process of law; nor shall private property be taken for public use without just compensation."

Mr. Benson thought the committee could not agree to the amendment in the manner it stood, because its meaning appeared rather doubtful. It says that no person shall be tried more than once for the same offence. This is contrary to the right heretofore established; he presumed it was intended to express what was secured by our former constitution, that no man's life should be more than once put in jeopardy for the same offence; yet it was well known, that they were entitled to more than one trial. The humane intention of the clause was to prevent more than one punishment; for which reason he would move to amend it by striking out the words "one trial or."

Mr. Sherman approved of the motion. He said, that as the clause now stood, a person found guilty could not arrest the judgment and obtain a second trial in his own favor. He thought that the courts of justice would never think of trying and punishing twice for the same offence. If the person was acquitted on the first trial, he ought not to be tried a second time; but if he was convicted on the first, and any thing should appear to set the judgment aside, he was entitled to a second, which was certainly favorable to him. Now the clause as it stands would deprive him of that advantage.

Mr. Livermore thought the clause very essential; it was declaratory of the law as it now stood; striking out the words, would seem as if they meant to change the law by implication, and expose a man to the danger of more than one trial. Many persons may be brought to trial for crimes they are guilty of, but for want of evidence may be acquitted; in such cases, it is the universal practice in Great Britain, and in this country, that persons shall not be brought to a second trial for the same offence; therefore the clause is proper as it stands.

MR. SEDGWICK thought, instead of securing the liberty of the subject, it would be abridging the privileges of those who were prosecuted.

The question on MR. BENSON's motion being put, was lost by a considerable majority.

MR. PARTRIDGE moved to insert after "same offence," the words "by any law of the United States." This amendment was lost also.

MR. LAWRENCE said this clause contained a general declaration, in some degree contrary to laws passed. He alluded to that part where a person shall not be compelled to give evidence against himself. He thought it ought to be confined to criminal cases, and moved an amendment for that purpose; which amendment being adopted, the clause as amended was unanimously agreed to by the committee, who then proceeded to the sixth clause of the fourth proposition, in these words, "Excessive bail shall not be required, nor excessive fines imposed, nor cruel and unusual punishments inflicted."

MR. SMITH, of South Carolina, objected to the words "nor cruel and unusual punishments;" the import of them being too indefinite.

MR. LIVERMORE.—The clause seems to express a great deal of humanity, on which account I have no objection to it; but as it seems to have no meaning in it, I do not think it necessary. What is meant by the terms excessive bail? Who are to be the judges? What is understood by excessive fines? It lies with the court to determine. No cruel and unusual punishment is to be inflicted; it is sometimes necessary to hang a man, villains often deserve whipping; perhaps having their ears cut off; but are we in future to be prevented from inflicting these punishments because they are cruel? If a more lenient mode of correcting vice and deterring others from the commission of it could be invented, it would be very prudent in the Legislature to adopt it; but until we have some security that this will be done, we ought not to be restrained from making necessary laws by any declaration of this kind.

The question was put on the clause, and it was agreed to by a considerable majority.

The committee went on to the consideration of the seventh clause of the fourth proposition, being as follows: "The right of the people to be secured in their persons, houses, papers, and effects, shall not be violated by warrants issued without probable cause, supported by oath or affirmation, and not particularly describing the place to be searched, and the persons or things to be seized."

MR. GERRY said he presumed there was a mistake in the wording of this clause; it ought to be "the right of the people to be secure in their persons, houses, papers, and effects, against unreasonable seizures and searches," and therefore moved that amendment.

This was adopted by the committee.

MR. BENSON objected to the words "by warrants issuing." This declaratory provision was good as far as it went, but he thought it was not sufficient; he therefore proposed to alter it so as to read "and no warrant shall issue."

The question was put on this motion, and lost by a considerable majority.

MR. LIVERMORE objected to the words "and not" between "affirmation" and "particularly." He moved to strike them out, in order to make it an affirmative proposition.

But the motion passed in the negative.

The clause as amended being now agreed to, the eighth clause of the fourth proposition was taken up, which was, "The enumeration in this constitution of certain rights shall not be construed to deny or disparage others retained by the people."

MR. GERRY said, it ought to be "deny or impair," for the word "disparage" was not of plain import; he therefore moved to make the alteration, but not being seconded, the question was taken on the clause, and it passed in the affirmative.

The committee then proceeded to the fifth proposition:

Article I. Section 10. between the first and second paragraph, insert "no State shall infringe the equal rights of conscience, nor the freedom of speech or of the press, nor of the right of trial by jury in criminal cases."

MR. TUCKER.—This is offered, I presume, as an amendment to the constitution of the United States, but it goes only to the alteration of the constitutions of particular States. It will be much better, I apprehend, to leave the State Governments to themselves, and not to interfere with them more than we already do; and that is thought by many to be rather too much. I therefore move, sir, to strike out these words.

MR. MADISON conceived this to be the most valuable amendment in the whole list. If there was any reason to restrain the Government of the United States from infringing upon these essential rights, it was equally necessary that they should be secured against the State Governments. He thought that if they provided against the one, it was as necessary to provide against the other, and was satisfied that it would be equally grateful to the people.

MR. LIVERMORE had no great objection to the sentiment, but he thought it not well expressed. He wished to make it an affirmative proposition; "the equal rights of conscience, the freedom of speech or of the press, and the right of trial by jury in criminal cases, shall not be infringed by any State."

This transposition being agreed to, and MR. TUCKER'S motion being rejected, the clause was adopted.

The sixth proposition, Article 3, Section 2, add to the second paragraph, "But no appeal to such court shall be allowed, where the value in controversy shall not amount to one thousand dollars; nor shall any fact, triable by a jury according to the course of the common law, be otherwise reexaminable than according to the rules of the common law."

MR. BENSON moved to strike out the first part of the paragraph respecting the limitation of appeals, because the question in controversy might be an important one, though the action was not to the amount of a thousand dollars.

MR. MADISON.—If the gentleman will propose any restriction to answer his purpose, and for avoiding the inconvenience he apprehends, I am willing to agree to it; but it will be improper to strike out the clause without a substitute.

There is little danger that any court in the United States will admit an appeal where the matter in dispute does not amount to a thousand dollars; but as the possibility of such an event has excited in the minds of many citizens the greatest apprehension that persons of opulence would carry a cause from the extremities of the Union to the Supreme Court, and thereby prevent the due administration of justice, it ought to be guarded against.

MR. LIVERMORE thought the clause was objectionable, because it comprehended nothing more than the value.

MR. SEDGWICK moved to insert three thousand dollars, instead of one thousand; but on the question, this motion was rejected, and the proposition accepted in its original form.

The committee then proceeded to consider the seventh proposition, in the words following:

Article 3, Section 2. Strike out the whole of the third paragraph, and insert, "In all criminal prosecutions, the accused shall enjoy the right to a speedy and public trial, to be informed of the nature and cause of the accusation, to be confronted with the witnesses against him, to have compulsory process for obtaining witnesses in his favor, and to have the assistance of counsel for his defence."

MR. BURKE moved to amend this proposition in such a manner as to leave it in the power of the accused to put off the trial to the next session, provided he made it appear to the court that the evidence of the witnesses, for whom process was granted but not served, was material to his defence.

Mr. Hartley said, that in securing him the right of compulsory process, the Government did all it could; the remainder must lie in the discretion of the court.

Mr. Smith, of South Carolina, thought the regulation would come properly in, as part of the judicial system.

The question on Mr. Burke's motion was taken and lost; ayes 9, nays 41.

Mr. Livermore moved to alter the clause, so as to secure to the criminal the right of being tried in the State where the offence was committed.

Mr. Stone observed that full provision was made on the subject in the subsequent clause.

On the question, Mr. Livermore's motion was adopted.

Mr. Burke said, he was not so much discouraged by the fate of his former motions, but that he would venture upon another. He therefore proposed to add to the clause, that no criminal prosecution should be had by way of information.

Mr. Hartley only requested the gentleman to look to the clause, and he would see the impropriety of inserting it in this place.

A desultory conversation arose, respecting the foregoing motion, and after some time, Mr. Burke withdrew it for the present.

The committee then rose and reported progress, after which the House adjourned.

Tuesday, August 18, 1789.

AMENDMENTS TO THE CONSTITUTION

Mr. Gerry moved, "That such of the amendments to the constitution proposed by the several States, as are not in substance comprised in the report of the select committee appointed to consider amendments, be referred to a Committee of the whole House; and that all amendments which shall be agreed to by the committee last mentioned be included in the report."

Mr. Tucker remarked, that many citizens expected that the amendments proposed by the conventions would be attended to by the House, and that several members conceived it to be their duty to bring them forward. If the House should decline taking them into consideration, it might tend to destroy that harmony which had hitherto existed, and which did great honor to their proceedings; it might affect all their future measures, and promote such feuds as might embarrass the Government exceedingly. The States who had proposed these amendments would feel some degree of chagrin at having misplaced their confidence in the General

Government. Five important States have pretty plainly expressed their apprehensions of the danger to which the rights of their citizens are exposed. Finding these cannot be secured in the mode they had wished, they will naturally recur to the alternative, and endeavor to obtain a federal convention; the consequence of this may be disagreeable to the Union; party spirit may be revived, and animosities rekindled destructive of tranquility. States that exert themselves to obtain a federal convention, and those that oppose the measure, may feel so strongly the spirit of discord, as to sever the Union asunder.

If in this conflict the advocates for a federal convention should prove successful, the consequences may be alarming; we may lose many of the valuable principles now established in the present constitution. If, on the other hand, a convention should not be obtained, the consequences resulting are equally to be dreaded; it would render the administration of this system of government weak, if not impracticable; for no Government can be administered with energy, however energetic its system, unless it obtains the confidence and support of the people. Which of the two evils is the greatest would be difficult to ascertain.

It is essential to our deliberations that the harmony of the House be preserved; by it alone we shall be enabled to perfect the organization of the Government—a Government but in embryo, or at least but in its infancy.

My idea relative to this constitution, whilst it was dependent upon the assent of the several States, was, that it required amendment, and that the proper time for amendment was previous to the ratification. My reasons were, that I conceived it difficult, if not impossible, to obtain essential amendments by the way pointed out in the constitution; nor have I been mistaken in this suspicion. It will be found, I fear, still more difficult than I apprehended; for perhaps these amendments, should they be agreed to by two-thirds of both Houses of Congress, will be submitted for ratification to the Legislatures of the several States, instead of State conventions, in which case the chance is still worse. The Legislatures of almost all the States consist of two independent, distinct bodies; the amendments must be adopted by three-fourths of such Legislatures; that is to say, they must meet the approbation of the majority of each of eighteen deliberative assemblies. But, notwithstanding all these objections to obtaining amendments after the ratification of the constitution, it will tend to give a great degree of satisfaction to those who are desirous of them, if this House shall take them up, and consider them with that degree of candor and attention they have hitherto displayed on the subjects that have come before them; consider the amendments separately, and, after fair deliberation, either approve or disapprove of them. By such conduct, we answer in some degree the expectations of those citizens in the several States who have shown so great a tenacity to the preservation of those rights and liberties they secured to themselves by an arduous, persevering, and successful conflict.

I have hopes that the States will be reconciled to this disappointment, in consequence of such procedure.

A great variety of arguments might be urged in favor of the motion; but I shall rest it here, and not trespass any further upon the patience of the House.

Mr. MADISON was just going to move to refer these amendments, in order that they might be considered in the fullest manner; but it would be very inconvenient to have them made up into one report, or all of them discussed at the present time.

Mr. VINING had no objection to the bringing them forward in the fullest point of view; but his objection arose from the informality attending the introduction of the business.

The order of the House was to refer the report of the Committee of eleven to a Committee of the whole, and therefore, it was improper to propose any thing additional.

A desultory conversation arose on this motion, when Mr. VINING moved the previous question, in which, being supported by five members, it was put, and the question was, Shall the main question, to agree to the motion, be now put? The yeas and nays being demanded by one-fifth of the members present, on this last motion, they were taken as follows:

YEAS.—Messrs. Burke, Coles, Floyd, Gerry, Griffin, Grout, Hathorn, Livermore, Page, Parker, Van Rensselaer, Sherman, Stone, Sturges, Sumter, and Tucker.—16.

NAYS.—Messrs. Ames, Baldwin, Benson, Boudinot, Brown, Cadwalader, Carroll, Clymer, Fitzsimons, Foster, Gilman, Goodhue, Hartley, Heister, Huntington, Lawrence, Lee, Madison, Moore, Muhlenberg, Partridge, Schureman, Scott, Sedgwick, Seney, Sylvester, Sinnickson, Smith, of Maryland, Smith, of South Carolina, Thatcher, Trumbull, Vining, Wadsworth, and Wynkoop.—34.

So the motion was lost.

A message from the Senate informed the House that the Senate had passed the bill providing for expenses which may attend negotiations or treaties with the Indian tribes, and the appointment of commissioners for managing the same, with an amendment, to which they desire the concurrence of the House.

The House again resolved itself into a Committee of the whole on the subject of amendments, and took into consideration the 2d clause of the 7th proposition, in the words following, "The trial of all crimes (except in cases of impeachment, and in cases arising in the land and naval forces, or in the militia when in actual service in the time of war, or public danger,) shall be by an impartial jury of freeholders of the vicinage, with the requisite of unanimity for conviction, the right of challenge, and other ac-

customed requisites; and no person shall be held to answer for a
capital, or otherwise infamous crime, unless on a presentment, or
indictment, by a grand jury; but if a crime be committed in a
place in the possession of an enemy, or in which an insurrection
may prevail, the indictment and trial may by law be authorized
in some other place within the same State; and if it be committed
in a place not within a State, the indictment and trial may be at
such place or places as the law may have directed."

MR. BURKE moved to change the word "vicinage" into "district
or county in which the offence has been committed." He said this
was conformable to the practice of the State of South Carolina,
and he believed to most of the States in the Union; it would have
a tendency also to quiet the alarm entertained by the good citizens
of many of the States for their personal security; they would no
longer fear being dragged from one extremity of the State to the
other for trial, at the distance of three or four hundred miles.

MR. LEE thought the word "vicinage" was more applicable than
that of "district, or county," it being a term well understood by
every gentleman of legal knowledge.

The question on MR. BURKE's motion being put was negatived.

MR. BURKE then revived his motion for preventing prosecutions
upon information, but on the question this was also lost.

The clause was now adopted without amendment.

The 3d clause of the 7th proposition, as follows, "In suits at
common law, the right of trial by jury shall be preserved," was
considered and adopted.

The 8th proposition in the words following, was considered,
"Immediately after Art. 6, the following to be inserted as Art. 7:"

"The powers delegated by this constitution to the Government
of the United States, shall be exercised as therein appropriated, so
that the Legislative shall not exercise the powers vested in the
Executive or Judicial; nor the Executive the power vested in
the Legislative or Judicial; nor the Judicial the powers vested in the
Legislative or Executive."

MR. SHERMAN conceived this amendment to be altogether unnecessary, inasmuch as the constitution assigned the business of
each branch of the Government to a separate department.

MR. MADISON supposed the people would be gratified with the
amendment, as it was admitted that the powers ought to be
separate, and distinct; it might also tend to an explanation of some
doubts that might arise respecting the construction of the constitution.

MR. LIVERMORE, thinking the clause subversive of the constitution, was opposed to it, and hoped it might be disagreed to.

On the motion being put, the proposition was carried.

The 9th proposition, in the words following, was considered, "The powers not delegated by the constitution, nor prohibited by it to the States, are reserved to the States respectively."

Mr. Tucker proposed to amend the proposition, by prefixing to it "all powers being derived from the people." He thought this a better place to make this assertion than the introductory clause of the constitution, where a similar sentiment was proposed by the committee. He extended his motion also, to add the word "expressly," so as to read "the powers not expressly delegated by this constitution."

Mr. Madison objected to this amendment, because it was impossible to confine a Government to the exercise of express powers; there must necessarily be admitted powers by implication, unless the constitution descended to recount every minutia. He remembered the word "expressly" had been moved in the convention of Virginia, by the opponents to the ratification, and, after full and fair discussion, was given up by them, and the system allowed to retain its present form.

Mr. Sherman coincided with Mr. Madison in opinion, observing that corporate bodies are supposed to possess all powers incident to a corporate capacity, without being absolutely expressed.

Mr. Tucker did not view the word "expressly" in the same light with the gentleman who opposed him; he thought every power to be expressly given that could be clearly comprehended within any accurate definition of the general power.

Mr. Tucker's motion being negatived,

Mr. Carroll proposed to add to the end of the proposition, "or to the people;" this was agreed to.

The tenth proposition: "That Art. 7 be made Art. 8" was agreed to.

The committee then rose, and reported the amendments as amended by the committee.

Mr. Tucker then moved that the following propositions of amendment to the constitution of the United States, be referred to a Committee of the whole House, to-wit:

Art. 1. Sec. 2. clause 2. at the end, add these words, "Nor shall any person be capable of serving as a Representative more than six years, in any term of eight years."

Clause 3. at the end, add these words, "From and after the commencement of the year 1795, the election of Senators for each State shall be annual, and no person shall be capable of serving as a Senator more than five years in any term of six years."

Sect. 4. clause 1. strike out the words, "But the Congress may at any time, by law, make or alter such regulations, except as to the places of choosing Senators."

Sect. 5. clause 1. amend the first part to read thus, "Each State shall be the judge (according to its own laws) of the election of its Senators and Representatives to sit in Congress, and shall furnish them with sufficient credentials, but each House shall judge of the qualification of its own members; a majority of each House shall constitute," etc.

Clause 2. strike out these words, "And with the concurrence of two-thirds expel a member," and insert the word "and" after the word "proceedings."

Sect. 6. clause 2. amend to read thus, "No person having been elected, and having taken his seat as a Senator or Representative, shall, during the time for which he was elected, be appointed to any civil office under the authority of the United States, and no person," etc.

Art. 1. sect. 8. clause 1. at the end, add these words, "No direct tax shall be laid, unless any State shall have neglected to furnish, in due time, its proportion of a previous requisition; in which case Congress may proceed to levy, by direct taxation, within any State so neglecting, its proportion of such requisition, together with interest, at the rate of six per cent. per annum from the time it ought to have been furnished, and the charges of levying the same."

Clause 9. strike out the words "tribunals inferior to the Supreme Court," and insert the words "courts of admiralty."

Clause 17. at the end, add these words, "Provided that the Congress shall not have authority to make any law to prevent the laws of the States respectively in which such district or places may be, from extending to such district or places in all civil and criminal matters, in which any person without the limits of such district or places shall be a party aggrieved."

Sect. 9. clause 7. Strike out the words "Without the consent of the Congress," and amend to read thus, "Shall accept of any present or emolument, or hold any office, or title of any kind whatever from any king, prince, or foreign state; provided that this clause shall not be construed to affect the rights of those persons (during their own lives) who are now citizens of the United States, and hold foreign titles."

Sect. 10. clause 2. amend the first sentence to read thus, "No State shall lay any duties on imports or exports, or any duty of tonnage, except such as shall be uniform in their operation on all foreign nations, and consistent with existing treaties, and also uniform in their operation on the citizens of all the several States in the Union."

Art. 2. sect. 1. clause 5. at the end, add these words, "Nor shall any person be capable of holding the office of President of the United States more than eight years in any term of twelve years."

Sect. 2. clause 1. Strike out the words "be commander in chief," and insert, "have power to direct (agreeable to law) the operations."

Clause 3. at the end, add these words, "He shall also have power to suspend from his office, for a time not exceeding twelve months, any officer whom he shall have reason to think unfit to be entrusted with the duties thereof; and Congress may, by law, provide for the absolute removal of officers found to be unfit for the trust reposed in them."

Art. 3. sec. 1. from each sentence strike out the words "inferior courts" and insert the words "courts of admiralty."

Sect. 2. clause 1. strike out the words "Between a State and citizens of another State," etc. to the end and amend to read, "between a State and foreign State, and between citizens of the United States claiming the same land under grants of different States."

Art. 6. clause 3. Between the words "No" and the word "religious," insert the word "other."

On the question, Shall the said propositions of amendments be referred to the consideration of a Committee of the whole House? it was determined in the negative.

Wednesday, August 19, 1789.

AMENDMENTS TO THE CONSTITUTION

The House then took into consideration the amendments to the constitution, as reported by the Committee of the whole.

MR. SHERMAN renewed his motion for adding the amendments to the constitution by way of supplement.

Hereupon ensued a debate similar to what took place in the Committee of the whole, (see page 734;) but, on the question, MR. SHERMAN's motion was carried by two-thirds of the House; in consequence it was agreed to.

The first proposition of amendment (see page 734) was rejected, because two thirds of the members present did not support it.

MR. AMES then brought forward his motion respecting the representation suggested, (see page 756.) A desultory conversation took place, and several amendments of the motion were attempted; but the House adjourned without coming to any determination.

Thursday, August 20, 1789.

AMENDMENTS TO THE CONSTITUTION

The House resumed the consideration of the report of the Committee of the whole on the subject of amendment to the constitution.

MR. AMES's proposition was taken up. Five or six other members introduced propositions on the same point, and the whole were, by mutual consent, laid on the table. After which, the House proceeded to the third amendment, and agreed to the same.

On motion of MR. AMES, the fourth amendment was altered so as to read "Congress shall make no law establishing religion, or to prevent the free exercise thereof, or to infringe the rights of conscience." This being adopted,

The first proposition was agreed to.

MR. SCOTT objected to the clause in the sixth amendment, "No person religiously scrupulous shall be compelled to bear arms." He observed that if this becomes part of the constitution, such persons can neither be called upon for their services, nor can an equivalent be demanded; it is also attended with still further difficulties, for a militia can never be depended upon. This would lead to the violation of another article in the constitution, which secures to the people the right of keeping arms, and in this case recourse must be had to a standing army. I conceive it, said he, to be a legislative right altogether. There are many sects I know, who are religiously scrupulous in this respect; I do not mean to deprive them of any indulgence the law affords; my design is to guard against those who are of no religion. It has been urged that religion is on the decline; if so, the argument is more strong in my favor, for when the time comes that religion shall be discarded, the generality of persons will have recourse to these pretexts to get excused from bearing arms.

MR. BOUDINOT thought the provision in the clause, or something similar to it, was necessary. Can any dependence, said he, be placed in men who are conscientious in this respect? or what justice can there be in compelling them to bear arms, when, according to their religious principles, they would rather die than use them? He adverted to several instances of oppression on this point, that occurred during the war. In forming a militia, an effectual defence ought to be calculated, and no characters of this religious description ought to be compelled to take up arms. I hope that in establishing this Government, we may show the world that proper care is taken that the Government may not interfere with the religious sentiments of any person. Now, by striking out the clause, people may be led to believe that there is an intention in the General Government to compel all its citizens to bear arms.

Some further desultory conversation arose, and it was agreed to insert the words, "in person" to the end of the clause; after which, it was adopted, as was the fourth, fifth, sixth, seventh, and eighth clauses of the fourth proposition; then the fifth, sixth, and seventh propositions were agreed to, and the House adjourned.

Friday, August 21, 1789.

AMENDMENTS TO THE CONSTITUTION

The House proceeded in the consideration of the amendments to the constitution reported by the Committee of the whole, and took up the second clause of the fourth proposition.

MR. GERRY then proposed to amend it by striking out these words, "public danger," and to insert "foreign invasion;" this being negatived, it was then moved to strike out the last clause, "and if it be committed," etc. to the end. This motion was carried, and the amendment was adopted.

The House then took into consideration the third clause of the seventh proposition, which was adopted without debate.

The eighth proposition was agreed to in the same manner.

The ninth proposition MR. GERRY proposed to amend by inserting the word "expressly," so as to read "the powers not expressly delegated by the constitution, nor prohibited to the States, are reserved to the States respectively, or to the people." As he thought this an amendment of great importance, he requested the yeas and nays might be taken. He was supported in this by one-fifth of the members present; whereupon they were taken, and were as follows:

YEAS.—Messrs. Burke, Coles, Floyd, Gerry, Grout, Hathorn, Jackson, Livermore, Page, Parker, Partridge, Van Rensselaer, Smith, (of South Carolina,) Stone, Sumter, Thatcher, and Tucker.—17.

NAYS.—Messrs. Ames, Benson, Boudinot, Brown, Cadwalader, Carroll, Clymer, Fitzsimons, Foster, Gale, Gilman, Goodhue, Hartley, Heister, Lawrence, Lee, Madison, Moore, Muhlenberg, Schureman, Scott, Sedgwick, Seney, Sherman, Sylvester, Sinnickson, Smith, (of Maryland,) Sturges, Trumbull, Vining, Wadsworth, and Wynkoop.—32.

MR. SHERMAN moved to alter the last clause, so as to make it read, "the powers not delegated to the United States by the constitution, nor prohibited by it to the States, are reserved to the States respectively, or to the people."

The motion was adopted without debate.

MR. BURKE.—The majority of this House may be inclined to think all our propositions unimportant, as they seemed to consider that upon which the ayes and noes were just now called. However, to the minority they are important; and it will be happy for the Government, if the majority of our citizens are not of their opinion; but be this as it may, I move you, sir, to add to the articles of amendment the following: "Congress shall not alter, modify, or interfere in the times, places, or manner of holding elections of Senators, or Representatives, except when any State shall refuse or neglect, or be unable, by invasion or rebellion, to make such election."

MR. AMES thought this one of the most justifiable of all the powers of Congress; it was essential to a body representing the whole community, that they should have power to regulate their own elections, in order to secure a representation from every part, and prevent any improper regulations, calculated to answer party purposes only. It is a solecism in politics to let others judge for them, and is a departure from the principles upon which the constitution was founded.

MR. LIVERMORE said, this was an important amendment, and one that had caused more debate in the Convention of New Hampshire than any other whatever. The gentleman just up said it was a solecism in politics, but he could cite an instance in which it had taken place. He called upon gentlemen to recollect the circumstance of MR. SMITH's (of South Carolina) election, and to ask if that was not decided by the State laws? Was not his qualification as a member of the Federal Legislature determined upon the laws of South Carolina? It was not supposed by the people of South Carolina, that the House would question a right derived by their representative from their authority.

MR. MADISON.—If this amendment had been proposed at any time either in the Committee of the whole or separately in the House, I should not have objected to the discussion of it. But I cannot agree to delay the amendments now agreed upon, by entering into the consideration of propositions not likely to obtain the consent of either two-thirds of this House or three-fourths of the State Legislatures. I have considered this subject with some degree of attention, and, upon the whole, am inclined to think the constitution stands very well as it is.

MR. GERRY was sorry that gentlemen objected to the time and manner of introducing this amendment, because it was too important in its nature to be defeated by want of form. He hoped, and he understood it to be the sense of the House, that each amendment should stand upon its own ground; if this was, therefore, examined on its own merits, it might stand or fall as it deserved, and there would be no cause for complaint on the score of inattention.

His colleague (MR. AMES) objected to the amendment, because he thought no Legislature was without the power of determining the mode of its own appointment; but he would find, if he turned to the constitution of the State he was a representative of, that the times, places, and manner of choosing members of their Senate and Council were prescribed therein.

Why, said he, are gentlemen desirous of retaining this power? Is it because it gives energy to the Government? It certainly has no such tendency; then why retain a clause so obnoxious to almost every State? But this provision may be necessary in order to establish Government of an arbitrary kind, to which the present system is pointed in no very indirect manner: in this way, indeed, it may be useful. If the United States are desirous of controlling the elections of the people, they will in the first place, by virtue of the powers given them by the 4th sect. of the 1st art. abolish the mode of balloting; then every person must publicly announce his vote, and it would then frequently happen that he would be obliged to vote for a man, or "the friend of a man" to whom he was under obligations. If the Government grows desirous of being arbitrary, elections will be ordered at remote places, where their friends alone will attend. Gentlemen will tell me that these things are not to be apprehended; but if they say that the Government has the power of doing them, they have no right to say the Government will never exercise such powers, because it is presumable that they will administer the constitution at one time or another with all its powers; and whenever that time arrives, farewell to the rights of the people, even to elect their own representatives.

Mr. Stone called upon gentlemen to show what confederated Government had the power of determining on the mode of their own election. He apprehended there were none; for the representatives of States were chosen by the States in the manner they pleased. He was not afraid that the General Government would abuse this power, and as little afraid that the States would; but he thought it was in the order of things that the power should vest in the States respectively, because they can vary their regulations to accommodate the people in a more convenient manner than can be done in any general law whatever. He thought the amendment was generally expected, and therefore, on the principles of the majority, ought to be adopted.

Mr. Smith (of South Carolina) said, he hoped it would be agreed to; that eight States had expressed their desires on this head, and all of them wished the General Government to relinquish their control over the elections. The eight States he alluded to were New Hampshire, Massachusetts, New York, Pennsylvania, Maryland, Virginia, North Carolina and South Carolina.

Mr. Carroll denied that Maryland had expressed the desire attributed to her.

Mr. Fitzsimons.—The remark was not just as it respected Pennsylvania.

MR. SMITH (of South Carolina) said, the Convention of Maryland appointed a committee to recommend amendments, and among them was the one now under consideration.

MR. STONE replied there was nothing of the kind noticed on the journals of that body.

MR. SMITH (of South Carolina) did not know how they came into the world, but he had certainly seen them. As to Pennsylvania, there was a very considerable minority, he understood one-third, who had recommended the amendment. Now, taking all circumstances into consideration, it might be fairly inferred that a majority of the United States were in favor of this amendment. He had studied to make himself acquainted with this particular subject, and all that he had ever heard in defence of the power being exercised by the General Government was, that it was necessary, in case any State neglected or refused to make provision for the election. Now these cases were particularly excepted by the clause proposed by his honorable colleague; and therefore he presumed there was no good argument against it.

MR. SEDGWICK moved to amend the motion, by giving the power to Congress to alter the times, manner, and places of holding elections, provided the States made improper ones; for as much injury might result to the Union from improper regulations, as from a neglect or refusal to make any. It is as much to be apprehended that the States may abuse their powers, as that the United States may make an improper use of theirs.

MR. AMES said, that inadequate regulations were equally injurious as having none, and that such an amendment as was now proposed would alter the constitution; it would vest the supreme authority in places where it was never contemplated.

MR. SHERMAN observed, that the Convention were very unanimous in passing this clause; that it was an important provision, and if it was resigned it would tend to subvert the Government.

MR. MADISON was willing to make every amendment that was required by the States, which did not tend to destroy the principles and the efficacy of the constitution; he conceived that the proposed amendment would have that tendency, he was therefore opposed to it.

MR. SMITH (of South Carolina) observed, that the States had the sole regulation of elections, so far as it respected the President. Now he saw no good reason why they should be indulged in this, and prohibited from the other. But the amendment did not go so far; it admitted that the General Government might interfere whenever the State Legislature refused or neglected; and it might happen that the business would be neglected without any design to injure the administration of the General Government; it might be that the two branches of the Legislature could not agree, as happened he believed in the Legislature of New York, with respect to their choice of Senators at their late session.

MR. TUCKER objected to MR. SEDGWICK's motion of amendment, because it had a tendency to defeat the object of the proposition brought forward by his colleague, (MR. BURKE.) The General Government would be the judge of inadequate or improper regulations; of consequence they might interfere in any or every law which the States might pass on that subject.

He wished that the State Legislatures might be left to themselves to perform every thing they were competent to, without the guidance of Congress. He believed there was no great danger, but they knew how to pursue their own good, as well when left to their discretion, as they would under the direction of a superior. It seemed to him as if there was a strong propensity in this Government to take upon themselves the guidance of the State Governments, which to his mind implied a doubt of their capacity to govern themselves; now his judgment was convinced that the particular State Governments could take care of themselves, and deserved more to be trusted than this did, because the right of the citizen was more secure under it.

It had been supposed by some States, that electing by districts was the most convenient mode of choosing members to this House; others have thought that the whole State ought to vote for the whole number of members to be elected for that State. Congress might, under like impressions, set their regulations aside. He had heard that many citizens of Virginia (which State was divided into eleven districts) supposed themselves abridged of nine-tenths of their privilege by being restrained to the choice of one man instead of ten, the number that State sends to this House.

With respect to the election of Senators, the mode is fixed; every State but New York has established a precedent; there is, therefore, but little danger of any difficulty on this account. As to New York, she suffers by her want of decision; it is her own loss; but probably they may soon decide the point, and then no difficulty can possibly arise hereafter. From all these considerations, he was induced to hope MR. SEDGWICK's motion would be negatived, and his colleague's agreed to.

MR. GOODHUE hoped the amendment never would obtain. Gentlemen should recollect there appeared a large majority against amendments, when the subject was first introduced, and he had no doubt but that majority still existed. Now, rather than this amendment should take effect, he would vote against all that had been agreed to. His greatest apprehensions were, that the State Governments would oppose and thwart the general one to such a degree as finally to overturn it. Now, to guard against this evil, he wished the Federal Government to possess every power necessary to its existence.

MR. BURKE was convinced there was a majority against him; but, nevertheless, he would do his duty, and propose such amendments as he conceived essential to secure the rights and liberties of his constituents. He begged permission to make an observation or two, not strictly in order; the first was on an assertion that had been repeated more than once in this House, "That this revolution or adoption of the new constitution was agreeable to the public mind, and those who opposed it at first are now satisfied with it." I believe, sir, said he, that many of those gentlemen who agreed to the ratification without amendments, did it from principles of patriotism, but they knew at the same time that they parted with their liberties; yet they had such reliance on the virtue of a future Congress, that they did not hesitate, expecting that they would be restored to them unimpaired, as soon as the Government commenced its operations, conformably to what was mutually understood at the sealing and delivering up of those instruments.

It has been supposed that there is no danger to be apprehended from the General Government of an invasion of the rights of election. I will remind gentlemen of an instance in the Government of Holland. The patriots in this Country fought no less strenuously for that prize than the people of America; yet, by giving to the States General powers not unlike those in this constitution, their right of representation was abolished. That they once possessed it is certain, and that they made as much talk about its importance as we do; but now the right has ceased, all vacancies are filled by the men in power. It is our duty, therefore, to prevent our liberties from being fooled away in a similar manner; consequently we ought to adopt the clause which secures to the General Government every thing that ought to be required.

MR. MADISON observed that it was the State Governments in the Seven United Provinces which had assumed to themselves the power of filling vacancies, and not the General Government; therefore the gentleman's application did not hold.

The question on MR. SEDGWICK's motion for amending MR. BURKE's proposition was put and lost.

The question was then put on MR. BURKE's motion, and the yeas and nays being demanded by the constitutional number, they were taken as follows:

YEAS.—Messrs. Burke, Coles, Floyd, Gerry, Griffin, Grout, Hathorn, Heister, Jackson, Livermore, Matthews, Moore, Page, Parker, Partridge, Van Rensselaer, Seney, Sylvester, Smith, (of South Carolina,) Stone, Sumter, Thatcher, and Tucker.—23.

NAYS.—Messrs. Ames, Benson, Boudinot, Brown, Cadwalader, Carroll, Clymer, Fitzsimons, Foster, Gale, Gilman, Goodhue, Hartley, Lawrence, Lee, Madison, Muhlenberg, Schureman, Scott, Sedgwick, Sherman, Sinnickson, Smith, (of Maryland,) Sturges, Trumbull, Vining, Wadsworth, and Wynkoop.—28.

So it was determined in the negative.

The House then resumed the considerations of the proposition respecting the apportioning of the representation to a certain ratio, proposed by MR. AMES.

When, after some desultory conversation, it was agreed to, as follows: "After the first enumeration, required by the first article of the constitution, there shall be one representative for every thirty thousand, until the number shall amount to one hundred. After which, the proportion shall be so regulated by Congress that there shall be not less than one hundred representatives, nor less than one representative for every forty thousand persons, until the number of representatives shall amount to two hundred, after which, the proportion shall be so regulated by Congress, that there shall not be less than two hundred representatives, nor less than one representative for fifty thousand persons."

After which the House adjourned.

Saturday, August 22, 1789.

AMENDMENTS TO THE CONSTITUTION

The House resumed the consideration of the amendments to the constitution.

MR. TUCKER moved the following as a proposition to be added to the same: "The Congress shall never impose direct taxes but where the moneys arising from the duties, imposts, and excise are insufficient for the public exigencies, nor then until Congress shall have made a requisition upon the States to assess, levy, and pay their respective proportions of such requisitions. And in case any State shall neglect or refuse to pay its proportion, pursuant to such requisition, then Congress may assess, and levy such State's proportion, together with the interest thereon, at the rate of six per cent. per annum, from the time of payment prescribed by such requisition."

MR. PAGE said, that he hoped every amendment to the constitution would be considered separately in the manner this was proposed, but he wished them considered fully; it ought to have been referred to the Committee of eleven, reported upon, and then to the Committee of the whole. This was the manner in which the House had decided upon all those already agreed to; and this ought to be the manner in which this should be decided; he should be sorry to delay what was so nearly completed on any account. The House has but little time to sit, and the subject has to go before the Senate, therefore it requires of us all the expedition we can possibly give it. I would prefer putting a finishing hand to what has been already agreed to, and refer this to the Committee of eleven for their consideration.

MR. TUCKER.—This proposition was referred to the committee, along with many others in the gross, but the Committee of eleven declined reporting upon it. I understood it to be in any gentleman's power to bring it forward when he thought proper, and it was under this influence that I proposed it, nor do I conceive it to be an improper time. The House is engaged in the discussion of amendments; they have made some progress, and I wish them to go on to complete what they have begun. This may be added without inconvenience, if it meet the sense of the House; but if it does not, I wish my constituents to be acquainted with our decision on the whole subject, and therefore hope it may be decided upon at this time.

MR. JACKSON.—The gentleman has an undoubted right to bring forward the proposition; but I differ greatly with respect to its propriety. I hope, sir, the experience we have had will be sufficient to prevent us from ever agreeing to a relinquishment of such an essential power. The requisitions of the former Congress were ineffectual to obtain supplies; they remain to this day neglected by several States. If a sense of common danger, if war, and that a war of the noblest kind, a contest for liberty, were not sufficient to stimulate the States to a prompt compliance, when the means were abundant, by reason of the immense quantities of paper medium, can we ever expect an acquiescence to a requisition in future, when the only stimulus is honesty, to enable the confederation to discharge the debts of the late war?

But suppose requisitions were likely to be, in some degree, complied with, (which, by the by, I never can admit,) in every case where a State had neglected or refused to furnish its quota, Congress must come in, assess, and collect it. Now, in every such case, I venture to affirm that jealousies would be excited, discontent would prevail, and civil wars break out. What less can gentlemen picture to themselves, when a Government has refused to perform its obligations, but that it will support its measures by the point of the bayonet.

Without the power of raising money to defray the expenses of Government, how are we to be secure against foreign invasion? What, can a Government exert itself, with its sinews torn from it? We can expect neither strength nor exertion; and without these are acquired and preserved, our Union will not be lasting; we shall be rent asunder by intestine commotion, or exterior assault; and when that period arrives, we may bid adieu to all the blessings we have purchased at the price of our fortunes, and the blood of our worthiest heroes.

Mr. Livermore thought this an amendment of more importance than any yet obtained; that it was recommended by five or six States, and therefore ought to engage their most serious consideration. It had been supposed that the United States would not attempt to levy direct taxes; but this was certainly a mistake. He believed nothing but the difficulty of managing the subject would deter them. The modes of levying and collecting taxes pursued by the several States are so various, that it is an insuperable obstacle to an attempt by the General Government.

He was sensible that the requisitions of the former Congress had not been fully complied with, and the defect of the confederation was, that the Government had no powers to enforce a compliance. The proposition now under consideration obviated that difficulty. Suppose one or two States refused to comply, certainly the force of the others could compel them, and that is all that ought to be required; because it is not to be supposed that a majority of the States will refuse, as such an opposition must destroy the Union. He hoped the States would be left to furnish their quotas in a manner the most easy to themselves, as was requested by more than half of the present Union.

Unless something more effectual was done to improve the constitution, he knew his constituents would be dissatisfied. As to the amendments already agreed to, they would not value them more than a pinch of snuff; they went to secure rights never in danger.

Mr. Page wished the proposition might be recommitted, for he was certain there was neither time nor inclination to add it to those already agreed upon.

He observed that the warmest friends to amendments differ in opinion on this subject; many of them have ceased urging it, while others have become strenuous advocates for the reverse. The most judicious and discerning men now declare that the Government ought never to part with this power. For his part, experience had convinced him that no reliance was to be had on requisitions, when the States had treated them with contempt in the hour of danger, and had abundant means of compliance. The public credit stood at this moment in the utmost need of support, and he could not consent to throw down one of its strongest props. He thought there was no danger of an abuse of this power, for the Government would not have recourse to it while the treasury could be supplied from any other source; and when they did, they would be studious of adapting their law to the convenience of the States. He hoped, when the gentleman returned home to New Hampshire, his constituents would give him credit for his exertions, and be better satisfied with the amendments than he now supposed them to be.

Mr. Sumter felt himself so sensibly impressed with the importance of the subject, that if he apprehended the proposition would not have a fair discussion at this time, he would second the motion of commitment, and had not a doubt that the House would acquiesce in it.

Gentlemen had said that the States had this business much at heart. Yes, he would venture to say more, that if the power was not relinquished by the General Government, the State Governments would be annihilated. If every resource is taken from them, what remains in the power of the States for their support, or for the extinguishment of their domestic debt?

Mr. Gerry thought if the proposition was referred, that it ought to go to a Committee of the whole, for he wished it to have a full and candid discussion. He would have something left in the power of every State to support itself, independent of the United States, and therefore was not satisfied with the amendment proposed. The constitution, in its original state, gives to Congress the power of levying and collecting taxes, duties, imposts, and excise. The fault here is that everything is relinquished to the General Government. Now, the amendment gives the same power, with qualification, that there shall have been a previous requisition. This by no means came up to his idea; he thought that some particular revenue ought to be secured to the States, so as to enable them to support themselves.

He apprehended, when this clause in the constitution was under the consideration of the several State conventions, they would not so readily have ratified it, if they had considered it more fully in the point of view in which he had now placed it; but if they had ratified it, it would have been under a conviction that Congress would admit such amendments as were necessary to the existence of the State Governments. At present, the States are divested of every means to support themselves. If they discover a new source of revenue, after Congress shall have diverted all the old ones into their treasury, the rapacity of the General Government can take that from them also. The States can have recourse to no tax, duty, impost, or excise, but what may be taken from them whenever the Congress shall be so disposed; and yet gentlemen must see that the annihilation of the State Governments will be followed by the ruin of this.

Now, what is the consequence of the amendment? Either the States will or will not comply with the requisitions. If they comply, they voluntarily surrender their means of support; if they refuse, the arms of Congress are raised to compel them, which, in all probability, may lay the foundation for civil war. What umbrage must it give every individual to have two sets of collectors and tax-gathers surrounding his door; the people then soured, and a direct refusal by the Legislature, will be the occasion of perpetual discord. He wished to alter this proposition in such a manner as to secure the support of the Federal Government and the State Governments likewise, and therefore wished the amendment referred to a Committee of the whole House.

Mr. TUCKER.—I do not see the arguments in favor of giving Congress this power in so forcible a light as some gentlemen do. It will be to erect an *imperium in imperio,* which is generally considered to be subversive of all Government. At any time that Congress shall exercise this power, it will raise commotions in the States; whereas, the mode of requisitions will operate in so easy a way, by being consonant to the habits of the people, that the supplies will be sooner realized in the treasury by this means than by any other. It will require a length of time to form a uniform system of taxation, that shall operate equally and justly through all the States; though I doubt the possibility of forming such a system. It has been said, that requisitions have not been complied with in former times, but it is to be hoped that there will not be so much difficulty in future. The supplies from the impost will greatly diminish the requisitions; besides, should any of the States refuse to comply, they will be liable to the exercise of the power of Congress in the very heart of their country. This power will be so disagreeable, that the very dread of it will stimulate the States to an immediate and prompt compliance with the requisitions. This amendment has been proposed by several of the States, and by some of the most important ones. For this and other reasons that have been offered on the subject, I hope the amendment will be adopted.

Several methods were proposed for disposing of this question for the present; but the motion for its lying on the table being put and negatived, Mr. PARTRIDGE, referring to his instructions, was solicitous that this amendment should not be too precipitately decided upon, and moved the previous question, which was negatived.

Mr. SEDGWICK said, that he believed his mind was as strongly impressed with the force of the instructions he had received from his constituents, as that of other gentlemen. But, sir, a Government entrusted with the freedom and the very existence of the people, ought surely to possess, in a most ample degree, the means of supporting its own existence; and as we do not know what circumstances we may be in, or how necessary it may be for Congress to exercise this power, I should deem it a violation of the oath I have taken to support the constitution were I now to vote for this amendment.

Mr. SHERMAN remarked, that if Congress should exercise this power, the taxes would be laid by the immediate representatives of the people; neither would it be necessary to adopt the uniform method of collecting direct taxes. The several States might be accommodated by a reference to their respective modes of taxation.

The question upon the paragraph being called for from every part of the House, the yeas and nays were taken.

YEAS.—Messrs. Burke, Coles, Floyd, Grout, Hathorn, Livermore, Van Rensselaer, Sumter, and Tucker.—9.

NAYS.—Messrs. Ames, Benson, Brown, Cadwalader, Carroll, Clymer, Fitzsimons, Foster, Gale, Gerry, Gilman, Goodhue, Hartley, Heister, Jackson, Lawrence, Lee, Madison, Matthews, Moore, Muhlenberg, Page, Parker, Partridge, Schureman, Scott, Sedgwick, Seney, Sherman, Sylvester, Sinnickson, Smith, (of Maryland,) Smith, (of South Carolina,) Stone, Sturges, Thatcher, Trumbull, Vining, and Wadsworth.—39.

MR. TUCKER proposed the following amendment to the constitution:

Article 1, section 8, clause 9, strike out the words, "tribunals superior to the Supreme Court," and insert the words "courts of admiralty."

And on the question being put, it passed in the negative.

He then moved for a further amendment to the constitution, as follows:

In the third section of the sixth article insert the word "other" between the word "no" and the word "religious."

And on the question that the House do agree to the said amendment, it passed in the negative.

MR. GERRY moved to add to the amendments already agreed to the following articles, to-wit:

"That Congress erect no company of merchants with exclusive advantages of commerce." And on the question that the House do agree to the said proposed article, it passed in the negative.

He introduced another motion, to add to the amendments already agreed to the following article, to-wit:

"Congress shall at no time consent that any person holding an office of trust or profit under the United States shall accept of a title of nobility or any other title or office from any King, Prince, or foreign State."

And on the question being put, it was negatived.

MR. BENSON introduced a resolution to the following purport:

Resolved by the House of Representatives of the United States in Congress assembled, That the following amendments to the constitution of the United States having been agreed to by two-thirds of both Houses, be submitted to the Legislatures of the several States; which, when ratified, in whole or in part, by three-fourths of the said Legislatures, shall be valid to all intents and purposes as parts of the said constitution.

This resolution was referred to a committee consisting of Messrs. BENSON, SHERMAN, and SEDGWICK, who were directed to arrange the said amendments and make report thereof.

Monday, August 24, 1789.

MR. BENSON, from the committee appointed for the purpose, reported an arrangement of the articles of amendment to the Constitution of the United States, as agreed to by the House on Friday last; also, a resolution prefixed to the same, which resolution was twice read and agreed to by the House, as follows:

Resolved by the Senate and House of Representatives of the United States of America in Congress assembled, (two-thirds of both houses deeming it necessary,) That the following articles be proposed to the Legislatures of the several States as amendments to the Constitution of the United States, all or any of which articles, when ratified by three-fourths of the said Legislatures, to be valid to all intents and purposes as part of the said Constitution.

Ordered, That the Clerk of this House do carry to the Senate a fair engrossed copy of the said proposed articles of amendment, and desire their concurrence.

Thursday, September 10, 1789.

A message from the Senate informed the House that the Senate have agreed to the resolution of this House, of the second ultimo, containing certain articles to be proposed by Congress to the Legislatures of the several States, as amendments to the Constitution of the United States, with several amendments; to which they desire the concurrence of this House.

Saturday, September 19, 1789.

The House then took into consideration the amendments to the Constitution, as amended by the Senate; and after some time spent thereon, the business was postponed till tomorrow.

Monday, September 21, 1789.

The House then resumed the consideration of the amendments proposed by the Senate to the several articles of amendments to the Constitution of the United States; some of which they agreed to, and disagreed to others, two-thirds of the members present concurring in each vote: whereupon, a committee of conference was desired with the Senate on the subject-matter of the amendments disagreed to; and Messrs. Madison, Sherman, and Vining, were appointed managers on the part of the House.

Thursday, September 24, 1789.

Amendments to the Constitution

The House proceeded to consider the report of a Committee of Conference, on the subject-matter of the amendments depending between the two Houses to the several articles of amendment to the Constitution of the United States, as proposed by this House: Whereupon, it was resolved, that they recede from their disagreement to all the amendments; provided that the two articles, which, by the amendments of the Senate, are now proposed to be inserted as the third and eighth articles, shall be amended to read as follows:

Art. 3. Congress shall make no law respecting an establishment of religion, or prohibiting a free exercise thereof, or abridging the freedom of speech, or of the press, or the right of the people peaceably to assemble, and to petition the Government for a redress of grievances.

Art. 8. In all criminal prosecutions, the accused shall enjoy the right to a speedy and public trial, by an impartial jury of the State and district wherein the crime shall have been committed, which district shall have been previously ascertained by law; and to be informed of the nature and cause of the accusation—to be confronted with the witnesses against him—to have compulsory process for obtaining witnesses in his favor, and to have the assistance of counsel for his defense.

And provided, also, that the first article be amended, by striking out the word "less" in the last place of the said article, and inserting, in lieu thereof, "more."

On the question that the House agree to the alteration of the eighth article, in the manner aforesaid, the yeas and nays were called, and are as follows:

YEAS—Messrs. Ames, Baldwin, Benson, Boudinot, Brown, Cadwalader, Carroll, Clymer, Contee, Fitzsimons, Foster, Gale, Gilman, Goodhue, Griffin, Hartley, Lee, Leonard, Madison, Moore, Muhlenberg, Parker, Partridge, Schureman, Scott, Seney, Sherman, Sylvester, Sinnickson, Smith, (of Maryland,) Smith, (of South Carolina,) Stone, Thatcher, Trumbull, Vining, White, and Wynkoop —37.

NAYS—Messrs. Bland, Burke, Coles, Floyd, Gerry, Grout, Hathorn, Jackson, Livermore, Matthews, Page, Van Rensselaer, Sumter, and Tucker—14.

On motion, it was resolved, that the President of the United States be requested to transmit to the Executives of the several States which have ratified the Constitution, copies of the amendments proposed by Congress, to be added thereto, and like copies to the Executives of the States of Rhode Island and North Carolina.

Friday, September 25, 1789.

DAY OF THANKSGIVING

MR. BOUDINOT said, he could not think of letting the session pass over without offering an opportunity to all the citizens of the United States of joining, with one voice, in returning to Almighty God their sincere thanks for the many blessings he had poured down upon them. With this view, therefore, he would move the following resolution:

Resolved, That a joint committee of both Houses be directed to wait upon the President of the United States, to request that he would recommend to the people of the United States a day of public thanksgiving and prayer, to be observed by acknowledging, with grateful hearts, the many signal favors of Almighty God, especially by affording them an opportunity peaceably to establish a Constitution of government for their safety and happiness.

MR. BURKE did not like this mimicking of European customs, where they made a mere mockery of thanksgivings. Two parties at war frequently sung Te Deum for the same event, though to one it was a victory, and to the other a defeat.

MR. BOUDINOT was sorry to hear arguments drawn from the abuse of a good thing against the use of it. He hoped no gentlemen would make a serious opposition to a measure both prudent and just.

MR. TUCKER thought the House had no business to interfere in a matter which did not concern them. Why should the President direct the people to do what, perhaps, they have no mind to do? They may not be inclined to return thanks for a Constitution until they have experienced that it promotes their safety and happiness. We do not yet know but they may have reason to be dissatisfied with the effects it has already produced; but whether this be so or not, it is a business with which Congress have nothing to do; it is a religious matter, and, as such, is proscribed to us. If a day of thanksgiving must take place, let it be done by the authority of the several States; they know best what reason their constituents have to be pleased with the establishment of this Constitution.

MR. SHERMAN justified the practice of thanksgiving, on any signal event, not only as a laudable one in itself, but as warranted by a number of precedents in holy writ; for instance, the solemn thanksgivings and rejoicings which took place in the time of Solomon, after the building of the temple, was a case in point. This example, he thought, worthy of Christian imitation on the present occasion; and he would agree with the gentleman who moved the resolution.

MR. BOUDINOT quoted further precedents from the practice of the late Congress; and hoped the motion would meet a ready acquiescence.

The question was now put on the resolution, and it was carried in the affirmative; and MESSRS. BOUDINOT, SHERMAN, and SYLVESTER were appointed a committee on the part of the House.

Monday, September 28, 1789.

DAY OF THANKSGIVING

A message from the Senate informed the House that they had agreed to the resolution desiring the President of the United States to recommend a day of general thanksgiving; also, to the resolution desiring him to transmit to the Executives of the several States of the Union, and also to the Executives of the States of Rhode Island and North Carolina, copies of the amendments agreed to by Congress, to the Constitution of the United States. They have also come to a resolution appointing a committee to join with such committee as this House shall appoint, to wait upon the President of the United States, and notify him of the proposed recess of Congress.

Whereupon, the House ordered that a committee be appointed to join with the committee of the Senate, for the purpose expressed in the last resolution; and named MESSRS. VINING, LEE, and GILMAN, accordingly.

HISTORY

of

THE PROCEEDINGS AND DEBATES

of

THE SENATE OF THE UNITED STATES,

AT THE FIRST SESSION OF THE FIRST CONGRESS,
BEGUN AT THE CITY OF NEW YORK,
MARCH 4, 1789,

UNDER THE CONSTITUTION SUBMITTED BY
THE FEDERAL CONVENTION IN PHILADELPHIA,
SEPTEMBER 18, 1787.

———

[This seems to be a proper place to notice a fact, which is necessary to account for the meagreness of the report of the Senate proceedings in the earlier days of the Government, viz: that the Legislative as well as Executive sittings of the Senate were held *with closed doors* until the second session of the third Congress, with the single exception of the discussion of the contested election of A. GALLATIN, as Senator from Pennsylvania, during which discussion the galleries were opened by a special order of the Senate. On the 20th February, 1794, the Senate came to a resolution that, after the end of that session of Congress, the galleries of the Senate should be permitted to be opened whilst the Senate should be engaged in its Legislative capacity, unless specially ordered otherwise. This, it will be perceived, was an important change in the constitution of the Senate.]

Tuesday, August 25, 1789.

Also, the resolve of the House of Representatives, "that certain articles be proposed to the Legislatures of the several States, as amendments to the Constitution of the United States;" and requested the concurrence of the Senate therein.

A message was received from the House of Representatives, with seventeen articles to be proposed as additions to, and amendments of, the Constitution of the United States. (Such of these articles as have been agreed to, and ratified, will be found in the appendix to this volume.)

Wednesday, September 2, 1789.

The resolve of the House of Representatives of the 24th of August, 1789, "that certain articles be proposed to the Legislatures

213

of the several States as amendments to the Constitution of the
United States," was taken into consideration; and, on motion to
amend this clause of the first article proposed by the House of
Representatives, to-wit: "After the first enumeration required by
the first article of the Constitution, there shall be one representative for every thirty thousand, until the number shall amount
to one hundred," by striking out "one," and inserting "two," between the words "amount to," and "hundred;"

The yeas and nays being required by one-fifth of the Senators
present, the determination was as follows:

YEAS—Messrs. Dalton, Gunn, Grayson, King, Lee, and Schuyler
—6.

NAYS—Messrs. Bassett, Butler, Carroll, Ellsworth, Elmer,
Henry, Johnston, Izard, Morris, Paterson, Read, and Wingate—12.

So it passed in the negative.

On motion to adopt the first article proposed by the resolve
of the House of Representatives, amended as follows: to strike out
these words, "after which the proportion shall be so regulated by
Congress, that there shall be not less than one hundred representatives, nor less than one representative for every forty thousand
persons, until the number of representatives shall amount to two
hundred; after which the proportion shall be so regulated by
Congress, that there shall not be less than two hundred representatives, nor less than one representative for every fifty thousand
persons;" and to substitute the following clause after the words
"one hundred:" to-wit, "to which number one representative shall
be added for every subsequent increase of forty thousand, until
the representatives shall amount to two hundred, to which one
representative shall be added for every subsequent increase of sixty
thousand persons:" it passed in the affirmative.

Friday, September 4, 1789.

The Senate proceeded in the consideration of the resolve of the
House of Representatives of the 24th of August, on "Articles to be
proposed to the Legislatures of the several States, as amendments
to the Constitution of the United States."

Monday, September 7, 1789.

The Senate resumed the consideration of the resolve of the
House of Representatives of the 24th of August, on "Articles
to be proposed to the Legislatures of the several States, as amendments to the Constitution of the United States."

On motion, to adopt the twelfth article of the amendments
proposed by the House of Representatives, amended by the addi-

tion of these words to the article, to-wit: "where the consideration exceeds twenty dollars;" it passed in the affirmative.

On motion to adopt the thirteenth article of the amendments proposed by the House of Representatives, it passed in the affirmative.

On motion to adopt the fourteenth article of the amendments proposed by the House of Representatives, it passed in the negative.

In the consideration of the fifteenth article proposed by the House of Representatives, on motion to add the following to the proposed amendments, to-wit: "That the General Government of the United States ought never to impose direct taxes, but where the moneys arising from the duties of impost and excise are insufficient for the public exigencies, nor then, until Congress shall have made a requisition upon the States to assess, levy, and pay their respective portions of such requisitions; and in case any State shall neglect or refuse to pay its proportion, pursuant to such requisition, then Congress may assess and levy such State's proportion, together with interest thereon, at the rate of six per cent, per annum, from the time of payment prescribed by such requisition;" it passed in the negative.

On motion to add the following to the proposed amendments, viz: "That the third section of the sixth article of the Constitution of the United States ought to be amended by inserting the word "other" between the words "no" and "religious:" it passed in the negative.

Tuesday, September 8, 1789.

The Senate proceeded in the consideration of the resolve of the House of Representatives of the 24th of August, "On articles to be proposed to the Legislatures of the several States as amendments to the Constitution of the United States." Several amendments were proposed, but none of them were agreed to. The subject was postponed till to-morrow.

Wednesday, September 9, 1789.

The Senate proceeded in the consideration of the resolve of the House of Representatives on the articles to be proposed to the Legislatures of the several States as amendments to the Constitution, and agreed to a part of them, and disagreed to others; of which they informed the House.

Monday, September 21, 1789.

A message from the House of Representatives brought up a resolve of the House of this date, to agree to the 2d, 4th, 8th, 12th,

13th, 16th, 18th, 19th, 25th, and 26th amendments, proposed by the Senate, to "Articles of amendment to be proposed to the Legislatures of the several States, as amendments to the Constitution of the United States;" and to disagree to the 1st, 3d, 5th, 6th, 7th, 9th, 10th, 11th, 14th, 15th, 17th, 20th, 21st, 22d, 23d, and 24th amendments; two-thirds of the members present concurring on each vote; and "that a conference be desired with the Senate on the subject-matter of the amendments disagreed to," and that MESSRS. MADISON, SHERMAN, and VINING, be appointed managers of the same on the part of the House of Representatives.

Friday, September 25, 1789.

A Message from the House of Representatives informed the Senate that the House of Representatives had passed a resolve requesting "the President of the United States to transmit to the Executives of the several States, which have ratified the Constitution, copies of the amendments proposed by Congress to be added thereto; and like copies to the Executives of the States of Rhode Island and North Carolina;" and that the House requested the concurrence of the Senate therein. It also informed the Senate, that the House of Representatives had passed a bill making appropriations for the service of the present year; to which concurrence was also requested.

Ordered, That the last mentioned bill be now read the first time.

Ordered, That this bill be read the second time to-morrow.

The Senate proceeded to consider the Message from the House of Representatives of the 24th, with amendments to the amendments of the Senate to "Articles to be proposed to the Legislatures of the several States, as amendments to the Constitution of the United States;" and,

Resolved, That the Senate do concur in the amendments proposed by the House of Representatives to the amendments of the Senate.

Saturday, September 26, 1789.

The Senate proceeded to consider the following resolve of the House of Representatives of the 25th instant, to wit:

"Resolved, That a joint committee of both Houses be appointed to wait on the President of the United States, to request that he would recommend to the people of the United States a day of public thanksgiving and prayer, to be observed, by acknowledging, with grateful hearts, the many and signal favors of Almighty God, especially by affording them an opportunity peaceably to establish a constitution of government for their safety and happiness.

"Ordered, That MESSRS. BOUDINOT, SHERMAN, and SYLVESTER be appointed of the said committee on the part of this House."

Resolved. That the Senate do concur in the above recited resolution, and that MESSRS. JOHNSON and IZARD be the committee on the part of the Senate.